T0274064

THE BOOK OF
Spells

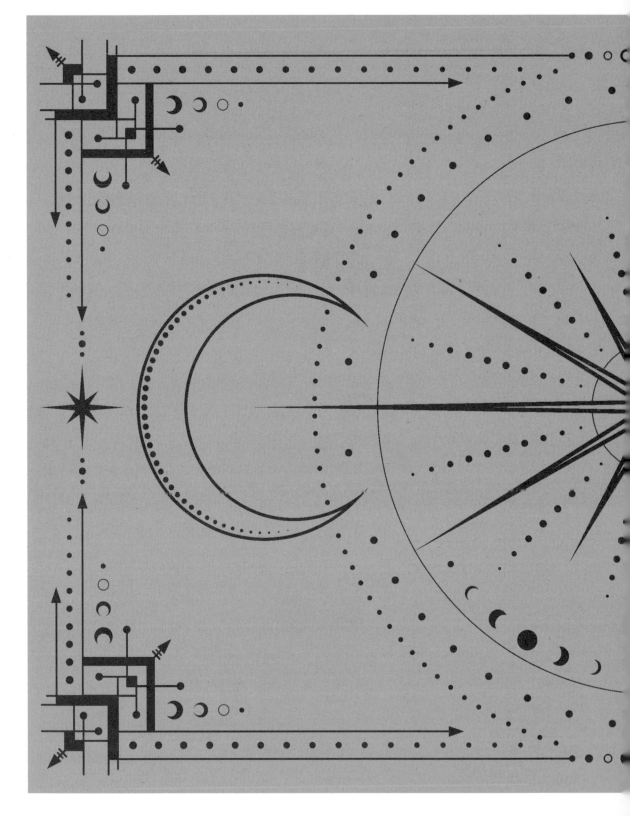

THE BOOK OF
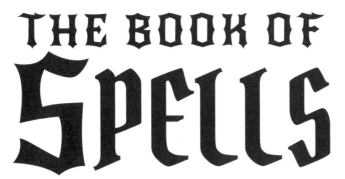
SPELLS

A MAGICAL TREASURY OF SPELLS, RITUALS AND BLESSINGS

MARIE BRUCE

SIRIUS

Illustrations courtesy of Shutterstock

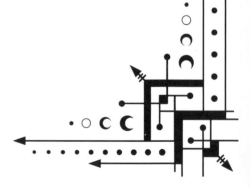

SIRIUS

This edition published in 2024 by Sirius Publishing, a division of
Arcturus Publishing Limited,
26/27 Bickels Yard, 151–153 Bermondsey Street,
London SE1 3HA

ISBN: 978-1-3988-2072-2
AD010235UK

Printed in China

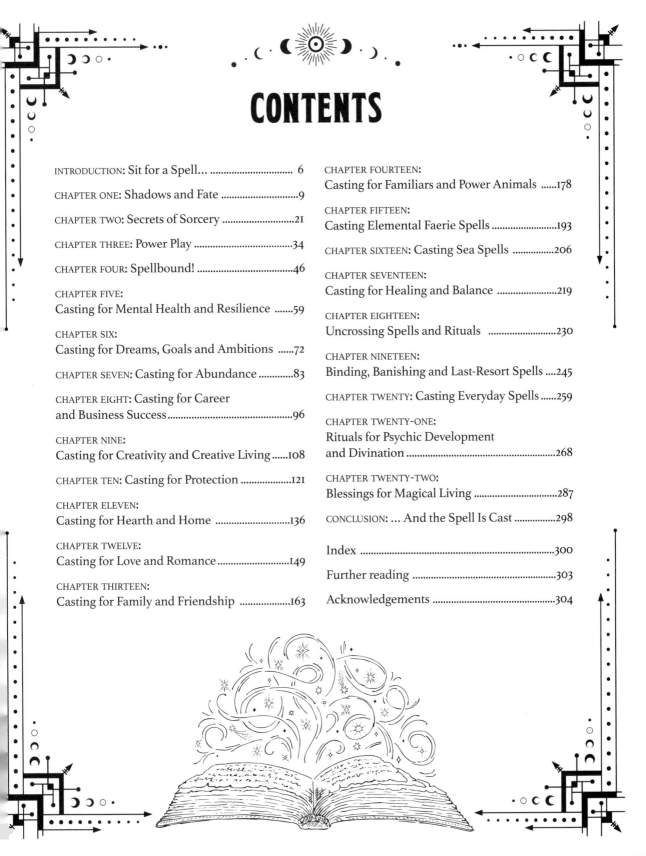

CONTENTS

INTRODUCTION

· · · · · · ◉ ◎ ◉ · · · · · ·

SIT FOR A SPELL...

Spell books have been around for centuries and, whether hand-made or traditionally published, most witches worth their salt have at least one volume of spells that they reach for in times of crisis. In Wiccan circles the spell book is known as the Book of Shadows, or BOS. In other circles, it is called a grimoire. Whatever its name, the spell book is a vital tool for magical practitioners, providing information, instruction, comfort and a sense of control when life gets messy.

Often, personal spell books are burnt after the practitioner's death, but there are still a few around if you know where to look. The Witchcraft Museum in Cornwall has a collection of spell books and grimoires, along with many other artefacts, which is worth a visit if you are curious. Many witches and practitioners like to create their own spell books, writing out their tried and trusted spells and rituals in a private journal. This is a good way to bring together all the spells that have worked especially well for you, so that you have them all in one place.

It should also be said that other witches prefer to work entirely from published books of spells, such as this one. These books can be a great time-saving device, as they tend to hold spells for all purposes and are easy to use. Of course, spells can always be adapted,

or used to inspire the practitioner to write their own original spells, so there is more than one way to utilize a book like this one.

In *The Book of Spells,* I have drawn together spells, rituals, meditations, visualizations, blessings and so on, to suit a variety of situations and circumstances. My intention is that this book will become a trusted resource, one which you reach for whenever you feel you need a little magical assistance to make your life run more smoothly. Here you will find spells for improving your career, life, love, family, pets, home and friendships, as well as rituals for working with elementals, power animals and nature in general. All the spells utilize easily sourced ingredients and the standard tools of magic, such as the pentacle, athame etc (see pages 49–50).

This book is for all those people who are tired of being buffeted by life and who want to steer their own course. It is for people who are fed up with feeling powerless and want to feel powerful instead. It is for those individuals who are looking for a life-enhancing way to develop personal autonomy, achieve goals and bring about a harmonious and successful life. Spell-craft is a powerful tool of choice for many modern witches, and now it can be your tool of choice too, helping you to meet challenges head-on and with a good dose of positivity, enchantment and, of course, magic!

This, then, is my gift to you: a comprehensive Book of Shadows with which you can navigate the ups and downs of life. So pour yourself a nice brew and sit for a spell as we dive into the fascinating world of witchery and spell-craft. Your magical journey is about to begin.

Blessed be,
Marie Bruce

CHAPTER ONE

SHADOWS & FATE

The image of a witch poring over a huge tome of spells is an iconic one in popular culture and it's not that far from the truth. Most witches do keep spell books on hand and they study their craft voraciously. However, today's witches are a far cry from the repulsive, horrific hags of the stereotype. Witchcraft is actually a very gentle practice, one which honours nature and respects all forms of life. It is a spirituality that celebrates the seasons, freedom of spirit, equality, diversity and tolerance.

Spell-casting is an art form and an intrinsic part of witchery. It takes time to learn but, as with any other craft, practice makes perfect. Given time, you will be able to whip up a spell in a few moments, once you have learnt how magical correspondences work and which phases of the moon are best for which types of magic. Casting 'on the fly', as it were, is a natural progression and adept witches often make up a spell in the moment, as and when the need arises.

To begin with, though, we all had to learn the basics. Magic is something that requires serious commitment and attention to detail. It must be approached with respect and a certain amount of reverence, for you are tapping into universal energies of great power and potential. You can't practise effective magic if you scorn it, or if you

think that it is all so much mumbo-jumbo. Applying knowledge with reverence is the key to making effective magic and changing your life for the better using spell-craft.

THE NEOPHYTE WITCH

A neophyte witch is a trainee magical practitioner. In a sense, this is a time of darkness before enlightenment, when the seeds of spiritual curiosity are sown. Neophyte witches tend to immerse themselves in a period of intense study and spell-craft. Gradually, they learn how to tap into, direct and release their inner magic, bringing about positive change. This first level of magical training often involves some kind of initiation. This could be a formal initiation into a coven, a self-initiation ritual, or perhaps some kind of life-centred initiation, usually brought about through the catalyst of change or chaos and also known as a baptism of fire.

This does not mean that any prior magical knowledge you might have is disregarded or useless. Quite the contrary, as any previous magical training will provide a great foundation on which to build your knowledge. What it does mean is that we must all return to the humble state of novice from time to time, for life is a series of lessons and opportunities to begin again. Approach the teachings of this book with an open mind and the fresh outlook of the novice, regardless of magical experience, because there is always something new to learn if we are open to it.

Living a magical life requires the practitioner to turn inwards, exploring motivations and limitations, and delving into the deeper reaches of the mind to find where your personal strengths and magical talents lie. By coming to know who you are on the inside, you will be in a better position to craft a future that suits you and helps you to thrive, rather than creating the kind of life that is fashionable in the moment and yet leaves you feeling unfulfilled. Use spell-craft to meet your true needs, not to keep up with trends. In that way you will glean the most benefit from your magical skills.

TALL POPPIES

Witches tend to stand out in a crowd because they get things done and make things happen. They are not passive by nature. They are active participants in their own lives and in society. Everyone has an inner power and a strength of will that they can tap into, but lots of people don't use this power. Instead, they live in a state of apathy and complaint. This type of passive indifference towards life is a personal choice, not an inability.

Witches take a different approach, prioritizing personal responsibility and willpower to change their lives for the better. If we don't like something, we change it, or we change our attitude towards it. Witches cast spells and perform rituals regularly and because of this they are very tuned in to their own sense of empowerment. This positive force of will is what strengthens a witch, enabling them to take life's hard knocks on the chin and bounce back quickly. You can't keep a good witch down for long!

Having a deep connection with their personal power also means that witches tend to achieve their goals and ambitions and make their dreams come true. Eventually, people will start to notice this and might even ask you how you always get what you want. Witches are like tall poppies and occasionally someone might try to cut you down to size. However, your ability to bounce back will ensure that you continue to succeed in spite of them. Anyone can follow the crowd and it is easy to be average, but witches choose to walk a different path and no one has the right to cut you down to size because of it.

WHAT IS A SPELL?

A spell or magic ritual is the ability to cast an influence over the events of one's life, using willpower and the powers of the natural world combined. It is a technique used by witches to facilitate a specific outcome, or to bring into being the desire of the witch. Spells are not evil and magic is neither black nor white. It is simply energy that is directed towards an intention. Whether that intention is for good or ill is down to the individual witch, but the power of spell-craft itself is always neutral.

I have often described spell-casting as *'prayer with props'* because that is essentially what it is. Witches are working with the powers of the universe to attract their desired outcome. We use tools such as candles, incense, incantations, written intentions, crystals, plants and so on, to help us maintain our focus and to bring in aspects of the natural energies with which we work.

Spell-casting is a collaboration between you and the universe, and you have to practise in alignment with the universal tides in order to cast an effective spell or ritual. Most spells, but not all, incorporate some kind of incantation – that is a series of words that are spoken out loud. Sometimes the incantation takes the form of a repetitive chant or a song. Its purpose is to state the intention of the spell.

being very sceptical about magic in general, can delay the outcome, or even sabotage it completely. You cannot fool the mirror of the universe and it will always reflect back the attitude you hold in your heart and mind, so stay positive!

HOW DO SPELLS WORK?

Spells work by attracting your intention towards you, using the magnetic fields of the universe. Think of the universe as a huge mirror that is designed to reflect your intentions back at you, like for like. This means that what you focus on is what you get. Keeping your thoughts positive will bring good things into your life, while allowing your thoughts to become negative will attract more things for you to complain about!

To make positive and effective magic, it is important to have a clear intention and a positive attitude towards the outcome. You must expect good things to come to you, and in a good way. This keeps your personal vibration on a high frequency, which results in positive manifestation of your intentions. Having doubts that your magic will work, or

MODERN MAGIC

Over the past few years, magic has had something of a facelift and has made its way into the mainstream of society, rebranded in turn as cosmic ordering, the law of attraction or the manifestation technique. Call it whatever you are most comfortable with, as all these techniques are basically the same thing. They are all ways to connect with the power, or magic, of the universe in order to bring about a desired outcome.

If you are already familiar with the law of attraction, then you will have a good idea as to how magic works. Try to incorporate your law of attraction practices with your spell-craft to give yourself the best chance of success. Feel free to use affirmations, visualizations, vision boarding and so on, as a back-up to your spells and vice versa. In this way, you are surrounding yourself with positive intentions and your spells should manifest more quickly as a result. The magic of the universe is very real and you can experience it for yourself whenever you choose to tap into it. Spells and rituals are a traditional route to this power, but the modern manifestation paths work too. Using both these techniques in conjunction with one another will make your witchery a force to be reckoned with.

MAGIC TAKES WORK

Although the film and TV industry would have people believe that magic is simply a wave of the wand and any dream will come true, in reality magic takes work. If you are casting for a big goal, then one spell might not be enough. You will need to layer up the magic by working several spells over a period of time, in order to bring about a successful outcome.

Other spells are designed to be cast daily or weekly. Protection spells, for instance, are cast on a regular basis to keep the magical boundary they create as strong as possible. This is also true for spells for good health or positive family relations. If you are casting to *maintain* something, then you will also need to maintain the magic with regular spell work. It takes time and it can be difficult at first to fit magic into your life. Most witches cast some kind of simple spell every week. Not only does this maintain the level of magic that surrounds them on a daily basis, it also keeps their skills sharp. Skills can fade over time and magic is no exception to this rule. As with anything else, regular practice will keep your abilities honed to a high degree.

That said, spells don't have to be complicated to be effective. Simple spells can work just as well, so if all you can do is light a small birthday candle or a stick of incense, then – providing your intention is clear – there is no reason why such spells shouldn't be just as effective as full rituals. As life is so busy for many people, simple spells can sometimes be the best option. The main thing to remember is that magic is cast regularly to keep the good vibes flowing into your life and to minimize any negative events.

BACK UP YOUR SPELLS

You must always be prepared to back up your spells in the mundane world. You can't expect magic to do all the work for you. As I said

before, witches are not passive or apathetic, they are active participants in their own lives, which means that for every spell they cast, they will take action in the real world to help the magic to manifest.

What does this mean in practice? It means that if you are casting spells for financial freedom, you will need to stop racking up debts. It means that if you cast for a new job, you need to apply for positions and brush up your interview technique, and if you are casting for love, then you need to be open to meeting new people.

Apathy, meaning a state of indifference, is passive by nature and sadly we live in quite an apathetic society. Apathy is exhausting. It makes you feel drained and leaves you in a state of inertia – doing nothing, sleeping too much, complaining often. It is the opposite of living a magical life, because magic is proactive, so to get the most out of your spells you must actively back them up in some way.

Every time you cast a spell, ask yourself how you are going to support the magic in the mundane world. Do you need to make a phone call, send an email, apply for a new post, stop spending on frivolous things, join a club, book a trip? What can you do that will show the universe that you are serious about your goal and that you are willing to put yourself out there along with your magic?

taking you back down to earth again. You will know which half of the cycle you are on by noticing the main events of your life in recent months or years.

An upwardly mobile cycle brings promotions, great experiences, new lovers and friends, opportunities, abundance, lovely holidays and all the good things life has to offer. In this stage of the cycle, it will seem as if everything is just coming to you, as you realize your dreams and enjoy life to the full.

THE WHEEL OF FORTUNE

The Wheel of Fortune is at work in all our lives, all the time. You are either on your way up or on your way back down, but it is a pattern that is clearly felt by all of us. It is constantly turning, allowing each of us to experience the highs and lows of life. In the tarot deck, the Wheel of Fortune is the tenth card of the Major Arcana. It reminds us that change is the only constant and it frequently signifies a change in luck or a reversal of fortune.

The Wheel of Fortune is like a cosmic big wheel. For someone to enjoy the view at the top, someone else has to be at the bottom. With each cycle the Wheel draws you higher and higher, until it is your turn at the top, but then inevitably, it also begins its descent,

A downward cycle, however, tends to strip things away from you, so you experience bereavements, divorce, job loss, poverty, rifts with family and friends etc. Delayed starts, false endings, obstacles and the

derailment of plans are all signs that you are on the downward cycle. It can be frustrating, upsetting and debilitating. But the Wheel of Fortune doesn't take anything away that you were meant to keep – rather it removes that which has been holding you back, or which has served its purpose in your life. When you are on a downward cycle, it can feel as if your life has been emptied out completely and there is nothing left but the void of what used to be, but take heart, because when you feel that you are at your lowest ebb, that is a sign that you have reached the bottom of the Wheel and the worst is over.

Like any big wheel in a funfair, the Wheel of Fortune allows you time to enjoy both the pinnacle at the top and the doldrums at the bottom. You need this breathing space to

assess how far you have come on the climb, to enjoy the fruits of your labour, or to come to terms with the losses. It isn't about being punished – it's about being *prepared* for the next turn of the Wheel.

You are far from powerless, because you can use the two poles of the Wheel's journey to make plans for the next half of the cycle. So when you're at the top, you can start cushioning yourself ready for the downward journey, by setting money aside in savings or retraining to improve your qualifications etc. When swinging in the doldrums, you can rest and recover, seek counselling for support with the losses and make goals for your next upward cycle so you know what you want the Wheel of Fortune to offer you.

These seemingly small actions will keep you proactive in your life and set the Wheel swaying a bit. Before you know it, you will feel the jolt as it shifts gears and moves on once more, taking your day-to-day life along with it. That is the purpose of the Wheel of Fortune – it keeps you moving. It teaches you that everyone has ups and downs and no one's life is perfect. It makes you stronger, more resilient and ready to accept that change is necessary and that it can be a good thing. It prepares you, making you ready for the fresh start it brings, as you ride on into the next upwardly mobile cycle of life.

But what does the Wheel of Fortune have to do with spell-casting? Quite a lot, actually, because once you have identified how the Wheel is turning in your life right now, you can then use the right sort of spells to reap the most benefit from the journey. So if you are on the upwards cycle, use spells to ensure the Wheel of Fortune brings you the opportunities and things you really want. If you are on a downwards cycle, then you can use damage-limitation and healing spells to make the process easier to bear.

It must also be said that many people come to magic through a sense of sheer desperation, when life is going wrong for them and they don't know which way to turn or what to do about it. They may have tried conventional means of support and found little benefit from them. For people in such situations, magic seems like their last hope and frequently becomes a new way of life, as they begin to harness their inner power and make positive changes to their lives.

Whatever way you might have found this path and this book, whether you are in dire straits or if you are a seasoned magical practitioner, know that you are welcome here and that for the time being, we share this magical journey together.

UNIVERSAL TIDES

Just as the Wheel of Fortune governs the patterns of your personal life, so the universe is governed by tides of its own. Like the sea tides, the universal tides are designed to ebb and flow, and they are made up of pure energy. It is these energetic tidal waves that bring the manifestation of your spell.

Have you ever noticed that sometimes lots of great things just come to you, all at once? It could be a pay increase, a promotion, a new lover, a pet etc. As like attracts like, when good things are snowballing into your life it means that the universal tides are coming in. If you are in the habit of casting spells, this is when they will start to manifest or, as the saying goes, this is when your ship will come in.

When the universal tide is out, however, you are more likely to notice how quiet things are, because this is a fallow period of rest. It is a good time to determine what you want to focus on next and begin casting for those goals. The results might not manifest in the very next incoming tide, but at some point, the tides will bring your desire to you.

Universal tides are linked to the phases of the moon, which acts as a visual cue for witches when working magic. We will be looking at how the lunar cycle affects magic in a later chapter, but for now, try to become

more aware of the subtle patterns in your own life. Are the tides in or out, ebbing or flowing towards you? Does this link up with where you currently sit on the Wheel of Fortune? Can you identify any correlation between the two?

Witches learn to keep track of all the subtle shifts in the energy that surrounds them, and they know how to tap into these shifts and spirals for a higher purpose. Keeping a journal is a good way to identify the energies around you and to see how and when your goals manifest. You can start a magical journal at any time, using a notebook or a computer file, whatever works best for you. Track whenever something good happens for you, or when you have experienced a loss or a disappointment. In this way you are getting to know how the tides of life are influencing the events of your life and you can learn to work with them in your spells and rituals, knowing that you will be working *with* nature, not against her, and so your spells will have a better chance of success.

A PROCESS OF ENLIGHTENMENT

Magic is a journey towards enlightenment. It will teach you that there is far more to the world than you might at first imagine. When you step out onto the magical path,

you may be a little sceptical, and this is understandable. A certain amount of scepticism is healthy, for it prevents you from becoming gullible. As you start to see your goals manifest, however, you will find that your belief in magic grows stronger, and the stronger your belief, the more powerful your spells will be.

The first time a spell manifests in your life, it can come as a bit of a shock. You might be surprised that you have the power to alter the course of your life. It might feel strange to you that the powers of the universe are there to help, so when a spell works, it can be a little unnerving. The power you are working with is directed by you, so providing your intentions are good, there is no need to worry that you have unleashed something that cannot be controlled. Enjoy the success of your magic!

That said, it can also be tempting to start casting spells for everything, including things that you can just as easily achieve without magical assistance. It is important not to take advantage of the universal power, because that will stop the flow of magic from working. Before you cast a spell, ask yourself if it is absolutely necessary, or if you can achieve this goal on your own. Even witches don't use magic for everything, so be sensible with what you cast for and what assistance you require from the universe. Magic is not an excuse for laziness!

In the next chapter we will be looking at different types of spells and how to identify if they are working or not, plus what you should do if you think a spell has gone wrong.

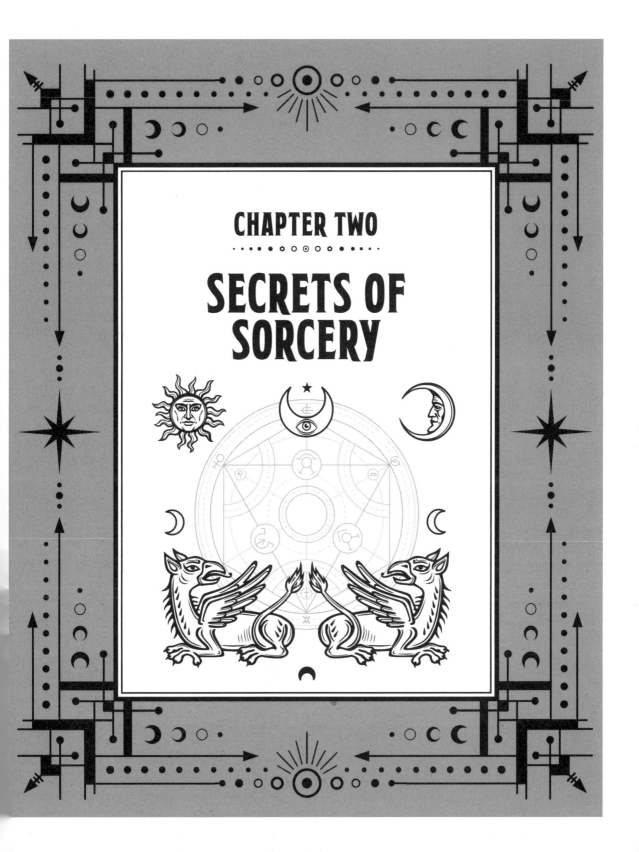

CHAPTER TWO

SECRETS OF SORCERY

Magic is far from new. It has been around for centuries, though we might not always recognize it as such. Many of the things we take for granted and have an understanding of today, such as modern medicine or the laws of chemistry, for instance, would have been viewed as feats of magic or alchemy in the past. Times change, superstitions are proven to be unfounded and our understanding of the world develops over time. We only need to think of technology to see how fast our world is changing, growing and developing. So the things that people once viewed as magic are now a part of our everyday lives.

What hasn't changed, however, is the human need to believe in powers greater than ourselves, our quest for knowledge and for a deeper understanding of the world around us. When you stop and really think about it, it *is* miraculous that the springtime comes round again every year, or that there is a vast universe out there that we know little about. All of this is magical. All of it is enchanting and for witches, it is all source material for spell-casting.

Why do witches cast spells? Well, there are lots of reasons, but the main one is that it gives us a sense of personal power and control over our lives. It is also a way to help others. It can be a great comfort to light a candle and say a few words when a loved one is ill and you are feeling helpless. It can be a source of strength to cast protection spells around your property when there has been a spate of burglaries in the area. It can be a healing experience to mix up a bath potion to use after a long day at work, or a great relief to hear the cat meowing at the door shortly after you have cast a safe-return spell.

To put it in the simplest of terms, casting spells can make you feel better. It makes you feel as if you've done something to address whatever situation you find yourself in – and you have! Spell-casting is a powerful technique, one which even the more orthodox religions use, though they would never refer to it as magic! Have you ever gone into a church and been invited to light

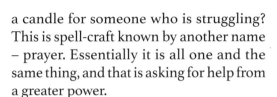

a candle for someone who is struggling? This is spell-craft known by another name – prayer. Essentially it is all one and the same thing, and that is asking for help from a greater power.

Becoming adept at spells and rituals means that you need never feel helpless again, because there is always something you can do. Even in the worst of times, such as bereavement, you can cast for strength and healing to help with the grieving process. There is nothing that cannot be improved with a little sprinkling of magic, no sticky situation that cannot benefit from a spell to smooth it out. So why wouldn't you want to make magic in your life, knowing that in turn, your life will become more magical?

SERENDIPITY AND COINCIDENCE

When magic is afoot there is no such thing as coincidence, because magic works by coming along the path of least resistance. This means that the magic will manifest in the easiest way possible, so if you are casting for a new job, it could be that you hear of a position from a friend or family member, who puts in a good word for you. It also means that you are more likely to trust the outcome of the magic when it manifests in your life, because it has come via a path that is already familiar to you, i.e. someone you know.

Rarely does magic show up full of bells and whistles. It's more of a 'blink and you'll miss it' scenario. Although occasionally it does come out with a big bang, it is more usual for spells to manifest in quite a routine way. It could be some time later before you realize that your spell has worked and you got exactly what you wanted, but it came in such a mundane way that you didn't immediately correlate the results to the spell. This is a natural oversight to make, especially if you are new to magic.

It might be that you have noticed many more coincidences happening around you since you started to practise spell-craft. Again, this is a sign that the magic is working. It is important not to dismiss such coincidences,

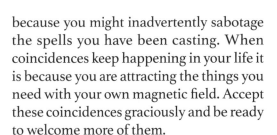

because you might inadvertently sabotage the spells you have been casting. When coincidences keep happening in your life it is because you are attracting the things you need with your own magnetic field. Accept these coincidences graciously and be ready to welcome more of them.

Serendipity is also a feature of a magical life. This is when a series of chance events lead to a happy ending. It is a sudden change in fortune for the better, or a run of good luck. While coincidence is linked to circumstances and situations, serendipity usually links to people, so think chance encounters, sudden meetings and bumping into people at exactly the right time. Serendipity is all about connections, networking and building your team, so introductions, interviews, invitations and so on are all at play here.

Again, try not to dismiss these encounters because they have been brought about for a reason. Of course, you should be careful and keep your personal safety in mind at all times, but try not to reject people out of habit, as you could be rejecting the results of your spells! Serendipity is a little louder than coincidence and has a habit of just dropping the right people into your life, seemingly out of the clear blue sky, right when you need them most. Magical meetings feel very different to mundane ones, so trust your intuition and see where these new

acquaintances take you. Trust that these people have come into your life for a good reason, and vice versa – they might need you just as much as you need them.

WHEN SOMEONE ELSE GETS WHAT YOU WANT

Another clear sign that you are heading in the right direction with your magical endeavours is when someone close to you gets exactly what *you* want. This is a sign that manifestation is close, though not yet guaranteed, because this situation is also a test of character from the universe. Can you be happy for that person, even though you are still waiting for it to happen? A classic example of this is if you are looking for love or trying to start a family, when a sibling or close friend suddenly announces they're getting married or having a baby. It can feel like a kick in the teeth and it can trigger a lot of envy, but you should be gracious and congratulate them on their exciting news. If you act upon the jealousy, by being spiteful, sulky or competitive, this could derail your spells, because you have proven that you are not coming from a place of love, gratitude and abundance, but from a place of envy, poverty and ego.

Just because someone achieves something you want doesn't mean that you can no longer achieve it too. There is enough success for everyone and the world is an abundant place. Their achievement hasn't taken anything away from you, but if a scarcity mind-set leads you to act enviously towards them, then you are only sabotaging your own success for the future. Instead, be grateful that your goal is now so close! Take it as a sign that you are on the right track, that you are putting out the right spells and vibrations for manifestation to occur.

Being close to someone who gets what you want is never an easy path to tread, but by being kind and gracious towards them, you will prove to the universe that you too are ready for the success of your spells and the achievement of your goals. Be as happy for them as you would want them to be for you. Some goals are so common that there

are bound to be others who get there first, so try not to take it personally.

Bear in mind that jealousy will only prevent your own progress. It is a poison you feed to yourself and it will do nothing to derail the success of those around you, so be happy for them and take it as a sign that your own success isn't that far behind.

CAN SPELLS GO WRONG?

Sometimes a spell might not work very well, or it might not work in the way that you envisioned it would. Often this is simply a case of rewording and tweaking the original spell. For magic to be effective, you need to be very clear and specific as to what you are casting for. As an example, if you cast a spell to bring a new companion into your life, then you might find that you manifest a new pet rather than a new lover! If it is a lover you want, that is what your spell should focus on. Likewise, if all you want is a casual fling then make this clear in the spell, or you might end up attracting someone who is looking to settle down. 'Heart-breaker' is never a good moniker!

Being specific is the key to a successful spell. Focus on exactly what you want. Don't leave it open to interpretation, because the universe doesn't understand nuance or vague suggestions. Be clear, be specific and be bold. Magic will usually manifest *something*, so clarity is essential. It is rare that a spell has no effect whatsoever, because you are sending energy out into the universe and that energy has to transform and come back to you in some way.

If you think that your spell simply hasn't worked, then check that all your correspondences etc. were in alignment with one another and with your goal. If they are, then you can always recast the spell. As mentioned earlier, some big goals need spells to be repeated over time to bring about manifestation. If the spells still don't seem to be working, it could be that what you are asking for isn't for your highest good. If this is the case, then another path will be offered to you instead, one that suits you much better, so don't lose heart. The universe really *is* on your side.

HOW TO MANAGE
THE POWER OF MAGIC

Everyone holds a spark of magic within them, a personal source of power that they can use to manifest their goals and ambitions. When you cast a spell, you are weaving together your own personal power with the greater power of the universe or nature. These two powers combined are what creates magic and manifestation. This magical power is a form of energy, so it can never be diminished,

it simply changes shape and form. You send energy out into the world when you cast a spell and that energy changes form, returning to you as the manifestation of your goal. This is why your spells should be cast with a positive mind set, to bring back positive results.

Some spells take more energy than others. A spell to manifest a new house would take significantly more power than a spell to bring about a quiet day at work. This is why large goals require repeated spells, because they need more energy. Likewise, several people working together in a coven can do more with one spell than a solitary practitioner can, again because there is more energy involved.

Managing energy is all part of being a witch or magical practitioner. As you cast a spell you will feel the energy and excitement build, until the spell is released in some way. This could mean burning, burying or scattering spell ingredients, to release the power of the magic. Building energy is an intrinsic aspect of spell-casting and it has its own guidelines, known as the Law of the Power, which is:

1. To Know
2. To Dare
3. To Will
4. To Be Silent

What this essentially means is that you must know what type of spell you are going to cast and for what purpose. You must then have the courage to cast the spell and will it into being. The final rule can be the hardest to follow for some people, because you must remain completely silent about what you have done.

Witches do not discuss the spells they are casting until manifestation has occurred. The reason for this is that talking about the spell is thought to reduce the power and the possibility of it working. Have you ever told someone of an exciting new opportunity or romance, only to have the whole thing fall through, as if you had somehow jinxed the outcome? That is why it is important to remain silent about the spells you have cast. Don't diminish the power of the spell by gossiping about it. After all, it is no one else's business what you get up to with a candle! It's your magic, your spell and your business. Magic works best in secret, so maintain the Law of the Power. We will be looking at the ethics of magic in the next chapter, but for now ensure that you work with good intentions and you won't go far wrong.

IT'S NOT A BLACK AND WHITE ISSUE

True magic is pure energy. It is neither black nor white, good nor bad. Although some people might describe themselves as white or black witches, this is really just to let others know where their intentions lie. A white, or good, witch would be someone who casts spells to help others, while the black, or bad, witch would cast with a harmful intent, such as spells for revenge. There are also racial connotations here which cannot be ignored and for that reason, many modern practitioners are steering clear of terms like black and white magic.

However, the power of magic remains the same. It is the intention of the practitioner which determines whether a spell is cast for good or ill. Magic has often been likened to electricity, which can be used to power life-saving hospital equipment or the electric chair, depending on how it is directed. The same is true of magical power – it can be used to heal or to harm, depending on how the practitioner directs it, but it is essentially a neutral energy.

TYPES OF MAGIC AND SPELLS

There are many different kinds of magic, and different witches prefer different spells. Some like to work with candles, others prefer to use living plants in the garden. Hedge Witches work predominantly with herbs, Kitchen Witches with potions and food spells, Green Witches with the earth and the forest, and Scribe Witches with runes, sigils (magic symbols) and the written word. It must be said, however, that most witches work with most types of magic, we just have our preferences for certain tools and spells. Here are some of the most popular types of magical spell.

PETITION SPELLS

By far the easiest and most popular spells to perform, petition magic involves writing down your intention and then releasing the spell by destroying the paper, either by burning it and scattering the ashes or ripping it up and disposing of it. Petition magic is the preferred spell of the Scribe Witch, who might also choose to incorporate runes and sigils as part of the spell. It is a very simple spell to perform and requires only a pen and a sheet of paper, so it is perfect for quick on-the-go spells that need to be cast in the moment. It requires little preparation and can be performed anywhere. It works by setting down your intention, in ink on paper, and then releasing it to the universe. In this way you are petitioning the universe with a particular aim in mind, just as you might petition a politician to bring about certain policies. You can use this type of spell by itself, or in conjunction with other kinds of magic, such as candle or poppet magic (see below). It is extremely effective and versatile.

POPPET SPELLS

Poppet magic is a type of sympathetic magic, which basically means that like attracts like, so whatever happens to the poppet should have an impact on the person it represents. We have all seen extreme examples of poppet magic in horror films, where someone is sticking pins in a voodoo doll to cause harm, but in truth poppet magic is a very gentle practice, most often used in healing or love spells. To begin with, some kind of poppet – a doll or puppet – is fashioned by the witch. This can be as elaborate or simple as you like. Poppets can be made from dough (think gingerbread man), clay, wool, string, a hanky, cardboard or paper. One thing all poppet spells have in common, however, is the tag-lock – something which

links it to the person it is meant to represent. This is usually a bit of hair from a hairbrush or comb, which is then added to the doll's stuffing or fixed to the poppet's head. Once the doll has been tagged with the hair, it represents a real person and can be used in positive spells for healing that individual. Obviously this kind of spell can be misused, so it should only be used for positive spells that will benefit the individual concerned and with their express permission.

CANDLE SPELLS

Candle magic is a staple in most magical spells and rituals, largely because the candle represents all four elements in one. The wax represents earth, the flame is fire, the melting wax is water and the smoke is air. This means that candle magic is very powerful indeed and it is a core ingredient of most spells. Different-coloured candles are used to represent different things. Large candles can be burnt over a period of time to bring about a big goal, while a simple tea-light can be burnt each day to maintain the light of love or abundance in your life. Candles are also a great base for other forms of magic. You can make candle spells as simple or as complex as you want. You can inscribe words, runes or sigils into the wax to incorporate scribe magic, or anoint them in essential oils and roll them in dried herbs to incorporate

hedge witchery. There is a lot of power in candle spells and there are many of them for you to try in this book. No witch worth her wand would ever run out of candles and tea-lights because they are so useful. In a pinch, magic can be made with a basic white candle and nothing else, so the box of candles you keep under the sink in case of a power cut could be all that you need.

CORD SPELLS

Cord spells are also called *witches' ladders*. They are a form of magic that uses a long length of cord or ribbon, in which knots are tied to manifest something or bind it to you. Traditionally nine knots would be tied into the cord to form the witches' ladder, as an incantation is spoken with each knot tied. Cords can also be used in banishing spells, to cut something from you, using a cord to represent that which no longer serves you. Cord rituals to manifest something are kept safe until manifestation has occurred, when the knots are released and the cord is cleansed ready to use again. In banishing spells, the severed cord is usually buried in the earth, while in binding spells it is left permanently in place.

CONTAINMENT SPELLS

Containment spells are used to bring together a variety of spell ingredients in order to bring about a certain goal. Often they use small jars or pouches which are filled with crystals, herbs, charms and the written petition for the goal. These jars are then kept in a special place, for example on the witch's altar, by the front door or hearth, or beside the bed, depending on what the purpose of the spell jar is. Pouches can be carried by the witch to manifest a specific outcome. Containment spells can also be used to negate any negative energy that is coming your way, by placing a representation of that energy in a container, adding a binding agent such as glue or ice, and then hiding the container from sight.

VISUALIZATION SPELLS

While all spells require a certain amount of visualization, in that you must be able to keep your goal in mind as you cast the spell, there are some which rely on this skill more than others. Spells that help you to connect with the elementals, or fey spirits, are one example, while power animal spells usually require strong visualization techniques too. If you have difficulty with visualization, just think of it as magical daydreaming, for that is what it is. So long as you can hold an image in your mind as you cast the spell or make an invocation, there is no reason why your elemental and totem spells should not work.

SCRIBE MAGIC

Scribe magic is the art of writing for manifestation. This kind of spell involves written affirmations and incantations, runes and magical alphabets, or drawing out symbols to represent your goal. Keeping a magical journal is also a form of scribe magic because you are documenting your magical journey for future reference. Scribe magic can be anything from writing out your goals, affirmations and petitions to dreaming up your ideal life on the page. It could be the process of writing a Book of Shadows or magical poetry. Basically scribe magic is the art of writing out your goal as if it has already happened, so you are in effect writing out

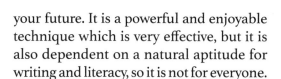

your future. It is a powerful and enjoyable technique which is very effective, but it is also dependent on a natural aptitude for writing and literacy, so it is not for everyone.

NATURAL MAGIC

Natural magic, or folk magic as it is also known, is a type of spell that uses elements of nature such as seashells, pebbles, pine cones, acorns, crystals, leaves, flowers, snow, rainwater and so on. Most spells incorporate some aspect of natural magic and it is the linchpin of all witchcraft.

As you can see from this by-no-means exhaustive list, there are many types of spells and usually they all work well together. In this book you will find examples of the spells mentioned here, often in combination with one another to build up the power. You can take aspects from here and there to build up a complete ritual, or use snippets to create your own unique spells. Magic is always experimental, and what works for you might not work for someone else. This is because we each have our own natural abilities when it comes to magic, so while scribe magic works well for me, you might prefer herb spells instead. Go with your instincts and don't be afraid to try new things, as that is the only way you will discover where your own magical skills lie.

CHAPTER THREE
· · · · · ◦ ◉ ◦ · · · ·
POWER PLAY

You have the potential to blaze a path of magic right through your life, using spell-craft to influence your choices, decisions and dilemmas. You can use the craft of magic to attract the right kind of people to you and to open doors to the right places and opportunities. Before you do any of this, however, you need to understand your obligations as a practitioner of magic.

Like any other kind of power and authority, magic comes with the weight of responsibility. It will give you autonomy over your own life, but you must ensure that your magic doesn't interfere with the lives of other people. Therefore, there are certain guidelines that you should follow in order to get the most from your spells, whilst also safeguarding the free will of others.

ETHICS OF MAGIC

Before you cast any kind of ritual or spell, you should ask yourself if it will have an impact on anyone other than yourself. Witches do not cast spells on other people, but we do weave a web of magic around ourselves in order to attract the things we want. What does this mean in practice? Well, it means that you should never cast spells for another person without their permission. This includes magic for healing the sick and helping someone who is dealing with addiction. It can be difficult watching someone you care about struggle, but unless you have permission to cast spells for them, try to help in more mundane ways instead.

There is a good reason for this and it is all about free will. In casting spells without permission you are effectively tampering with someone's free will. You could also be preventing them from learning a spiritual or life lesson with your interference. By all means have a chat with them and test the ground to see how they feel about magic, but unless you have permission to work spells on their behalf, stick to casting only for yourself. While this might seem selfish, it is really the kindest and most ethical option. If someone you love is sick, but you know they wouldn't like the idea of magic, then instead of casting healing spells for them, cast spells for strength and service around yourself, so that you can be there when they need you, and so that you are more inspired to help in a way that they find most comforting.

Another example would be that of love spells. You should only cast spells upon yourself in order to attract more love into your life. Love cannot be forced, even by magic. It is a gift that must be offered freely, without conditions attached. So if you want more romance in your life, cast a spell to attract more romantic situations towards you, rather than one to turn your partner into Casanova! Always bear in mind the ripple effect of any spells you cast and try to ensure that they do not encroach on the free will of anyone else.

THE THREEFOLD LAW

One of the reasons witches are such sticklers for protecting free will is because of the Threefold Law, which states that whatever you send out magically, will come back to you with three times the force and three times the consequences. This is why you should never cast in the spirit of envy, vengeance or spite, because essentially, you are only hurting yourself in the long run, when all those emotions are directed back at you in some way.

The Threefold Law means that whatever you send out will come back to you, so if you are sending out positive, happy vibrations, you will receive positive and happy opportunities in return. Likewise, if you are sending out negative, complaining vibes then you are attracting more negative things to complain about. In short, do good deeds and good things will come to you. Do bad deeds and ... well, I wouldn't want to be in your shoes when they return!

In Wiccan belief we often refer to the Threefold Law as the Harm None rule, which simply states: *'An it harm none, do what you will.'* This little mantra reminds us to make sure we keep our thoughts, words, deeds and magic positive in nature, so that we are not inadvertently encroaching on someone's free will, or causing harm to another living creature. It is a very life enhancing law to live by, for it means that we are always mindful of how our actions might impact other people, animals and the natural world around us.

EMOTIONS

Your emotions are the fuel to your spells. How you are feeling when you cast a spell can have an impact on how well it works. Likewise, so can your state of health. Generally speaking, the more positive and upbeat you are when you cast a spell, the better it will work. But what about those occasions when you cannot

be upbeat, but you need a little magic on your side?

Say you have suffered a bereavement, or you have the flu – what then? At such times as these, it is best to work only gentle spells, rather than full rituals. Simple acts of petition, crystal or candle magic can give you the boost you need, without taking too much of your energy, because remember that effective magic requires your energy to work. Try not to cast big spells if you are very sick, because you need your energy to recover. Instead, light a candle or hold a crystal and ask for healing energies to surround you.

All emotions can be fuel for magic, so long as they are directed in the right way. While some witches believe that you should not cast in anger, others claim that this is vibrant energy that should be directed to

your goal, providing you adhere to the Harm None rule. Imagine that your house was burgled. You would understandably be quite angry about such a violation of your space and privacy, but instead of directing this anger towards the perpetrators of the crime in a spell for vengeance, you could channel it into a powerful protection spell around your home, or a spell for justice so that the police can catch the burglars. In this way, you turn a negative event into positive spell-craft. Just because an *emotion* is considered negative doesn't mean that the *magic* you make with it will be. You can turn a negative emotion into a positive outcome by channelling it as fuel and directing it towards a positive goal. Just keep the Harm None rule at the forefront of your mind as you release these emotions into your magic.

SET YOUR INTENTION

We talked about intentions a little earlier. If emotion is the *fuel* for your magic, then intention is the *vehicle* in which it travels. You do need both to cast an effective spell, otherwise, like a car without petrol or petrol without a car, the magic is going nowhere. Where many neophyte witches fall down, however, is to assume that you state your intention once and the job is done. It isn't quite that simple.

Intention is all about mind-set, belief

and behaviour. You can state the intention that you will find love, but unless you also *believe* that you are loveable and *act* from a loving heart, the intention falls flat. This is because your actions and behaviours are not in alignment with your magical goal. In short, you are not backing up your spell with complementary actions that support your intention.

To set a true intention, you must first of all believe that it is possible for you to have what you are casting for. You must know deep in your heart that you are worthy of it and that you deserve to have it. You must act as if it is already coming to you and feel a sense of certainty that you will have it. Finally, you must make yourself ready to receive it by making space for it in your life. This process is the same regardless of the goal.

If setting an intention were as simple as just writing it down on a piece of paper, then we would all be manifesting our heart's desires all the time! Writing down your intentions does help, especially if you can see it every day, as this will help to keep you on track with regards to your mind-set, but it is really just a visual cue to set the intention internally, within your heart, mind and soul. Only when you have achieved this, when you are living and breathing your intention on a daily basis, only then will manifestation of your spell occur, because you are giving the

universe a full picture of what you want it to reflect back at you.

For magic to be effective, your intention must be clear and strong. Self-doubt can slow down your spells or stop them from working altogether. If you cannot imagine yourself juggling the responsibilities of self-employment, then your spells to become a full-time business owner are likely to fall flat, especially if you've never even set up shop, as it were. It is essential that you take steps to live in alignment with your magical goal, even before it has manifested. This is how you teach yourself to believe that it is possible.

Setting an intention is not just a case of daydreaming or wishful thinking. It is the act of committing to a specific goal, of knowing what your motivations are and how you need to change your behaviour in order to accomplish that goal. It is about living proactively and moving closer to your goal on a daily basis, or at least keeping it at the forefront of your mind. It is about knowing why you want something and what you hope to gain from having it. It is about mentally and emotionally stepping into your future, even before that future exists in reality. Most importantly, it is a shift in your mind-set towards greater possibility for yourself, as you begin to live your life in alignment with that goal.

It is your intention that helps to support the magical process and you cannot cast effective spells without it. Think carefully about how you word your intention for each spell you cast and what you need to do to back it up in your day-to-day actions and behaviours.

As you can see, setting your intentions is a ritual in its own right and it can be quite time-consuming until you become used to doing it. Once your spells start to work and you realize that you can co-create your reality with the help of the universe and a little magic, then it will soon become second nature, but to put it in the simplest of terms;

Emotion + Intention
= Magical Manifestation

TIMING

When you perform your magic will have an effect on how well it works. While emergency spells can and should be cast as and when the crisis occurs, for all spells that are planned in advance, you will need to ensure that you are casting them at the right time. All the spells in this book clearly state when they should be cast, but once you begin to create your own spells and rituals, you will need to have a working knowledge of magical timing and how it works.

THE LUNAR CYCLE

Magic is created in accordance with the phases of the moon. This is the most important aspect of magical timing, because the magnetic pull of the moon works with

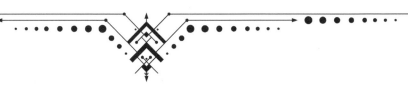

the universal tides to either pull something towards you or take it away. That being the case, your spells to manifest something should be cast during the period from new to full moon, whereas spells that banish something should be cast from full to waning moon. Below is a brief overview of how the different phases of the moon can be used in your magic.

New Moon

This is the beginning of the lunar cycle, although the moon cannot actually be seen in the sky until a few days after the new moon. For this reason, the start of the new moon phase is sometimes known as dark moon and is typically a time of rest. As soon as the first sliver of light appears – a delicate crescent moon that looks like a backwards C shape – it is time to start thinking about what you want the next lunar cycle to bring you. The new moon is a time for sowing seeds of new projects, weighing up the pros and cons of a situation, assessing the need for a change in your patterns etc. Remember that all seeds are sown in darkness, to grow with the light. Now is the time to decide what you want.

Waxing Crescent

The light increases as the crescent moon fills leftwards. This is the time when you set your intention – set your mind on exactly what it is you want. You don't need to know how you will achieve the goal, just set your intention and allow the universe to work out the details for you.

First Quarter Moon

In this phase the moon looks as if it has been cut in half – half of it is illuminated by the sun, the other half remains in darkness. Now is the time to take action on your intentions, so brush up your CV or start applying for jobs if a career change is your goal. Make a positive start on a new project. Get out more and meet new people if you want to draw friends to you. Make a start on your goal, even if only in a small way.

Waxing Gibbous

The moon now appears to be three quarters full, with most of it brightening our night sky. Now is the time to start walking your talk. It's not enough to have a goal, you need to take consistent action and work towards it. The lunar energies won't do the work for you! It is a collaboration and you need to put the effort in too. At this time, the energies are growing stronger and magnetically pulling in your intention, so help it along with positive action.

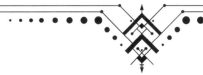

Full Moon

The full moon lights up the night sky and her effect can be felt by everyone, all over the world. This is a time of abundance, of goals coming to fruition and labouring on long-term ambitions. The full moon offers a boost of energy if you are flagging on your aspirations, lending much-needed energy to your goal. The energy of the full moon can be felt for three nights in a row – the night before, the night of, and the night after the moon is full. This is also the most powerful time for all kinds of magic, divination and spell-casting, so don't waste it!

Waning Gibbous

As the moon begins to wane, now is the time to show gratitude for what this lunar cycle has brought you so far. Reflect on what worked and what projects are still in progress. Big ambitions take more than one lunar cycle to manifest, so use this time to assess where you are on the path to achievement and reflect on what your next steps should be. Think about what has worked well for you and what you would like to change or do better at in the next lunar cycle.

Last/Third Quarter Moon

This is the time to start releasing anything that no longer serves you. Let go of old grudges, bad relationships, mistakes made, toxic habits and so on. In this phase, the moon requires you to be honest with yourself, to identify the toxic behaviours and bad habits that might be contributing to a negative situation, so that you can release those too.

Waning Crescent/Balsamic Moon

This phase marks the end of the lunar cycle, when the moon shows up in our skies as the classic fairy-tale C-shaped crescent. It is a time to reflect and move deeper into self-awareness. This is a good time to cast banishing spells as the moon's energy helps to pull things away from you (the word 'balsamic' in its name refers to its restorative nature). Slowly the light will fade out, night by night, until we are back at the dark moon and the cycle begins once more, so it is never too late for a fresh start and each moon cycle offers a new opportunity to begin again.

DAYS OF THE WEEK

Each day of the week is associated with a planet and it therefore has its own energies that you can tap into magically. Although you don't have to wait for a given day to perform a spell, casting on a particular day can give your spells an added boost of power, so if you *can* cast on the right day then do so.

Sunday

Ruled by the Sun, this is a golden day to cast for success, abundance, growth, happiness, joy and greater achievement or acknowledgement of your accomplishments. Sunday is the day to cast spells that are designed to get you noticed for all the right reasons.

Monday

Ruled by the Moon, this is the day for spells of intuition, dreams, ambition, psychic ability, protecting innocents and goal setting. It is a good day to cast glamour spells or enchantments and to create an air of mystery around yourself.

Tuesday

Ruled by Mars, Roman god of war, this is the day to work towards conflict resolution, self-defence, protection and boundary setting. Mars's energy can help you to speak your mind and stand up for yourself and others, but use it cautiously or it could lead to aggressive behaviour. Aim for peace, rather than victory at any cost.

Wednesday

Ruled by Mercury, Roman god of communication, this is the day to cast spells of communication, partnerships, collaborations, creativity, arts and crafts, reunions and reconciliations. This is the best day to send off CVs, apply for jobs or set up interviews and business meetings. If you need help with confidence in your communications, make Mercury your friend.

Thursday

Ruled by the mighty Jupiter and associated with the Norse god Thor, Thursday is a great day to cast for all aspects of financial control, career and business growth, wealth building, decision making and stability. With Thor on side, you can also work magic to protect your interests and defend against any saboteurs who might be trying to move against you – for example, to prevent being gazumped in a house sale. This is a day for practicalities, but also for standing strong, staking and maintaining your claim.

Friday

Ruled by Venus and associated with the Norse goddess Freya, Friday is the day for all matters of the heart, be they romantic or familial. This is the day for spells of love, passion, sexuality, friendships, family bonds, pets and so on. Basically, if it tugs at your heart strings, Friday is the day to work magic for it.

Saturday

Ruled by Saturn, Saturday is the day of banishment and sometimes melancholy. This is the day to cast spells to remove things from your life that no longer serve you, or to come to terms with feelings of depression and low mood. Saturn is also associated with the Roman winter feast of Saturnalia, which was held between December 17th and 23rd, and is the origin of a good Saturday night out, so this is the best day to cast for fun, frolic and adventure.

HOW LONG WILL IT TAKE?

If you are new to magic, you might be wondering how long it will take for your spells to work and manifestation to occur. This all depends on what you are casting for. In general, larger goals and spells take longer to work than smaller ones and repeat casting is usually needed, but that doesn't mean that they're not working. Often there will be signs that your magic is in play, as we mentioned earlier, so be on the watch for these and don't lose heart. If you just want some indication that you have the ability to cast an effective spell, then cast for something small and simple, such as an easy parking space or a free cup of coffee, and see how long that takes to manifest in your life. Such small spells usually work in a day or two and will offer the reassurance you need that your magic is effective.

Medium goals, say for attracting new friends or opportunities, can take a full lunar cycle before you begin to see any signs that they are working, while big life goals, such as starting a family, moving to a new location or changing careers, will take several months before they start to manifest. Just keep the faith and repeat the spells for larger goals. If it is something that is meant for you, it will always find its way to you, and if it's not, then trust that something even better will come along instead.

HOW TO WRITE YOUR OWN SPELLS

As you progress in your craft, you will inevitably want to begin writing your own spells. This is a very positive sign and a key component of your progress on the magical path. While the spells that you find in this book can and do work, and are a great starting point, they will never be as effective as the spells you create for yourself. This is because you are adding your powers of creativity and manifestation to the magic. It makes the spell more personal when it is tailor-made by you. Another advantage is that you can create a spell based on the materials you already own and have in the house, rather than having to go out and buy something.

When you come to write your own spells and rituals, remember that all spells carry the same components, as follows:

- A notion of whether the spell is for manifestation or banishment.
- An acknowledgement of the phases of the moon and days of the week.
- Ethics – does it uphold the Wiccan Rede (see page 246)?
- Use of specific correspondences, herbs, colours, oils etc. tailored to the spell.
- A clear and defined intention.
- A charge of power, often via a spoken incantation.
- A release of the spell.

You will need to know if you are working to bring something towards you or to remove it from your life. This will in turn help you to determine which moon phase you use, bearing in mind that new to full moon is for manifestations and full to dark moon is for banishing.

Check your ethics and make sure that you are not tampering with anyone's free will. Do you have a defined intention? What is the purpose of the spell and the desired outcome? Next, you will need to decide which correspondences you want to use, so what colours, crystals and herbs etc. are going to be part of your spell? How will you charge it? Are you going to leave it on the pentacle, or in the light of the sun or moon to charge, or are you going to write an incantation, or all three? Finally, how do you plan on releasing the spell so that it can work its magic – burn it, bury it, carry it with you?

Once you can answer all these questions, you will have the framework of a well-thought-out spell. This framework might be something you choose to add to your own Book of Shadows for future reference, so that you can write spells with confidence and enjoy your practice.

In the next chapter we will be looking at all the tools you can use and preparations you should make to create effective magic.

CHAPTER FOUR

SPELLBOUND!

Casting a spell is similar to conducting a science experiment. You gather the apparatus required, use your knowledge and instincts to guide you, and then make a note of what worked well and what didn't, what needs tweaking and so on. Then you repeat the process until you get the results you want, or until you learn something new. Like any other scientific experiment, magic involves certain preparations and it has its own tool kit.

No two practitioners will experience exactly the same results, even if they are casting the same spell. This is because magic utilizes your own unique energy and so the way it manifests will be as unique as you are. Don't worry if you get slightly different results to your friend. Your magic will work in the way that is best for you.

ELEMENTS OF MAGIC

Most spells combine your own power with that of nature and the universe, using the four elements of earth, air, fire and water. These elements make up the whole of the natural world around us, so adding them into spellcraft is a very powerful approach and one that witches have used for centuries. If you look carefully at any spell book, including this one, you will see these four elements pop up time and again. This is because our survival depends on them, and each is

essential to us in its own way. Each element also represents a particular kind of magic. In general, a spell will incorporate at least one of these elements in some form or another. The main tools of magic also link back to one or other of the elements.

Earth

The Earth is our mother and the planet on which we reside so we should take steps to care for and protect her. Earth power is green and growing, ever changing and renewing. It is the strength of the trees and forest, the growth of plants, the blooming and blossoming of flowers, the darkness of caves and coves, the majesty of mountains. It is alive with potential. In magic, earth power is represented with herbs, plants, leaves,

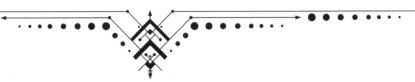

cones, crystals and so on. Earth spells tend to focus on growth, abundance, expansion, transformation and grounding.

Air

Air is vital for our survival: we cannot live without it. Like the wind, the powers of air can be soft and gentle as a summer breeze, or strong and raging as a winter gale. It can be a tricky power to work with, being so changeable. It is seen in the clouds drifting by, or the flight of birds. It can be felt in the soft brush of falling leaves, blossom and feathers. In magic, the power of air is represented with burning incense, smudge bundles, feathers, fans and images of birds or clouds. Air spells tend to be cast for inspiration, creativity, communication, ambition, momentum and the arts. Music is particularly associated with the powers of air, especially wind instruments.

Fire

The fire of the sun keeps our planet habitable and abundant with fruitful growth. Fire power can be felt on a hot summer's day, or in the first rays of sunshine after a long winter. A careful balance must be struck when using fire in spells, because it has the power to destroy and consume everything in its path. In general, fire magic is contained within a heat-proof vessel such as an iron cauldron, to keep it from getting out of hand. We have all felt the pull of this element, for it is very alluring. We feel its power when we gaze into the flame of a candle, or when warming ourselves by the fire on a cold winter's day. In magic, it is naturally represented by burning candles and tea-lights, but it can also be channelled through fiery coloured crystals, combining the powers of earth and fire in one. Fire spells are cast for passion, love and desire, but due to this element's all-consuming nature, fire magic is used in banishing spells too. If you want to be free of something, then a fire spell will usually do the trick.

Water

Water is the most healing of all the elements. You need only spend a day at the coast to feel its power improving your well-being. Water accounts for 71 percent of the Earth's surface and up to 60 percent of the human body, so it is an element that is close to all of us. Again, like the power of air, water can be a gentle stream or a destructive tidal wave, a light shower of rain or a heavy downpour. This element can be temperamental to say the least! Rivers, streams, brooks, burns, lochs, lakes and oceans are all great places to cast water spells. Rain, ice and snow water can also be used, as can your bath and shower at home. In magic, water is represented with a chalice of water or wine, seashells, pebbles, images of fish and marine life. Driftwood and seaweed can also be used, thus combining the elements of water and earth. Water spells are usually cast for matters of emotional balance, healing, dreams, intuition, psychic ability, cleansing and purifying.

TOOLS OF MAGIC

Although spells can be successfully performed with relatively few tools, there are several items that most witches keep handy. You will need to gather a set of these tools, but most can be found around the house and adapted to magical use, so there is no need to spend a lot of money.

Athame

This is a magical knife. It is used to direct energy, or to carve sigils and words into spell candles. Traditionally it should have a black handle and the blade should be dulled to render it harmless. You can use any knife that you find appealing, however, from a basic kitchen knife to a fancy letter opener. The athame is attuned with the element of fire.

Wand

A wand can be used as an alternative to the athame, for directing energy. It can be made of crystal or wood and is attuned with the element of air.

Pentacle

This is a round disc depicting a pentagram or five-pointed star upon it. It is probably the most useful tool of spell-craft, as witches place candles, crystals and so on on the pentacle to charge them up with magical energy. It is attuned with the element of earth. You can make one yourself by drawing a five-pointed star on a plate or disc of modelling clay.

Chalice

Your chalice can be any stemmed drinking vessel of your choice. There are lots of magical chalices available, from pretty silver ones to ornate pewter goblets, but a simple

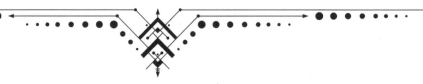

wine glass will also suffice. The chalice is attuned with the element of water and used to hold ritual wine.

Broom/Besom

Yes, witches do use broomsticks! A traditional broom is used in cleansing rituals to sweep away negative energy. They are usually decorated with ribbons, feathers and carvings down the stave, and simple ones can be bought quite inexpensively around Halloween, or from garden centres, which you can decorate in your preferred style.

Cauldron

An iron cauldron is typically used to contain fire. This means that you can safely burn fire spells in it, or place a candle in it as part of a ritual celebration. It can also be used as a divination tool. Like the chalice, it represents the element of water. You can pick up iron cauldrons in antique shops, but for the time being, any fire-proof pan will do.

Cloak and Crown

These are by no means essential and are reminiscent of high ceremonial magic, such as Wicca, but some magical practitioners do like to wear a special robe, gown or cloak when they are in a ritual setting. Crowns were used to denote hierarchy in a coven, but a simple flower or moon crown can be

worn and can help the practitioner to step into a magical frame of mind. Cloaks can be useful when conducting spells and rituals outdoors, especially on cold evenings. It must be stressed, however, that this is down to personal preference and is not a necessary tool of magic.

Consumables

Most of the spells in this book utilize some kind of consumable ingredients, such as herbs, candles, oils, crystals, ribbons and so on. If you are on a budget, this is where you should focus your magical spending, as all the other tools can be found around the home and adapted to magical use, but the basic ingredients of the spells are essential. You will find a list of consumables and their magical correspondences later in this chapter, so you will be able to switch one ingredient for another if you need to.

CREATING A MAGICAL ALTAR

Once you have gathered your tools, you are ready to create an altar in your home and dedicate it to your magical practice. This can be a shelf, windowsill or work surface. If you are keeping your craft private, your altar can be hidden away in a cupboard or bureau. If you are open about your interests in spell-craft, you can choose to have your altar on display.

Traditionally, the altar should be placed in the north or east of a room. While every witches' altar is different and unique, they always represent the four elements, plus divinity, and there are certain standard items that should be placed on it.

You should stand two white candles at either side, towards the back of the altar.

These represent the element of fire.

Between the two candles, place something that represents divinity to you. This could be a statue of a goddess or a god, or both. It could be a picture of a deity in a nice frame, or it could be something more abstract, such as a beautiful crystal or a plant.

An incense holder of some kind is very useful, as you can use it to represent the element of air, and also to burn incense sticks as an offering of thanks and gratitude, even when you don't plan on casting a full ritual. Place the incense holder to the east or right side of the altar.

Water is usually represented by a chalice. This can be any stemmed drinking vessel, placed at the west or left side of the altar. As an alternative, you can use a beautiful seashell or pebble.

Finally, you should add something to represent the element of earth. This could be a plant, crystal, flowers or your pentacle, which belongs front and centre of the altar.

Other items that you might like to use as decoration for your altar include crystals, seashells, feathers, pine cones or a jar of salt for purification. Make it as magical and beautiful as you can, and place your Book of Spells close by. Be aware that your altar will evolve over time, growing as you grow into your magic.

SYMBOLS OF MAGIC

Certain symbols and sigils are seen time and again in magic, each one with its own special meaning. Below is a list of the most common symbols used in magical practice, though this is by no means exhaustive. There might also be symbols that you feel drawn to and which do not feature on this list, but you should feel free to experiment with those too.

Pentagram

This is the magical five-pointed star, not to be confused with the Star of David which has six points. The pentagram is the most common symbol used in magic. It is carved upon the pentacle disc, into candles, written on spell papers and so on. It represents the forces of positive magic, with each point of the star being associated with one of the elements, the top point representing the energy of the universe or the light of spirit and divinity.

Reverse Pentagram

Thanks to horror films, the reverse pentagram has something of a bad reputation, being much maligned in popular culture; non-magical people tend to associate it with negative types of magic. In Wiccan circles, however, the reverse pentagram – two points upwards and one point facing downwards – has nothing to do with negative magic or evil influences. If you look closely at the reverse pentagram, you will see that the shape suggests the horns and beard of the Horned God of Wicca, so it is used to attune with the male aspect of nature and divinity. There is nothing at all sinister about this symbol and it can be used in positive magic or in meditation to reflect on the reverse energies of nature, such as darkness, decay and winter. That said, the pop-culture associations are well known in society, so be mindful of these negative associations and use the reverse pentagram carefully, as it can make people a little nervous.

The Triple Goddess

The sigil of the Triple Goddess is used in magic to connect spells with the divine

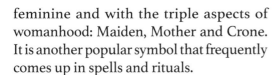

feminine and with the triple aspects of womanhood: Maiden, Mother and Crone. It is another popular symbol that frequently comes up in spells and rituals.

The Triquetra

This is another symbol of trinity and the divine female, yet it can also be used to represent the past, present and future, symbolizing the interwoven thread that links all three together.

Ankh

This Egyptian symbol is often seen in magical circles and has become a popular sigil, used to represent immortality, reincarnation, afterlife and the sacred journey of the undying, eternal spirit.

Eye of Horus

Another Egyptian symbol, this time associated with wisdom, clarity, the spiritual vision of the third eye, psychic ability and the realms of the unseen. It is often used as a protection device, to guard against all harm, both seen and unseen.

Equal-Armed Cross

This sigil symbolizes the meeting of the four directions, the four winds and the four elements. It is also used to represent the four seasonal thresholds of Spring Equinox,

Midsummer, Autumnal Equinox and Midwinter. It is used in magic for grounding and stability. It is associated with polarity and duality.

Celtic Cross

The Celtic Cross embodies all the symbolism of the Equal-Armed Cross, yet it also has the protective powers of the sacred circle, making this a very powerful symbol indeed.

MAGICAL CORRESPONDENCES

Any tool that is used in spell-craft is called a correspondence. There are correspondences for all different types of magic and you will need to know what these are when you come to start writing your own spells. Below is a list of Magical Correspondences for the most popular types of magic, so that if you do not

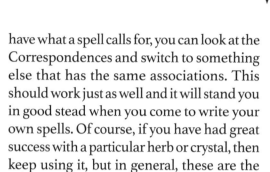

have what a spell calls for, you can look at the Correspondences and switch to something else that has the same associations. This should work just as well and it will stand you in good stead when you come to write your own spells. Of course, if you have had great success with a particular herb or crystal, then keep using it, but in general, these are the Correspondences that work well for these types of magic.

Magical Correspondences for Love

Colours: red, pink, lilac, white
Crystals: carnelian, rose quartz, ruby, diamond, clear quartz, citrine
Herbs: rose, rosemary, peony, lavender, lilac, elderflower, myrtle, ivy
Oils: rose, geranium, ylang ylang, lavender, neroli
Incense: rose, strawberry, ylang ylang, night queen, sandalwood

Magical Correspondences for Prosperity

Colours: green, gold, silver, white
Crystals: aventurine, jade, iron pyrite, clear quartz
Herbs: basil, bay, cinnamon, tea leaves, sage, mint, sunflower
Oils: patchouli, frankincense, sunflower, rape seed
Incense: cinnamon, frankincense, night queen, patchouli, dragon's blood

Magical Correspondences for Protection

Colours: black, grey, dark blue, purple, dark red, white
Crystals: haematite, onyx, amethyst, sodalite, smoky quartz
Herbs: thistle, rosemary, basil, holly, turmeric, garlic, mugwort, foxglove
Oils: tea tree, bergamot, eucalyptus, cedar wood, pine
Incense: pine, sage, night queen, patchouli, dragon's blood, black pepper

Magical Correspondences for Power

Colours: black, purple, red, white
Crystals: haematite, amethyst, clear quartz, smoky quartz, snowy quartz
Herbs: lavender, rosemary, basil, sage, mugwort
Oils: tea tree, patchouli, eucalyptus, pine
Incense: pine, sage, night queen, patchouli, dragon's blood

CREATING A SACRED SPACE

Most practitioners of magic cast their spells in a special space that has been ritually constructed and cleansed. This need not be an elaborate or large space; a small area of a room or a quiet, sheltered spot out of doors are both more than adequate. This space should give you access to the altar, or enable you to set up an altar on the ground

realms of existence. Some practitioners refer to the circle as being on the *Astral Plane*, which again refers to the fact that it is in neither this world nor the next, but somewhere in between.

The purpose of the circle is to contain the energy that you raise as you work magic, so that it doesn't leak away from the spell. In this way the magical energy is only released when the practitioner directs and wills it to be so. The circle also acts as a boundary of protection around you as you work. A magic circle can be cast as a protective device around your home, your car or yourself too, so it is a handy skill to acquire.

if you prefer to work outside. To begin with, smudge the area with incense, by wafting an incense stick or a smudge bundle around the entire sacred space. This acts as a ritual cleansing.

All magic is performed within the protective space of this type of cast circle, which is a visualization exercise. The circle of magic is a realm between the worlds, which means that it hangs in the ether, deep within the womb of sacred creativity, creating a portal which allows the magic of transformation to be birthed. The circle is where all magic begins and the seeds of manifestation are sown. It is often referred to as being *between the worlds*, meaning that it is of both the magical and mundane

Casting a Circle

To cast a circle, you will need your athame, wand or finger. Stand before your altar and walk, or turn if the space is small, in a circle with your wand (or whatever) held out. Move three times in a clockwise direction, visualizing a blue or white light coming from your athame, wand or finger and creating a circle all around you and your altar. As you do so, say:

I conjure this circle of sacred power
Protect my magic this witching hour
In the great void of darkness, I conjure
*   this shield*
In my magical fortress, this circle is sealed

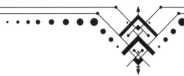

Calling the Quarters

Each quarter of the circle is governed by one of the elements. These elements should also be called, or invoked, before any magic is performed. As spell-craft is all about attuning with nature, we invoke the four elements that make up our world – earth, air, fire and water. To begin the invocations, go to the north of your circle, raise your arms high in invocation and say:

Elemental guardians of the north
Powers of abundance and growth
I invoke your presence and ask you to
  protect this sacred space

Move to the east of the circle and repeat the process, saying,

Elemental guardians of the east
Powers of creativity and communication
I invoke your presence and ask you to
  protect this sacred space

Move to the south of your circle and this time say,

Elemental guardians of the south
Powers of love and passion
I invoke your presence and ask you to
  protect this sacred space

Finally, go to the west of the circle and invoke the final quarter, saying,

Elemental guardians of the west
Powers of intuition and emotion
I invoke your presence and ask you to
  protect this sacred space

Move to the middle of the circle and say,

Welcome, spirits and guardians four
To this world between worlds of magical
  lore

You are now ready to work rituals with your chosen deities, cast the spells of your choice or perform divinations. Once you have completed your magical tasks, you will need to release all the guardians that you have invoked. Do this by going in reverse order, starting in the west, and saying to each quarter,

The spell is cast, the magic is bright
Guardians I release you
In peace, love and light

To Take Down the Circle

Once the magic is complete and the element guardians have been released, you need to take down the magic circle that you have created. This is an indication that your spell has been released into the world so that it can begin to manifest. Taking down the circle is easy. Simply walk three times around your sacred space in an anti-clockwise direction, imagining the light of the circle fading out as you say:

*The wise words of spell-craft have now
   been spoken
This circle is open, but never broken*

You can now go about your normal daily routine, knowing that you have added a touch of magic and enchantment to your life.

EMERGENCY SPELLS

There might be occasions when you simply do not have the time to gather lots of tools or when it isn't convenient to cast a full circle and call in the quarters. In an emergency, magic can still be made and made effectively with very few tools and little ceremony. If, for example, you were at a hospital having been taken ill or injured, you can cast a healing spell using a cup of water, by focusing your intention on the water and visualizing the healing benefits of that element, then drinking the water to activate the spell. This is a simple form of magic that will not use much energy and which can be performed in public, with those around you being none the wiser.

However, most emergency spells are cast in the privacy of your own home. Tea-lights are the best tool for the job. Like all candles, they represent all four elements in a single tool, so they are ideal for emergency spells. Hold one between your palms and focus on the intention and the outcome you are trying to manifest. This could be a simple home repair, a better day at work or time to pay an unexpected bill. Once you can clearly see the goal in your mind, light the tea-light and allow it to work its magic for you. State that you are casting an emergency spell as you light the flame, saying:

*In a fix I find myself, in dire straits of woe
I resolve the issue with this spell and let
   the magic go*

Emergency spells are usually quick to resolve an issue, but don't be afraid to cast them daily if needs be, until a resolution is achieved. In a pinch, or while on the go, you can also use the flame of a lighter to cast such spells. Have faith that you have set magic in motion and that your circumstances will now improve.

SILENT SPELLS

Throughout the following chapters of this book you will find silent spells. While most of my spells incorporate incantations designed to be spoken out loud, not everyone is comfortable with this kind of chanting. For that reason, I have included special spells that do not involve speaking at all. It should also be said that any of the spells

in this book can be turned into silent spells simply by omitting the incantations. It is nice, however, to have some magic that is specifically designed to be worked in silence.

Many spiritual disciplines use silence as a form of worship and communion. It helps to turn the mind inwards, to communicate more readily with our higher selves and with divinity. Silent worship gives space for messages to come through our subconscious, into our conscious mind. These messages might otherwise be lost amid the chatter that we habitually surround ourselves with on a daily basis. Spiritual silence is a way of feeling closer to divinity. It can help to deepen your understanding of yourself and the natural world around you. It can open up the channels of communication between you and your spirit guides.

Maintaining silence isn't always easy, so the silent spells are deliberately short and sweet. Take special note of anything that you are drawn to do during these spells, any inspiration that comes to you amid the silence. If you suddenly feel that you should spend more time meditating or out in nature, then heed these messages. Enjoy the new forms of communication that silent magic can alert you to, whether this be birdsong or the sound of the wind. In this way, silent spells can be a form of prayer and reverence, as well as magical manifestation.

CHAPTER FIVE

CASTING FOR MENTAL HEALTH AND RESILIENCE

One of the most important things you can ever do as a magical practitioner is work on your mental health and robustness. This is because you need a calm and balanced mind in order to cast effective spells. A wise witch is a strong witch, and strong witches do not crumble at the first hurdle or disappointment. They know who they are and what they want from life. They have an awareness of their own faults and they work steadily to try and improve them. They know what they expect from themselves and from others. This is not to say that they are perfect and never have a bad day. Of course they do, but they understand that they have a role to play in resolving any issues that come up.

Mental health is a vital aspect of overall happiness and well-being. Without a certain level of resilience, you might convince yourself that life is out to get you. Life isn't out to get anyone, it is simply a pattern of days, weeks, months and years. While some people do have greater troubles than others, it is how we deal with those troubles that determines whether we are increasing our resilience or falling into a victim mentality.

We have all known people who complain about everything. They find drama in every situation and they are not afraid to be the one who creates it! Some people are living with personality disorders, such as narcissism, that make them behave this way, while others are just looking for an audience to complain to. It is one thing to be *unaware* of one's faults, but another thing entirely to be fully aware of them and yet have no interest in addressing them, because the payoffs are too great.

What do we mean by payoff? Well, we live in a society where people can opt out of most things they find uncomfortable or disagreeable, simply by citing a mental health issue. This is because very little is expected of those who are clinically depressed, or who suffer from high levels of anxiety. They might not have to go to work or school, or they might enjoy the additional attention the illness provides. This can be a hard habit to break. When people have been labelled with a condition, it isn't always easy to shake

off that label and return to a more normal, healthy life pattern of working, living independently and meeting responsibilities. We call this *learned helplessness* and it lies at the root of our so-called 'snowflake' culture within society.

The main problem with such medical labels is that they frequently stick like glue, when they are usually meant to be temporary. This is because mental health fluctuates, in exactly the same way that physical health does. Just because you had the flu last month doesn't mean that you still have it. The illness passes and a state of good health returns. It is the same with mental health. The fact that you were once depressed doesn't mean that you will be depressed for the rest of your life. Mental health does vary, meaning that you will have some bad days and some good days. Even for people with long-term conditions, some days are better than others. This is perfectly normal.

Mental health is about ensuring that you have more good days than bad ones, and that you build up a resilience so that you can cope with the darker days more effectively. It is about restoring a level of balance, both in your moods and in your daily habits. You need to feel productive for your own self-esteem, but you also need time to rest on the bad days when your mental health takes a knock.

Restoring this balance in your mental health can be further enhanced with spell-craft and positive exercises designed to help you move forwards at a steady pace. This isn't about denying the issues you might be facing, or telling you to just get a grip – it is about acknowledging that you have a particular challenge, be it anxiety, depression or low self-esteem, and offering coping strategies to help you deal with it. While a detailed exploration of mental health and self-care is beyond the scope of this chapter, you can learn more about facing these difficult issues from my book *A Wiccan Guide to Self-Care*. Here, however, we will explore magical ways for you to increase your overall resilience and robustness, and to restore the balance of your mind-set for greater mental well-being.

IDENTIFYING POSITIVE VS NEGATIVE THOUGHT SPIRALS

The mind can play cruel tricks on us sometimes, making mountains out of molehills and catastrophizing everything. Frequently this happens without you being fully aware of it, as most people pay little attention to their own self-talk – that is, until that little voice in your head is screaming death threats at you, by which time panic has set in and you've become entirely reactive to an imaginary event!

Thoughts can often spiral out of control if you let them. This is as true for positive though spirals as it is for negative ones. Have you ever sat daydreaming at work about what you would do if you won the lottery? This can take you out of yourself for a while, lifting your spirits from your mundane surroundings at work, helping you to envision a brighter, more affluent future for yourself. While it is harmless in small doses, or in the correct setting, too much daydreaming at work could eventually get you fired, so you need to keep it in check.

In much the same way, a negative spiral can also get out of hand, and with much more damaging effects. When your self-talk tells you how worthless, useless and stupid you are, this leads to low self-esteem and under-confidence, which can lead to mistakes. Over

time, it becomes a self-fulfilling prophecy as you begin to believe that negative voice in your head and your behaviour changes accordingly.

The key to control is to take notice of your self-talk. Check in with yourself on a regular basis, say every couple of hours. What was the last thing that inner voice said to you? Was it positive or negative? Did it make you feel good or insulted? Try to catch your inner voice right at the beginning of any negative self-talk, so that you can stop it from spiralling out of control. Take the negative and turn it into a positive, by visualizing yourself doing the opposite of the negative thought, so if you told yourself that you are stupid, visualize yourself winning academic accolades and achievements or

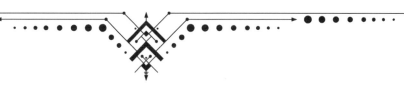

being congratulated on your clever idea and performance. Sometimes you won't notice the negative spiral until you are catastrophizing with every breath. When that happens, cast this spell in the moment to release the negativity.

Dark Crystal Spell to Absorb a Negative Thought Spiral

Items required: a black obsidian or smoky quartz crystal

Timing: perform as needed and in the moment you identify a negative thought spiral

First of all, remove yourself from the situation and find a quiet space. Keep a black crystal with you if you know that you are prone to negative thought spirals. Once in your quiet place, take the crystal and hold it close to your lips. Breathe out all the negative emotions, and visualize the dark crystal absorbing those energies. These darker crystals are very good for absorbing negativity and neutralizing it, so keep breathing your panic into the crystal until a state of calmness is restored. Immediately afterwards, rinse the crystal in cold running water to cleanse away all the negativity and make the crystal ready for next time you need it. As an alternative, if you don't have a black crystal handy, you can breathe the negative panic into a tissue and then flush it away.

Spell to Turn a Negative into a Positive

Items required: a black or white board, chalk or a dry-wipe marker pen, a cloth

Timing: best performed during the dark moon

On the board, write out a word that sums up your main negative self-talk, so you might write worthlessness, friendless or stupid. Write the word in big letters. Sometimes you need to see something written down to fully understand its impact on you. Sit for a moment and look at that word. This is what you are telling yourself every day. Imagine if someone was saying that to someone you love, what would you do? How would you defend that person? What would you say to make them feel better? What words would you use? Come up with a single word which is the opposite of the one currently written on the board. Using the examples given above, you might choose worthy, popular or intelligent. As the final step, rub out the negative word and replace it with the positive one, then set the board where you can see it every day. Each time you catch yourself using negative words to, and about, yourself, replace them with positive ones. You can repeat this spell as a visualization exercise whenever you need to – just imagine the board in your mind and rub out the negative words to replace them with more positive ones.

DEALING WITH ANXIETY

Anxiety is the *result* of a negative thought spiral. It is the emotional response to the mind's catastrophizing. Sometimes anxiety is natural and valid. If you are having a job interview, for instance, it is natural to feel a little apprehensive. The problem occurs when anxiety becomes prolonged or habitual, and shows up uninvited for no good reason.

Anxiety is a part of the survival instinct so it is a very useful cog in the human psyche. We all experience it from time to time. It is what alerts us to a potential threat or warns us to be on our guard and take care. It triggers the fight, flight or freeze response and it is basically designed to keep you alive. This is all very well when

anxiety is only experienced when you are in imminent danger, but when it becomes your day-to-day mind-set, it can be a huge problem, often preventing you from living your life or doing the things that you enjoy.

No one should have to live their life in a state of perpetual panic, but this is what a high level of anxiety does to people. It turns a simple trip to the shops into a high-risk action movie, in which you think you might need to fight for your life at any given moment! Obviously this is not a realistic assessment of the threat, so to deal with it you need to learn how to reassess your situation and talk yourself down from the ledge. To do this you must examine the situation more carefully, by answering the following questions:

- Where are you?
- Are you in any danger right now?
- Who is with you?
- Are you in a public place?
- Has anyone threatened you?
- Do you have your phone handy and can you call someone you trust?
- Where is the exit? Can you reach it safely?
- Do you have a safe mode of transport home?
- Is the threat real or is it the perceived result of high anxiety?

Once you have answered these questions you should have a more realistic picture of your current situation. Often high anxiety tricks people into believing that they are in danger when in fact there is no threat. Understanding this can help you to calm down and make the decision whether to continue with your daily activities or go home. As you go through this mental assessment repeatedly, in different situations, you will begin to take control of the anxiety, rather than letting it control you. You will also be retraining it to only show up when there is an actual threat to your safety.

Also, just because something feels *uncomfortable* doesn't mean that it is a threat, or that you should not do it. Giving a presentation as part of a university degree is quite an uncomfortable experience for most people, but it is in no way a threat to life and it should be experienced because it improves confidence and self-esteem. The fact that something routine gives you anxiety doesn't mean that you should not participate in that event. Simply assess the situation with a more realistic viewpoint and identify the actual threat levels.

A Restorative Lavender Bath Potion

Items required: a voile pouch, muslin cloth or hanky, two teaspoons of dried lavender, one teaspoon of dried camomile flowers, a lavender ribbon, lavender essential oil

Timing: use this spell whenever you are feeling particularly stressed, but it works all the better at a full moon

Stress is a part of daily life and one that we must take steps to minimize and counteract. However, when you are feeling particularly stressed, you probably won't have the energy to work a full ritual. That's where bath potions come in. They can be made up in advance and kept in an airtight jar, ready for use when you need them most. For this restorative bath potion, you will need two parts dried lavender, mixed with one part dried camomile flowers. Both these herbs are well known for their healing and restful properties. If there is a more restful way to de-stress than soaking in a fragrant lavender bath, I haven't found it yet! This is one of my staple remedies.

First make the bathroom enticing. Light candles if you want to and run a hot bath. Place the dried herbs into the pouch, or in the middle of the hanky and tie it tightly using the ribbon. As the bath fills, swirl the pouch of herbs in the water in a clockwise direction, scenting the hot water with fragrance. Imagine that once you sink into the water, all your cares will float away on lavender clouds. Tie the pouch to the tap so that it hangs in the water. As a final step, add ten drops of lavender essential oil to the water just before you sink into the depths. Relax and breathe in the fragrance. Allow the herbal scent to calm you and let go of any stressful thoughts. Remain in the water for as long as you can, making the most of the restful energies of the herbs. When you are ready, dry off and empty the wet herbs into the earth, giving back what you have taken. Enjoy the remainder of your day and do calming, gentle activities to maintain your sense of peace. You can also use this pouch in a shower, hanging it by the shower head and letting the steam release the scents.

DEALING WITH DEPRESSION

Depression is a deep sense of sorrow, usually accompanied by low self-worth. In extreme cases it can be triggered by a chemical imbalance in the brain, which you will need to consult a doctor about to seek treatment. However, most people will experience milder forms of depression at some point during their lifetime and, although it is not necessarily a bad thing, it is difficult to endure.

While prolonged clinical depression of the kind that requires medical intervention can be very debilitating, milder cases are usually a natural response to some kind of trauma or upheaval. If you can pinpoint the event that triggered the depression, such as a job loss, relationship breakdown or bereavement, then it is quite normal to feel depressed at such times. In fact, it is a fairly healthy response. This is because you need time to process what just happened and how your future has altered considerably. When life knocks you down with an unwelcome event such as a divorce, you're not meant to be happy about it or carry on as normal! You're meant to feel sad, to sit still for a time and process the turn of events, to absorb the shock of it, before you can begin to start moving forward. Depression allows this – it is like a mental and emotional time out and it is always rooted in a deep sadness.

That said, if it goes on for too long, or if there is no viable reason for it, it can become a problem. Depression can also become a habit and it is one the hardest medical labels to shake off. That might sound harsh, but the habits of depression – not going out, not exercising, eating too much, sleeping too much, self-medicating and so on – can all become learned behaviour patterns which in turn help to prolong the depression, so it becomes a very vicious cycle.

If anxiety is about fear of an imagined catastrophic future, then depression is about living in the past. It is an unhealthy nostalgia, a yearning for a time that has already passed and which you need to leave behind and let go of. This is easier said than done, of course, but for the most part, once you have absorbed the shock of the triggering event,

it is time to work through your feelings and let go of the past, though this takes time.

In some cases, depression comes about long after the event itself, and it is generally an indication that some trauma of the past is still unresolved. This means that you could be experiencing depression in adulthood due to something that happened when you were a child, when you didn't have the maturity or the emotional intelligence to be able to process it at the time. If this is the case, counselling might be helpful. In almost all cases of depression, it is worth going to see your doctor. There are also things that you can do yourself to help alleviate the symptoms of depression:

- Take the dog for a walk! Depression is often referred to as the Black Dog, so take it for a walk, get lots of fresh air and see if you feel marginally better afterwards. Make this a new daily habit.
- Enjoy a restorative bath or shower using the lavender potion above.
- Talk to someone, be it a friend, relative, doctor, therapist or all of the above.
- Allow your feelings to come out, don't bottle them up.
- Make plans for your future, even if it's just coffee with a friend next week.
- Start a new self-care ritual, such as playing an album of lovely music every

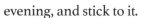

evening, and stick to it.

- Seek out things that make you laugh. Laughter really is medicine.
- Improve your diet.
- Join an exercise class or walking group, or take up a new hobby.
- Track your good and bad days in a diary, noticing any patterns.
- Give yourself a pat on the back for getting through a tough day.
- Give yourself small rewards – a favourite film, a new shower gel etc.
- Know that life is hard for everyone at times, so you're not alone.
- There are people who want to help, but you have to speak up to find them.

A Fire Spell to Alleviate Depression

Items required: a notepad, a pen, a lighter, a cauldron or heat proof bowl
Timing: during the waning moon

For this spell you will need some time in solitude. Have your phone handy, so you can call someone if you need to, but mute it so you are not disturbed. Take a moment and think about the depression you might be experiencing and try to identify the main event that triggered it. Write down an account of that event, how it makes you feel, what emotions come up for you when you remember it. Note down how

the feelings of depression and low mood are impacting on your life and self-image. Write it all out, whatever comes up. Get it all out on paper, where you can see it. This is all the stuff that you have been carrying around in your head and your heart. Release it onto the page. When you are done, read it through. Now roll up the paper, light it and allow it to burn in the cauldron. As you do so, say:

My past no longer binds me tight
From my woes I'm free
I let it go to set things right
As I will it so shall it be

Once the paper has burnt and cooled, throw the ashes out into the wind and let it all go.

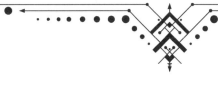

potted plant. It just needs to be someone or something that relies on you and depends on you. Something to look forward to is probably the easiest one to master as we can all plan a night out, a theatre trip or a holiday. Gratitude for all that you have and all that you enjoy should be a daily habit, because once you begin to notice these smaller moments of joy, that is when your happiness will grow and you will feel truly blessed. So take a moment right now and see if you can tick off all four criteria for happiness in *your* life.

THE TRICK TO HAPPINESS

Happiness is brought about through four things – something to do, someone to love, something to look forward to and gratitude for all of the above. It sounds like a very simple recipe, so shouldn't we all be happy every day? Too often, people tend to focus on the negatives instead, latching on to their disappointments when they should be making plans for new achievements and events.

Having something to do isn't only about a career or job, it can be a hobby, volunteering, caring for someone, an event to plan or anything else that gives you a sense of purpose. Someone to love could be a pet, an elderly neighbour, a tank of fish or even a

BUILDING RESILIENCE

If good mental health is all about robustness, how do you go about building up your resilience? Life is a fantastic teacher and

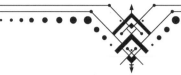

the lessons you most need to learn will just come to you. In Wiccan circles we believe that people are never given more than they can handle, but you might be stretched almost to breaking point. Crime, poverty, food insecurity, job losses, bereavements, illness and so on are all lessons and opportunities for you to increase your resilience. What doesn't kill you really does make you stronger, and you tend to find that those individuals who have never had any troubles and have been cosseted since birth are the ones who crack most easily when the pressure is on. The school of hard knocks is the most effective way of developing mental robustness and emotional intelligence. It's not easy, but after a few classes, you come to learn that there isn't much you *can't* cope with if you have to. Difficult times are when you are being smelted in the fire and made stronger. Try to lean into them and see how resilient you can become. In the meantime, cast this spell for greater strength and courage.

A Spell for Inner Strength

Items required: a thistle, a cord or ribbon on which to hang it, a thistle pendant
Timing: on the waxing moon

The thistle is the flower of Scotland and its motto is *None shall irritate me unscathed,*

meaning that it will inflict the swift retribution of its prickles to anyone who dares tamper with it! This is a good metaphor for developing inner strength and courage. No one can cause you lasting harm if you face them with courage and move forward in your life with resilience. On the night of the waxing moon, take a thistle flower and hold it to your heart. Bow your head in reverence and say:

> *I choose to live by the law of the thistle*
> *I make this promise by night*
> *To face each foe without fear*
> *To let my courage take flight*
> *From hardship and want I'll not waver*
> *From conflict I will not flinch*
> *As I wear my thistle favour*
> *My strength grows inch by inch*
> *So mote it be*

To complete the spell, tie the ribbon around the thistle and hang it upside down to dry, somewhere close to your altar, or your bed, if possible. Put on the thistle necklace and wear it as a talisman of inner strength.

A Silent Spell for Resilience

Items required: a small square of paper, a few pine needles or a small clipping from a fir tree or evergreen plant, sealing wax

Timing: best performed on the new moon
Gather the items together and sit for a while contemplating how it feels to be resilient. When troubles come, you can cope with them; when conflict appears, you can emerge victorious; when facing a challenge, you know that you are capable. Picture all of this in your mind and envision yourself as a strong, resilient, capable individual. Now place the pine needles or the evergreen in the centre of the paper. Evergreens can weather most storms – they bend in the wind rather than breaking, they show their true colours in the darkest time of winter – so they are a good representation of the kind of reliance you are casting for. Once the evergreens are in place, fold each of the corners of the paper inwards, covering the greenery and forming a small parcel. Seal the corners together by dripping sealing wax where they meet. This is your charm for resilience. Let it sit in the light of the moon for a full lunar cycle, then keep it close to you whenever you are going through a challenging time.

CHAPTER SIX

· · · ◦ ○ ◎ ○ ◦ · · ·

CASTING FOR DREAMS, GOALS AND AMBITIONS

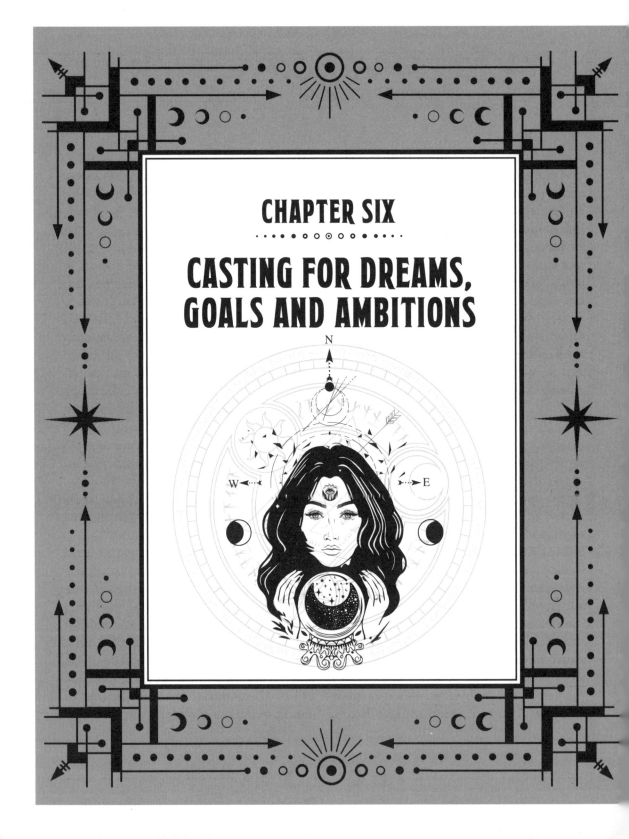

Having dreams, goals and ambitions is an important aspect of keeping your life moving forwards. Without a goal to aim for, life can become monotonous, routine and stagnant. As humans, we require a sense of growth and expansion to be happy and fulfilled. One of the leading causes of depression is not having enough to do. People who find themselves unemployed or under-employed often complain of having no sense of purpose, no reason to get up in the morning, so having something to work towards is essential for mental well-being. This is true for all of us. While downtime is needed to recharge, too much of it can be detrimental to your long-term success. As with anything else, striking a balance is the key.

Goal setting is an intrinsic part of spell-craft, but it should also be considered an intrinsic part of life. You need to know where you are heading and what you want from life before you can start casting for it. This goes back to the intention-setting techniques we looked at earlier. Without a clear direction, you will be buffeted around by the whims of others, and you might find yourself growing resentful when those around you achieve their dreams but you don't seem to be getting anywhere. This chapter will help you to determine what it is that you want from life and offer magical steps towards achieving it.

AMBITION IS A GOOD THING

Some people are naturally very ambitious. They show signs of high achievement from a very young age, doing well in school and activities, turning hobbies into income streams and generally getting on with things and steaming ahead. For other people, ambition has to be developed and worked up like a muscle. They might believe that dreams are a waste of time because good things never happen to them, or that people who are successful have just been very lucky. While a certain amount of luck does play a part in any success story, there is a science behind ambition which shows that those who set a goal are more likely to be successful than those who don't. It is also true that one success tends to lead on to the next, meaning that once you have achieved one goal, you are more likely to set and achieve other goals as well, leading to a snowball effect of achievement.

Ambition is very good for your mental health, providing it is realistic and within the realms of possibility. Not everyone can become an international pop star or an A-list actor, but most people can use their talents and interests to enhance their lives and maybe provide additional income. Some ambitions have nothing to do with money and are more about a personal sense of achievement. Sporting ambitions, such as running a marathon or climbing a mountain, would fall into this category. You can have ambitions for your career, relationships, fitness, health, self-image, creativity and many other things.

Ambition is also good for your self-esteem, because it often leads to achievement. Achievement gives your confidence a boost and proves that you are capable of realizing your goals, which in turn gives you the confidence to set more goals and work towards those too. This becomes a positive cycle of ambition, achievement, confidence, which leads you to create bigger and bigger goals, thereby creating a life you love.

So how do you know if you have ambition? One good indicator is how you respond to the success of others. Do you see their achievement as something *you* could do too if you put in the same amount of time and hard work, or do you view it as a threat and feel resentful towards them? If you feel inspired to take action on your own goals, then you probably have a natural sense of ambition and view your life through the lens of possibility. If you feel a touch resentful or envious, however, that could be a sign that you need to activate your own sense of personal ambition, so that you too can begin to realize your dreams. Cast the spell below to help you with this.

Spell to Light the Spark of Ambition

Items required: a gold or silver candle and suitable holder, your athame or carving tool, sunflower oil, a little saffron (optional)
Timing: cast at noon, during the time of the full moon for greatest power of sun and moon energy

Take the items to your altar and think about what it means to be ambitious. How would you feel if you believed that you could achieve anything; if you felt that you could have, be and do anything, if only you worked hard enough? What would your life look like, what would your future look like? Imagine how much confidence you would have. Try to dream up these feelings as you hold the candle in your hands.

Visualize yourself living out your dreams and achieving your goals. When you are ready, carve the word *Ambition* into the length of the candle, then anoint it by rubbing the sunflower oil all over it, imbuing the candle with the sun's energies. If you are using saffron, sprinkle a little onto some kitchen towel and roll the anointed candle through the saffron so that it sticks to the oil, pulling the candle towards you as you do so. You only need a small amount of saffron because it is very powerful. Place the candle into the holder and light the wick as you chant these words nine times:

Ambition burns bright in me
The light of success shines down upon me
The sunlight empowers me
The moonlight guides me
Opportunity finds me
Achievement delights me
By earth, moon and sun
This magic is done

Leave the candle in place to burn down naturally, which can take several hours, so make sure you cast this spell when you will be at home to watch over the flame.

if you never attend auditions! Remember that manifesting anything is a collaboration and you must play your part. Decide what you want most and start to work towards that goal. A smaller goal is usually achieved more easily, so start with something simple to increase your confidence and then work up to the bigger goals. Once you have a clear idea of your main goals, use that information to create a vision board.

WHAT DO YOU REALLY, REALLY WANT?

Half the fun of having ambition lies in deciding exactly what you want. This is where you get to dream up a variety of possibilities and see which one calls to you the loudest. If you could make your living in a fun way, what would you be doing? If you could live anywhere, with any lifestyle, what would that be? If you could meet one of your idols, who would you choose?

Spending time visualizing is all part of the creative, magical process. You have to be able to envision something before you can bring it into being or start living intentionally towards that goal. There is no point dreaming of being a professional dancer

Create a Magical Vision Board

Items required: a large piece of poster board, images that represent your ambitions, a glue stick, patchouli oil, a marker pen
Timing: create your board at the time of the new moon, to bring all good things towards you

Making a vision board is a traditional way to set your intention and have your goals in front of you on a daily basis. While you can make digital versions on a computer, you will need to anoint your board with oil, so the old-fashioned poster-board variety is necessary for this spell. Find images that represent the things you are working towards – this could be pictures of people working from home, travelling, enjoying a romantic dinner, getting married and so on. Gather a collection of images, so that all the main aspects of your life are represented. Alternatively, you can create a vision board that focuses on a single ambition or goal.

Using the marker pen, draw a pentagram on the back of the board. This will help to protect your dreams from negative energies and toxic influences. Take the patchouli oil, which represents success and abundance, and dab a little onto the four corners of the vision board. Next, glue all the images in place on the board and put it where you will see it every day. This board should act as a reminder to you, inspiring you to keep your dreams in mind and work towards them every day. As you achieve the goals on the board, use a red, silver or gold pen to tick them off. This will give you a boost, as you see that you are moving closer to your dreams, one step at a time. Once the board is full of ticks and you have checked off all the images, make a new board designed around your new goals.

NOTHING BUT A DRIFTER

Achieving your goals and living your dream requires daily action, dedication and determination. Of course, we can't plan for every event and sometimes life just happens to get in the way of our goals, but having no plan at all is a recipe for an unfulfilling existence. The worst thing you can do is allow yourself to drift through life without much of a plan, yet many people do just that. Why? Well, because it's the easy option.

Achievement takes a lot of effort. It's hard to commit to a three- or four-year academic degree and see it through to the point of graduation. It's hard to come home from a long day at work and then start working on a side hustle in the evenings. Some people simply don't want to give up their evenings and weekends to do yet more work, studying or training. They want to come home from a job that pays the bills and then call it a day. If that is what makes them happy, it's okay.

But if you want more from your life than a job or a lifestyle you don't particularly enjoy, then drifting is a form of self-sabotage. It is when you get in your own way, nurturing habits of laziness and apathy, making excuses for why you *can't* do something, when you should be making plans for why you *can* and taking action instead. There is no point in complaining that you can never get an opportunity if you are not actively seeking and applying for those opportunities. Setting a few goals is the first step to moving your life forwards.

A Silent Spell to Stop Drifting
Items required: a dried leaf
Timing: during a waning moon

This simple spell will help you to stop being buffeted by life and become more proactive. Find a fallen leaf and allow it to dry out. Imagine how it fell from the tree, blown here and there, at the mercy of the winds. This is how life can feel to someone who is drifting along, pushed in all directions by circumstances and buffeted by the will of other people. It is time to take back control! Once the leaf has dried out, hold it to your heart and allow your sense of powerlessness and apathy to sink into the leaf. Let go of fear of the future and know that you can direct your life in a positive way if you choose to do so. Be brave and see yourself making plans and following them through. Imagine how it feels to be in control of your life and to turn your dreams into reality. Forgive yourself for any laziness in your past and make a promise to be more proactive from now on. Kiss the leaf, then bury it in the earth, to ground it, so that it drifts no more.

Seven-Step Spell for Goal Manifestation
Items required: seven slips of paper, a special tea-light holder you love, tea-lights, a pen
Timing: at the time of the full moon

This is an ongoing spell that takes time to complete so you will need to include it in your day-to-day routine. It works best for bigger goals, such as changing careers, moving house, starting a family and so on. Gather the items needed and begin by visualizing the goal as if you were already living it. Enjoy this part of the process and indulge in a little daydreaming. What does your goal feel like to you? How does it make you act, dress, behave? Once you can see the goal clearly, break it down into seven manageable steps to get you there. These steps can be simple or complex. The first could be doing research into your topic, such as looking into homes for sale, followed by seeing a mortgage lender, viewing a house and so on. Once you have seven clear steps of varying complexity, write one step on each of the slips of paper. You now have seven pieces of paper which spell out what you need to do to achieve your goal. Take the first piece of paper and read the first step out loud. This is an instruction to yourself, a command to make the first move and to get the ball rolling.

Light a tea-light in the holder each evening and place all the spell papers close by. Each day, follow the command of the relevant step until you have achieved that aspect of the goal, then burn it in the flame of the tea-light. In burning the spell paper, you are indicating that you cannot go backwards, but can only move forwards towards your goal.

This spell is designed to keep you focused on your goal each day and to encourage you to live intentionally by having you achieve smaller steps towards a larger goal on a regular basis. Daily action is how manifestation occurs, because you are encouraging the universe to reflect your desire back at you as your future reality. Don't be afraid to dream big!

LUCKY, LUCKY, LUCKY

There is more to a successful ambition than just hard work and goal setting. At some stage, luck and good fortune will also play a part, putting you in the right place at the right time. There is also much to be said for knowing the right people and moving in the right circles, although not everyone has such connections. So how can you get ahead when you are still on the outside looking in, when your goal still seems like more of a pipe-dream? Here are a few mundane tips that you can use to start turning luck in your favour:

- **Be nice to the gatekeepers.** In all your dealings with your chosen industry or ambition, be nice to receptionists, personal assistants, secretaries and so on. They are the gatekeepers to the world you wish to join and they are the ones who can ensure your correspondence reaches the right people, so be nice. They can open doors you didn't even know existed!
- **Use a charm offensive.** Aim to be pleasant and personable in all your interactions, and your name is more likely to be remembered for all the right reasons when new opportunities are up for grabs.
- **Don't just offer your services.** You need to offer something concrete, rather than just the gift of your services, as this can come across as being condescending. Offer a business plan, a submission, a proposal, a demonstration – something that proves you have put some thought into how you can be an asset.

Think of all this as laying the groundwork. In any given day, you never know who you might meet and it only takes one person to like you for doors to start swinging wide open in welcome. That said, Lady Luck tends to bestow her gifts where she is most at home, so you need to believe that you are a lucky person and that fortune favours you, guarding you from making too many missteps.

Hard work will only get you so far. Luck alone can bring a fleeting success that burns bright in the moment, but soon burns out. However, hard work and good fortune working in tandem together is how lasting success is brought to pass. Give Lady Luck a warm welcome by casting the following spell.

A Spell for Good Fortune

Items required: an ace of diamonds playing card, frankincense oil, a pen
Timing: during a waxing moon

Playing cards have long been used in spell-casting, so it is always a good idea to have an extra pack around the house that you can use solely for this purpose. This spell calls for the ace of diamonds. Take the card and write your full name and date of birth on the front of the card. Dab it with a touch of frankincense oil on all four corners. Put

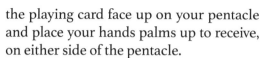

the playing card face up on your pentacle and place your hands palms up to receive, on either side of the pentacle.

Sit for a time and imagine lots of luck coming to you. Visualize meeting the right people, receiving invitations, having the right opportunities extended to you. Imagine winning streaks, lucky breaks, windfalls and blessings, all coming to you now. When you feel ready, chant the following words three times:

Lady Luck shines bright on me
All my dreams come true
In love and light there comes to me
Diamonds forged anew
Fate will open doors for me
This charm now paves the way
Opportunities now come to me
My luck is strong by night and day

How to Make Fortuna Oil

Items required: a 50ml (1¾fl oz) bottle and stopper, 40ml (1¼fl oz) sweet almond oil, frankincense, patchouli and citronella essential oils, three small threads of saffron, a small lodestone crystal (tiny enough to fit in the bottle), a Night Queen incense stick
Timing: prepare this oil at the time of the full moon

In Greek mythology, Fortuna was the goddess of luck and fortune. She was said to wear a blindfold which made her impartial to whoever received the luck she doled out. This magical oil can be used to anoint spell candles, cards, crystals and charms. You can also use a small amount of it as a bath oil.

On the night of the full moon, first cleanse the bottle by lighting the stick of incense and putting the smouldering tip into the jar. Let the vessel fill with cleansing smoke, then set the incense stick to one side to burn safely as you work. Next drop the lodestone, which is a natural magnet, into the bottle to attract great opportunities to you. Add the saffron threads to bring good fortune

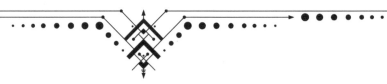

your way. Pour in the sweet almond oil, then add five drops each of the following essential oils: frankincense, patchouli and citronella. Put the stopper in the bottle to seal it. Then hold it in your hands and empower it to its purpose with the following incantation.

Lady Fortuna, goddess of old
Through lodestone and saffron more
* precious than gold*
Through citron, patchouli and incense
* of kings*
Your gift of good fortune this oil now
* brings*
Lady Fortuna, smile on me this night
That I may bring my ambitions forth
* into the light*
So mote it be

Silent Spell to Bottle Your Dreams

Items required: a small spell jar 2.5–5cm (1–2 inches) tall with a stopper, a tiny slip of paper, a pen, silver thread, a silver candle or sealing wax, dried basil, cinnamon and sage, a clipping of your hair, a Night Queen incense stick to cleanse
Timing: on the new moon

To being with, cleanse the jar using the stick of incense following the instructions above. Think of a single key word that sums up your main goal or dream. Write this on the slip of paper, then roll the paper into a small scroll and secure it with the silver thread. Drop it into the jar, add the hair clipping, then use equal amounts of the three dried herbs to fill the jar. Fix the spell in place with the stopper and seal it by dripping hot wax all around the neck and stopper of the jar. Keep the jar in a special place. Once your dream has manifested, break the seal and tip the contents of the jar into the earth and bury them, giving thanks for your good fortune. Wash the jar, cleaning off all the old wax, so that you can use it again for future containment spells. Remember to cleanse it with incense before you use it again.

The spells in this chapter can be used alone or in conjunction with other spells in this book. By layering up spell-craft in this way, you have a greater chance of success. When building a ritual, choose one of these generic spells for ambition and goal setting, along with a spell from the relevant chapter, say a love spell, to bring about the manifestation of your desire. Happy casting!

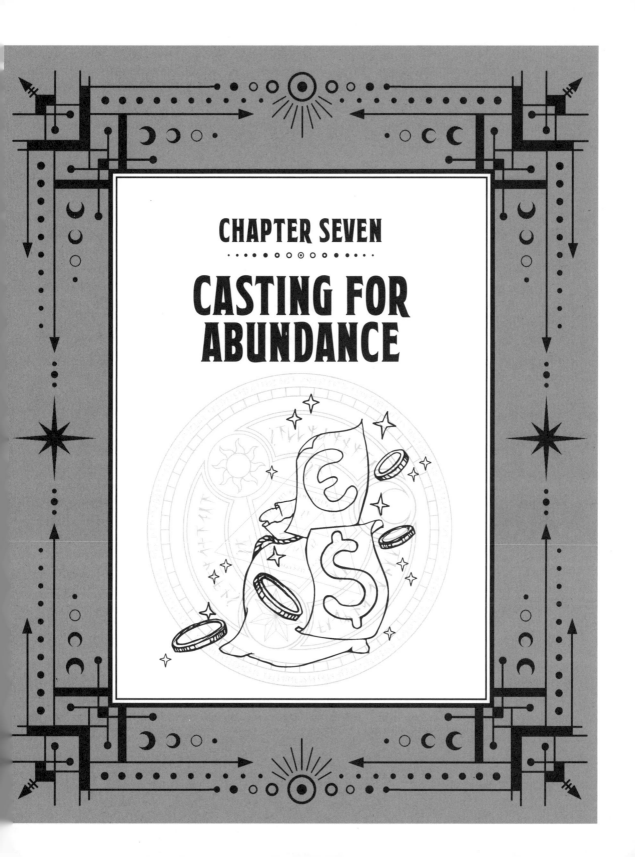

CHAPTER SEVEN

CASTING FOR ABUNDANCE

Money is an issue for many people. Too much of it can be overwhelming, while too little can lead to destitution. There are very few people who are entirely comfortable with the amount of money they have; most people have some degree of money stress to contend with. While money should never be thought of as the root of all evil, it can be troublesome at times. In this chapter we will explore how you can use magic to become more abundant and prosperous, so that your money worries are few and fleeting.

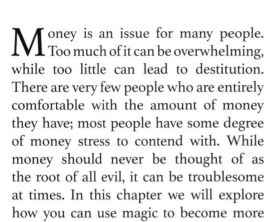

WHAT IS ABUNDANCE?

Abundance is a state of plenty. It is about knowing that you have enough for the needs of you and your family. It is the natural state of the world around us, as we watch the seasons change and the earth producing flowers, fruit and crops in great swathes. Although some years are leaner than others, in general Mother Nature provides for the needs of all her dependents and that includes us.

Living in a state of abundance means that you can pay all your bills with relative ease, you have food in the cupboards and some savings to fall back on should an unexpected expense arise, such as a car repair or the breakdown of a large appliance. Abundance offers peace of mind. When there is plenty of money in the bank, you don't need to worry too much about the state of the economy, because your own micro-economy is in good health and you have more than you need.

Charles Dickens referred to this little bit extra as 'a margin of happiness' and that is an excellent way to describe abundance. When you have more than you need, you feel calm and happy. When you have less than you need, you feel fraught and fearful. Developing your own margin of happiness is the key to personal abundance. Prosperity is always a very personal journey. The sum of money that makes one person feel wealthy might make someone else feel poor. Much of it is down to your own comfort levels around money. If you have been scratching to make ends meet, suddenly having savings of £500 (about US $660) might make you feel positively rich, while for someone who regularly spends thousands of pounds on luxury goods, being down to just £500 might make them feel destitute, so what makes you feel abundant is entirely subjective.

CASTING FOR MONEY AND PROSPERITY

It is an acceptable practice to cast spells for money, but there are a few things to bear in mind. First of all, you should cast money spells based on need, not greed, because the sense of urgency to get your needs met will make the spell more powerful. Casting to win a lottery jackpot with the vague notion that you would like to be rich is unlikely to succeed, because there is no genuine emotional need driving the spell. So cast for just a little bit more than you actually need for your margin of happiness.

Money spells can manifest in a myriad of ways – more overtime at work, a pay rise, a tax rebate, a windfall. It won't usually be 'free money' that comes to you out of the blue, but it will be money that you have either worked for or overpaid. That said, sometimes a windfall will come to you after a prosperity spell has been cast and this always feels very magical, but it is more usual that you will need to participate in acquiring additional cash, even with magic on your side.

As money can sometimes come through negative routes such as insurance pay-outs and compensation, it is always wise to add a simple caveat to all your money spells to ensure that any money coming your way comes through positive means and with harm to none. So at the end of every spell for abundance you should say:

I cast this spell with harm to none
For the good of all, so it be done

This will ensure that all your prosperity spells work in a nice, gentle manner and via a positive means of manifestation.

HOW MUCH DO YOU NEED?

It is surprising how many people don't actually know how much money they need to live on each month, or how much they spend on non-essentials. This is vital information and it is the first thing you need to determine before you begin casting money spells. There is no point in casting for more money if you have no clue where your current income is going. If money runs through your fingers like water, then you need to find out where it's going! Are you really not making enough to live on, or are you simply overspending?

So the first step is to work out exactly how much money you need to pay all your bills, keep the car running and buy groceries for the month. Add all these expenses together to come up with a single figure. This is your baseline, your survival money.

If your income is below this threshold, you are not making enough money. If it is above, but only just, you are still in a precarious position. If you have quite a bit more than your baseline but you struggle financially nonetheless, you are probably overspending and you need to work out where your frivolous spending zones are. It could be a habit of online shopping, or a tendency to eat out too often. Find the money drain and put a plug in it!

Once you have your baseline figure, you can work out how much you want to start saving for your margin of happiness, or towards a specific event such as a wedding, Christmas funds or a nice holiday. This in turn will determine how much extra money you need to bring in each month, which is the figure you should base your spell-casting around. Alternatively, you can cast for a sum of money to cover the cost of a large purchase such as a new appliance.

Spell to Make a General Prosperity Pouch

Items required: a green pouch, three silver coins, a lodestone crystal, half a cinnamon stick

Timing: on the new moon

This spell works to keep prosperity flowing towards you at all times. Place the items on your pentacle to charge overnight as the new moon first appears. The next day, hold the coins and the crystal in your hands and say:

Coins of silver shining bright
Bring forth to me by new moon light
The gift of great prosperity
This lodestone draws it here to me
In peace and plenty I will thrive
My increased wealth now comes alive!

Place the coins and crystal in the pouch, then using the cinnamon stick, trace a pound or dollar sign on the pouch and put the cinnamon stick inside to draw money to you. Keep this prosperity pouch near you as you sleep, to keep money flowing to you.

A Silent Tea of Plenty Spell to Ease Money Worries

Items required: a cup of peppermint tea
Timing: use this spell whenever you feel anxious about money

Peppermint is the herb of plenty, strongly associated with abundance and prosperity. Make a cup of peppermint tea in your favourite teacup or mug. Find a quiet place and sit with the tea. Breathe in the scent of mint and try to calm your money worries. Think back to times when you were just as worried about making ends meet as you are now, but you made it through. Know that you will find a way to get through any lean times you might experience and trust that something will always turn up to help you. Imagine paying all your bills easily and having plenty of food to eat. Feel an emotion of plenty filling you as you sip the peppermint tea and take its gifts of prosperity into yourself. You and the mint are one, it fills you with abundance and hope. It warms you through with its comforting heat, it refreshes you for the time ahead. When you are finished with the tea, scatter the mint leaves in a garden or potted plant and give it back to the earth, with thanks.

to you from all directions. Sprinkle a small amount of dried mint on a sheet of paper kitchen towel and roll the candle through the herb, pulling it towards you as you do so. Maintain your visualization throughout this process. Finally, place the candle in the holder, light the wick and say the incantation below, then allow the candle to burn out naturally.

Blessings of wealth come hither from there
I call forth abundance to fly through the
*   air*
Circle about and surround me with glee
The sum I require now comes to me!

A Prosperity Bath

Items required: a green pouch or hanky, dried mint, a cinnamon stick, a piece of ginger root, a few coins, a green ribbon
Timing: use this bathing spell on the night of the full moon

Spell for a Specific Sum of Money

Items required: a green candle and holder, athame or carving tool, patchouli oil, dried mint, paper kitchen towel
Timing: during new to full moon

If there is something you need a specific sum of money for, say a holiday or a special purchase, then cast this spell as the moon waxes from new to full. Visualize what you want the money for and see yourself enjoying that event or item. Take a green candle and carve into the wax the amount of money you require. Anoint the candle in patchouli oil, by rubbing the oil from the top to the middle of the candle, then from the bottom to the middle. This will help to bring the money

Place the coins in the pouch or the middle of the hanky. Add a teaspoon of dried mint, the cinnamon stick and ginger root. These are all associated with prosperity and abundance. Tie the pouch or hanky into a bundle and hang it from the hot tap as you draw a bath, letting the water run over the pouch and release the scents. You can also leave the pouch in the water to infuse if you want to. Enjoy a relaxing bath, soaking in the waters of prosperity. This will cloak you in the energies of abundance and as like attracts like, you will draw more prosperity to you like a magnet. To keep money flowing towards you, perform this bathing ritual every couple of months or so and at least once a quarter – that is, every three months.

Grow Your Own Abundance
Items required: a small mint plant, a nice plant pot, three aventurine crystals
Timing: on the new moon

Mint is one of the most powerful herbs for attracting prosperity, which is why it features in so many money spells. It is also remarkably easy to grow, either in your garden, if you have one, or on a sunny windowsill. You can buy mint plants quite inexpensively from garden centres and supermarkets. Once you have chosen your plant, pot it up and put the three aventurine crystals on top of the soil around the base of the plant. This will add to the abundance magic that you are creating. Care for the mint, envisioning it bringing wealth and plenty to you, and as it grows, your sense of abundance should grow with it. This ritual has the added benefit that you can use the mint for your money spells and in cooking too, so it is worth taking the time to cultivate some home-grown mint, as you will always have it to hand for your magic.

A Spell for Money Wisdom
Items required: a piece of iron pyrite, also known as fool's gold, a sage smudge bundle and lighter, your wallet or purse, all your bank cards, your pentacle

You work hard for your money and put it to good use, but frivolous spending habits can leave you feeling the pinch if you're not careful. Sometimes it's easy to get carried away and spend too much. However, being wise with your money and considering your purchases carefully before you buy anything

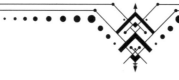

will lead to a greater sense of prosperity and control of your finances. Cast this spell to help you to achieve greater wisdom in your financial life.

Gather together all your cards, along with your purse or wallet. Place them on the pentacle, light the smudge bundle and waft the smoke all around the cards and purse to cleanse them of any negative money habits that you might have acquired. Imagine having the discipline to only buy essential purchases and to leave shops or close down web browsers without buying anything. Think of what you could do with the money you save, simply by being more discerning in your shopping habits. Imagine making wise investments with your money or having a healthy savings account. Keep smudging your cards as you envision yourself growing in financial wisdom. When you are ready, pick up the fool's gold and say:

A fool with money I shall not be
No longer spending frivolously
I keep these cards close to my chest
And with prosperity I am blessed

Keep the fool's gold in your purse or wallet to act as a reminder to be more careful with your money.

Magical Tips to Keep the Money Flowing In

- Put a bay leaf in your purse to ensure it is never empty.
- Carry a lodestone in your pocket to keep your pockets full.
- Carry a conker to draw natural abundance your way.
- Drink mint tea often to take prosperity into yourself.
- Keep aventurine crystals on your desk at work to increase earnings.
- Put the king and queen of diamonds playing cards in your wallet or purse to guard your wealth.

COPING WITH DEBT

The flip side of prosperity is debt, which can act as a block to your abundance. While not all debt is considered to be a bad thing, all debt can lead to anxiety and stress if you are having trouble keeping up with repayments. This includes 'good' debts such as mortgages and student loans. In general, consumer debts are the ones most people struggle to manage, so things like store cards, credit cards, catalogue accounts, hire-purchase debts, car finance and so on. Such debts generally have high interest rates, which means that you can find yourself struggling to keep up with repayments.

For people on a low income with no savings, debt is often a fact of life. It is usually the only way that they can replace a large appliance if it breaks down, or afford to pay an unexpected expense such as vet bills or car problems. But the fact that debt is commonplace doesn't make it any less stressful, and borrowing on tomorrow's salary to pay for something today is to be avoided if at all possible. This is because when the time to repay comes around, not only will you need to pay for all your baseline essential expenses but you will also need to pay back the debt that you have acquired, leaving less money to put into savings and an even smaller margin of happiness.

Debt can also become a habit. It's easy to get into a *treat yourself* mind-set, and if you have been working all month it might seem reasonable that you purchase something

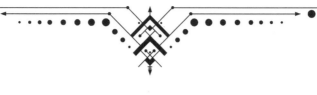

nice as a reward. This is fine, providing you can afford it, or if you only treat yourself using credit cards every now and then. However, if you are in the habit of going on expensive shopping sprees using store cards and catalogues, or splurging on a credit card, then eventually this can lead to money issues later on, particularly if you are carrying debt from month to month. Bear in mind as well that it is to the benefit of the credit card companies that you remain in debt, because they can keep charging interest on what you owe, which is why they might increase your credit limit if you are close to the existing limit.

That said, if you tell a company that you are struggling to make payments and are experiencing financial difficulty, they have a duty of care to help you come to a repayment agreement that you can afford, though if you default on one of these payments then they can demand the balance in full or pass the account to a debt collection agency who will add their own fees, thereby increasing the overall debt. Be aware that in the UK a consumer debt creditor cannot chase a debt if it has been more than six years since they last had contact with you or you made a payment.

So how do you cope if you are in this kind of situation and your debts are increasing rather than decreasing? First of all, try to automate as many of the payments as you can, by setting up direct debits for an agreed amount each month. This takes some of the pressure off because you won't need to think about making the payments. The debts will be paid automatically every month, and you won't need to worry about forgetting to pay. Next put all credit and store cards in a safe place, until you have got on top of the debts you currently owe. Keeping them in your purse just keeps temptation handy and you need to break the habit of acquiring debt. Finally, use the debt management spells below to put a little magic on your side and regain control of your finances, because paying off your debts is also a way of banishing poverty (but be aware that spells alone will not solve your problems; practical steps will be required too).

Silent Spell to Diminish Debt

Items required: two squares of card about 5cm (2 inches) square, a black pen, black electrical tape
Timing: during a waning moon

You can use this spell in two ways. Firstly, you can add up all the debts you own to various creditors to come up with your total amount of debt. Secondly, you can use the spell for a single creditor, dealing with one debt at a time. Whichever method you choose, write the amount you owe in black pen at the top of one of the squares of card, then copy out the sum, omitting the final digit in each line until you are left with nothing, like this:

£150,000.00
£150,000.0
£150,000
£150,00
£150,0
£150
£15
£1
£0

Once you have written out the debt in this way, place the second square of card on top of the first to cover the figures, then use the black tape to wrap around the card until it is fully covered. This will help to prevent the debt from increasing. Place the diminishing spell in a dark place and once the debt is paid, burn it, giving thanks.

A Spell for Desperate Times

Items required: a candle of any colour (use whatever you have in the house, as this is an emergency spell), a candle holder, black pepper, paper kitchen roll, sunflower oil or any oil you have handy
Timing: use in times of desperate need

Desperate times call for desperate measures and this emergency spell is perfect for those occasions when creditors are hounding you, bailiffs are due to come or you need more time to pay an essential bill such as rent, mortgage or fuel. Hold the candle in your hands and visualize your creditors being understanding and helpful to you, offering a payment plan that you can afford or giving you more time to pay. This spell is about giving you some breathing space – it won't make the problem go away, so you will need to be brave and communicate with your creditors. However, this spell should turn down the heat somewhat. Once you have visualized a positive resolution, anoint the candle in oil. Sprinkle the black pepper,

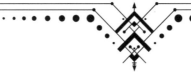

which has banishing properties, on the kitchen roll and push the candle through the pepper, pushing it away from you to banish the problem. Place the candle in the holder and light it. Allow it to burn for 30 minutes a day until the situation is resolved, which is usually before the candle has burnt to the end.

Spell to Freeze a Debt Collector

Items required: a letter from the debt collection agency, scissors, a plastic tub and lid, two sewing pins, spring water
Timing: during the waning moon, preferably on a Tuesday, the day of Mars, to resolve conflict

If you feel you are being unduly harassed by a debt collection agency, then use this spell to freeze them out of your life. Take the letter and cut away the agency's logo and address. This is the tag-lock for the spell. Place the two pins through the agency details, so that they form the shape of St Andrew's cross. Put the paper into the tub, fill the tub with water and put on the lid. Hold your hands firmly on top of the lid and say:

Hounded and harassed I will not be
No more from this day
I honour this debt with honesty
I know that I must pay

I ask for future clemency
Leave me be and go away!

Place the tub at the back of the freezer to ice out the agency and their collectors, but be sure to maintain any payment plan you have agreed to, or make one as soon as possible.

Spell to Call in a Debt

Items required: a small mirror, the amount of money that is owed to you written on a slip of paper, your pentacle
Timing: new moon

If someone owes you money, you can use this spell to call in the debt. This spell is helpful to get a large company to pay out money they owe you, or it can be used if you have loaned money to a friend or family member and you need it back. On the night of the full moon, take the items needed to your altar or to a quiet place. Write down the sum of money that is owed to you, or if you are unsure, write down something like *Return overpayments on my utility account* along with the name of the company. Set the mirror in the middle of the pentacle and place the piece of paper on top, face down with the sum of money towards the mirror. Now say the following incantation nine times:

> *That which is owed returns to me*
> *It comes with love and grace*
> *That which is owed comes back to me*
> *Reflected through this sacred space.*
> *So be it*

The debt should be repaid within a full lunar phase, so by the following new moon.

Magical Tips to Banish Debt

- Sprinkle black pepper around your house to keep debt from your door.
- Smudge all your bills with sage as they come in to prevent negative energy attaching to them.
- Pay your bills on a Thursday, the day of Jupiter, to maintain control of your finances.

- Automate as many payments and bills as you can to free up your head space and avoid late payment fees.
- Magically cleanse your purse and cards once a month using incense or a smudge bundle.
- Hold a rose quartz crystal in your hand when you talk to creditors to ensure a positive outcome and conversation.
- Remember that the main lesson of debt is that it has to be paid back at some stage, so avoid overspending and keep your debt levels to a minimum.

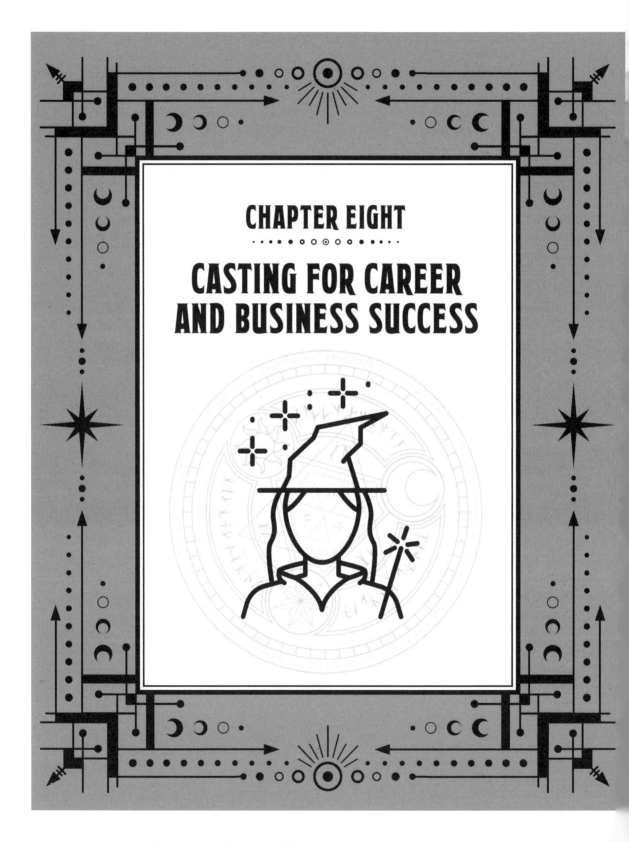

CHAPTER EIGHT

· · · · · ◉ ○ ◉ ○ ◉ · · · · ·

CASTING FOR CAREER AND BUSINESS SUCCESS

You spend approximately one third of your life at work so it is vital that you enjoy your job as much as possible. Sadly, this isn't always the case and lots of people feel tied to a job they hate or an employer who expects too much for too little. Unless you are in your dream job, working in a vocation you love, you might only be at work for the money, simply because you have bills to pay. This is certainly the case for many people and, while working for a living is a fact of life, it isn't always easy.

The workplace can often be a leading cause of stress, anxiety and depression, with enforced overtime, zero-hours contracts, disgruntled members of the public and difficult colleagues all playing a part in adding to the stress. It isn't easy to create a harmonious team when you have a clash of characters, cultures, beliefs and personalities. All workplaces bring together very different people who are expected to merge as one and work as a team, but this can sometimes prove to be quite challenging.

In an ideal world everyone would get along and work together towards a common outcome, but this isn't always the case. It is inevitable that at some stage in your career you will be forced to work with someone you don't like or can't get along with. It is likely that you'll have to work alongside someone who doesn't pull their weight or do their fair share, leaving you to pick up the slack. If you are a woman working in a male-dominated environment, or vice versa, then you might feel that you have to work twice as hard to prove that you are worthy of the job. Add to this the fact that employment contracts are usually skewed in the employers' favour, leaving the employee at a disadvantage, and it's not surprising that workplace stress is one of the leading causes of sickness and absenteeism.

In this chapter, we will look at what you can do magically to make your working life more enjoyable, including how you can leave a job you hate, gain a promotion or start a side hustle as a new business venture. Before we get to the magic, however, let's take a look at how psychological enslavement works and how employers use it to their advantage. Forewarned is forearmed!

PSYCHOLOGICAL ENSLAVEMENT AND THE WORKPLACE

Psychological enslavement is a term used by psychotherapists when someone's autonomy is being severely compromised. This can happen in any relationship, be it personal or professional. Usually this kind of enslavement takes place over a long-term relationship, or when there is an automatic power imbalance involved. It is not to be confused with the *Modern Slavery Act*, which is a different thing altogether, although the two things often run in tandem together. Psychological enslavement is a mind game and it is extremely insidious. It can become a negative aspect of any romance, employment or family life.

The main problem is that most people do not recognize when they are being psychologically enslaved. The enslavers themselves might not know what they are doing, or they might deny any wrongdoing. Confront any employer with an accusation of psychological enslavement and they will immediately point out the fact that they are not in breach of the *Modern Slavery Act*, but psychological enslavement is a completely different thing. Just because your employer isn't breaking the laws on Modern Slavery doesn't mean that they are not psychologically enslaving their employees by facilitating a controlling atmosphere. They may well be doing just that.

Psychological enslavement means that someone has put you into a mental cage. If you feel that you cannot act in any way without first consulting your boss, or that you cannot make plans because your employer expects you to be 'fully flexible and available at short notice', or that you have to check in with your line manager every day to see if they need you at work – then you have been psychologically enslaved to that relationship.

Furthermore, you are also likely to experience the symptoms of severe stress such as anxiety, high blood pressure, migraines, headaches, nosebleeds and so on. The longer this continues, the harder it becomes to extract yourself from the situation or change the relationship to a healthier dynamic. An enslaved relationship is a very unhealthy one and it will take its toll on both your mental and physical well-being. The workplace is one of the main arenas of psychological enslavement and this is where you are likely to feel your autonomy is most compromised, right down to how many toilet breaks you are allowed to take!

WORKPLACE VS WORKHOUSE

In any employment situation there is an unequal power dynamic because you are working *for* someone and they seem to hold all the cards. You may feel fortunate to have a job, but if your employer is trying

to enforce unfavourable working conditions, contractual changes or pay cuts, or telling you that if you don't like it you should just move on, knowing full well that the current jobs climate simply does not support that way of thinking, then you could be in an enslaved situation. This is even more likely to be the case if you work at the lower end of the pay-scale, where the competition for jobs is much greater and the rewards for working are smaller.

It could even be the case that some degree of psychological enslavement is actually written into your contract. If you are on a zero-hours contract or you are expected to phone your employer every morning to see if you are needed that day, then you are psychologically tied to that job and its uncertainty. Such contracts increase anxiety, as you never know how many hours you will be working and therefore if you will earn enough money to pay all your bills each month. Furthermore, you won't be able to take on a second job to increase your income, just in case your original employer calls you in to work and the two schedules clash. This is a very common way in which employers mentally enslave their employees.

Another form of contractual enslavement is a 'flexibility' or 'required overtime' clause, whereby your employer

expects you to remain fully flexible for the duration of your employment with them and they can call you in to work at the drop of a hat, despite the fact that you are not paid extra to be 'on call'. Again, this keeps you on tenterhooks, worried that your days off will be invaded by your employer and that your own time is not being respected.

Bear in mind, however, that in most modern countries an employer has no legal right to enforce you going in at a moment's notice on your day off, unless they are paying you extra money to be on call. For this there would be an 'on call' clause in your contract, whereby you would be on call for a certain period of time and you would be paid extra for the inconvenience. If this *isn't* in your contract, they cannot demand that you go to work on your days off with no notice – but they might try emotional manipulation instead, by saying how much they are struggling without your help. See this for what it is. Manipulation.

I should point out that neither of the above contractual clauses is actually illegal, and your employer is technically within their rights to include them, but such clauses are immoral and unfair to their employees, and are not conducive to a happy, healthy workforce. In addition, they tend to be found at the lower end

of the pay scale. Furthermore, they are designed to tilt the balance of power in the employer's favour, leaving the employee at an automatic disadvantage, fearing job loss if they refuse to comply.

Employment based upon this kind of contract can quickly start to feel like more of a workhouse than a workplace. Although we believe that workhouses are a thing of the past, I would venture to suggest that they have simply been given a facelift. These days, low-paid jobs with very long hours and a single 30-minute break for lunch, where even your days off are not guaranteed due to a flexibility clause in your contract, have become the modern-day workhouses of our society. Those who work in them often feel they have no choice and are trapped there, with little chance of escape. Sadly, this type of workplace has become common in our society. Little wonder then that 40 percent of all sickness from work is due to workplace stress!

In addition, any attempts by employees to address their situation might be dismissed as the employees' own negative attitude. Toxic positivity can be rife in the workplace, particularly within large global corporations. It is simply not in the employer's interests to even up the power imbalance, and the sad truth is that

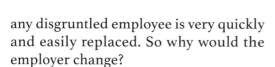

any disgruntled employee is very quickly and easily replaced. So why would the employer change?

That said, there are still things that you can do to alleviate your situation. First of all, find out if there is any scope for flexibility from your employer. Have a meeting and explain that the overtime is too much for you, or that you need to be free every Monday for childcare purposes or whatever. If your employer is willing to meet you halfway and accommodate your request, all well and good. If they are not, then they have demonstrated that they are completely rigid, while expecting full flexibility from their employees. This tilted situation is unlikely to change, but at least now you are aware that your workplace is skewed entirely to one side, which is not in your favour, so brush up your CV and start job hunting, because they are unlikely to change.

Another thing you can do is begin some kind of sideline business from home. A home-based business might be just the ticket to give your mind a bit of breathing space from the job. If it is creative, it has the added benefit of being relaxing and good for your overall mental health. It can give you something to look forward to and work towards, which in turn will take your mind off the stresses of work. Eventually you might

be able to give up the job and work on your business full time. Plenty of people have done it, and it is possible, but you won't get there if you don't make a start.

You should also do all you can to maintain your freedom on your days off by setting boundaries. You are entitled to time away from work without being disturbed by phone calls from bosses and colleagues, but many workplaces encourage employees to be constantly contactable, under the guise of being 'one big family'. To counteract this, limit the number of ways in which your employers can contact you. They simply should not be bombarding you with texts, calls and messages on social media in your own time. So limit the information you give to them. Decline to join any social media groups they have, such as WhatsApp or Facebook groups, so that they cannot use these platforms to invade your free time.

Also, be aware that your employer isn't contacting you in your free time so that *they* can do *you* a favour! With that in mind, it is in your own interests to have two phones, but only give them one number. During your free time, *turn that phone off!* This means that family and friends can still call you on your other, private number, but your employer is being forced to respect your boundaries and your free time.

Alternatively, choose a phone which filters out calls from certain numbers or blocks them completely at certain times, so that you are in charge of who can contact you and when, because your time is your own, your life is your own, and your workplace will only enslave you fully if you allow it to. Keep your mind above the fray, maintain strong boundaries around your personal time and know your rights. That way you can tread water in a bad job, while at the same time working on your plan of escape. Use the spells and rituals in this chapter to help make your working life more successful and fulfilling. Good luck!

Spell to Transition from a Bad Job to a Dream Job

Items required: a notebook and pen, a black candle, athame or carving tool, a white candle, two plates, black pepper and white rice
Timing: on the full moon

It can be very debilitating when you feel trapped in a job that you dislike. However, leaving might not be an option until you have found something else, so use this spell to make that transition a little easier. Write down all that you require from your ideal job, noting down everything you're looking for, from the hours and pay to the environment and kind of colleagues you prefer to work with. Next carve the words My Dream Job on the white candle and your current place of employment on the black candle. Set each of these candles on the plates, melting the bottoms of the candles so that they stand securely. Put the plates side by side. Sprinkle a circle of black pepper around the black candle to banish the negative influence of your current workplace, then sprinkle a circle of white rice for prosperity around the white candle to help manifest your dream job. Light the black candle and say:

My work is done within this place
My time here will soon be done

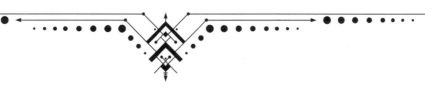

I walk away with joy and grace
Happy to be moving on!

Spend a few minutes visualizing your final day at your current workplace, with all your colleagues wishing you well for your future role. When you can see this clearly, light the white candle and say:

I summon my dream job to me
In a role that I enjoy
I call this opportunity
With the magic I now deploy

Finally, burn the slip of notepaper describing your dream job in the flame of the white candle. You can begin the transition by actively job hunting and seeking out new opportunities, but this spell should work within six months.

Silent Spell to Shine in an Interview

Items required: a pentacle, a small item that you will wear to the interview, a citrine crystal for luck and communication, a pen and paper
Timing: the day before the interview

Job interviews can be very nerve wracking and it can be easy to let them overwhelm you. Preparation is the key to success and the more interviews you do, the more comfortable you will become. Always do some research into the company you are interviewing with, because they will usually ask you if you know anything about them, so at the very least you should look at their website and try to pick up key phrases and mission statements etc. that you can use as part of your interview strategy. Bear in mind that an interview works both ways and you can use this time to figure out if it is a company that suits you. It is also a good idea to have a couple of examples ready from your current or previous work experience in order to demonstrate occasions when you went above and beyond your role, or when you feel you could have done better and what you would do differently in hindsight. Again, these tend to be standard questions asked by interviewers. Once you have prepared yourself in this way, you are ready to cast the spell. Take a small item that you plan to wear to the interview, such as a lipstick, tie or piece of jewellery, and place it on the pentacle. Add the citrine crystal, which is good for communication and success. On a slip of paper, write out the following charm:

Gracious, kind and sharp of mind
Success in my job interview I find

Put this paper beneath the crystal and memorize the words, so that you can mentally affirm them on the way to the interview and while sitting waiting to be called in. This will keep your mind active and your emotions positive. Leave all the items in place overnight to charge on the pentacle. The following day as you get ready, put on the lipstick or tie and see yourself conducting a great interview and coming across well to your prospective employers. Finally, put the slip of paper and the crystal into your pocket or purse, to carry the magic with you. If you get the job, burn the paper and give thanks. If you are unlucky, keep the spell in place on the pentacle and use it for future interviews as there is probably something better coming along you haven't seen yet.

Spell to Cope with Difficult Colleagues

Items required: an amethyst crystal or amethyst jewellery, a bottle of spring water
Timing: on the waning moon and then whenever you have to work with a difficult colleague, daily if needed

No matter how kind and patient you are, there will be times when a colleague gets on your nerves. Maybe they never stop talking and you need to try and concentrate through their verbal diarrhoea, or perhaps they are trying to draw you into gossip and office politics. Maybe they are lazy and you are fed up with doing their tasks as well as your own. Whatever the issue, use this simple spell to absorb their negative energy before it can bring you down. Take the amethyst crystal and let it sit in the light of the waning moon. You can also use a power bracelet of amethyst beads. Allow it to charge until the moon is dark, then take the crystals to work with you and place them between you and the difficult colleague, or keep them on your person, to absorb any negative energy coming your way. If a crystal is too obviously out of place on your desk, use the bottled water for the same purpose – pour a cup

of water and place it between you and the person you find challenging to work with. The water will help to absorb their negative energy. Just make sure that you don't drink it! Pour it away or cleanse the crystal under running water at the end of each working day.

Spell to Sweeten Up a Difficult Boss

Items required: a small spell jar and stopper, a small slip of paper and pen, sugar
Timing: at the new moon

Putting someone's name in the sugar is a traditional folk spell used to bring out their sweeter nature. If you have to work with a difficult boss it can be hard to stand up for yourself for fear of losing your job. Bear in mind that things like sexual harassment and workplace bullying should always be reported to your line manager or above. If your boss is simply grumpy, irritable or impatient, however, then try this spell to sweeten them up. Write their name on a slip of paper, roll it up and place it in the spell jar, then fill the jar with sugar. Put on the stopper and keep the jar safe at home, where it will not be found by nosy colleagues!

Chant for a Quiet Day at Work

Items required: none
Timing: when you first get in to work and mentally throughout the day

Sometimes we all need a more relaxed day at work, one when the phones are quiet, there are no emergencies to see to and the office is calm. This is a little affirmation chant that I have used successfully in many different roles. It shouldn't be used too often, but every now and then it can serve to bring about a much calmer working day and maybe even an early finish. When you first get to work, sit in the car or find a quiet space and repeat the affirmation several times, either out loud or in your head, then repeat as you will, throughout the day.

Bar the door, stop the phone
Bend the time, early home
Quiet office, calm in mind
A peaceful day at work is mine

Spell for a Raise or Promotion

Items required: an envelope, a green pen, three leaves of fresh mint, a sprig of rosemary, three heads of lavender flower, three silver coins, an aventurine crystal, a lock of your hair
Timing: at the new moon

Bear in mind that higher pay or a promotion generally comes with greater responsibility, so be certain this is what you want before

Once you have been granted the pay rise or promotion, empty the contents of the envelope into the earth, keeping the coins back for future prosperity spells. Give thanks for the new role by burning incense and dedicating it to your chosen deity.

you cast this spell. To bring about a pay rise, a promotion or both, take the envelope and write down the new job title and salary you are aiming for on the inside of the flap, using the green pen. Next fill the envelope with the following items: aventurine and mint for prosperity, lavender for luck, rosemary for growth and success, and three silver coins to increase your earnings. Add the tag-lock of your hair, seal the envelope and say:

Time to shine and room to grow
Greater success I wish to know
A promotion sealed within this place
It comes to me through time and space
By earth, moon and sun
By magic it is done

Spell for a Successful Business Venture

Items required: a green candle and holder, a few sunflower seeds, the name of your business or creative venture written down
Timing: during a waxing moon

Lots of people like to have a sideline business alongside their main job. Not only can this

provide an additional income stream, it can also offer stress relief from your normal job, giving you something else to focus on. Developing a side business has never been easier thanks to the internet, and you can set up shop online with relatively few expenses. All you need to do is work out what kind of sideline business you want to create. Once you have this in mind, write it down and place the paper beneath a green candle. Light the candle and place two or three sunflower seeds around the candle holder to signify the growth of your business venture. Light the candle and say:

With this light I find my way
To make my passion bear fruit
I start this venture from today
And for the stars I'll shoot!

Allow the candle to burn down naturally and then plant the sunflower seeds in the earth. These are the seeds of your dreams, so tend to them carefully as you set about making your business idea a reality. Good luck!

Spell to Keep Money Flowing into Your Business

Items required: three dried bay leaves, patchouli oil
Timing: on the full moon

To keep the finances of your business venture ticking over, anoint three dried bay leaves with a dab of patchouli oil – both bay and patchouli attract victory and abundance. Place the leaves in the cash register of your business, or wherever you keep all your business finances, say a cash box or a safe. If all your business dealings are online, keep the leaves under your computer to attract more business and financial success your way. Eventually, your sideline business could become your main job, so keep working at it.

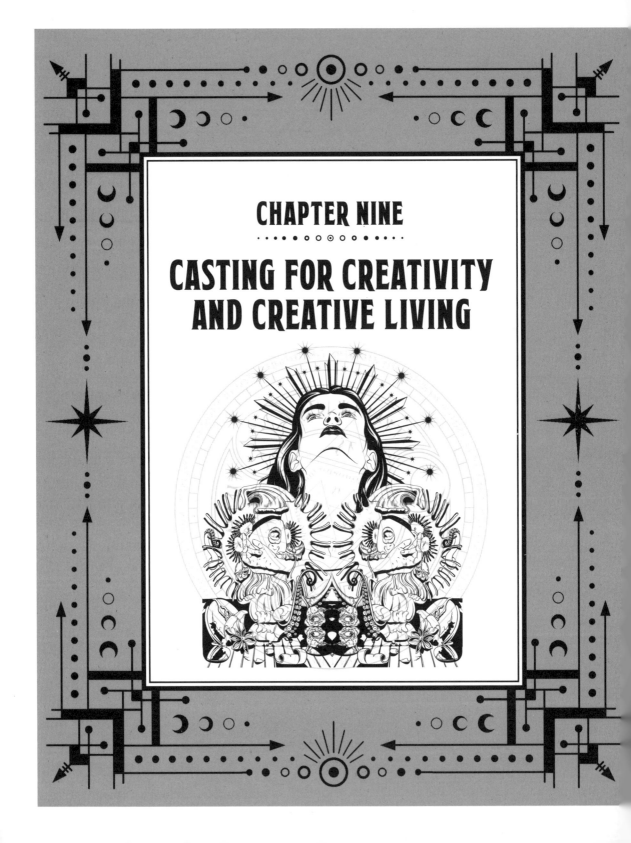

CHAPTER NINE

· · · · · ◦ ○ ◉ ○ ◦ · · · · ·

CASTING FOR CREATIVITY AND CREATIVE LIVING

e live in a time when it has never been easier to live a creative life. There are so many ways that you can be creative and so many different platforms through which you can share your work with the world. From video channels and podcasts to blogs and photographic platforms, you can create something in the comfort of your own home and quickly share it with a global audience.

This way of living is still so relatively new that some people aren't really sure what to make of it all. Yet the need to be creative is as old as the hills and we all feel it in some way. Whether your talent lies in baking, needlecraft, pottery, music, art, dance, writing, singing or something else, the spells in this chapter will help you to hone those skills and make creativity a natural aspect of your everyday life.

CREATIVE LIVING

Living a creative life comes easily to some people, and it is very rewarding. Whether you intend to share your work in a professional capacity at some stage or not, creating something from nothing is still a pleasurable experience. Having hobbies such as sketching, knitting, writing and so on offers a way to calm the mind in times of stress. Lots of creative pastimes involve working with the hands, giving the mind a chance to switch off completely.

In the past, women would spend their time spinning wool into yarn, sitting at the spinning wheel for hours on end, chatting and bonding through shared labour. The term *spinster*, meaning a single woman, comes from this traditionally female craft. The menfolk would work with wood or metal, mending fences and making homes ready for the winter. We can still see echoes of this in modern life, as people happily sit knitting together, making garments for a new baby, while others retreat to their garden shed to potter about with their tools. So creativity is just as much a part of modern life as it has always been, though sadly it is no longer held in such high regard and professions in the creative arts are often thought of as less valid than those in other sectors. That said, many people choose to live in a creative way. This could mean that they work in one of the creative industries such as publishing or media, or it could be that they like to spend all their free time painting or potting plants, ready to sell their wares at craft fairs. There are many ways to incorporate creative interests into your life and once you find a hobby that you love, you will probably never look back.

Ritual to Bless Your Creative Space
Items required: rose water, a little salt, a chalice
Timing: each new moon

Take the items to the area where you usually work on your creative projects. This could be a study, studio, easel, desk or comfy chair. Pour some rose water into the chalice and add a little of the salt. Swirl the chalice to help the salt dissolve. You can use this mixture to consecrate your space, allowing the salt to cleanse the area as the rose water purifies and brings positive energies. Moving in a clockwise direction, dip into the chalice and sprinkle the mixture from your fingertips all around your work area and the tools you use, saying:

Spirit of rose which blooms and grows
Let my creativity flow
As each petal opens brightly
I will not take my talent lightly
I hone my skills, my talent blooms
Whenever I work within this room
So mote it be

Blessing Jar for Inspiration
Items required: a large jar and lid, a small notepad and pen, your favourite incense
Timing: begin on the dark moon

It always seems to be when you are in the middle of a project that lots of new ideas keep bubbling up in your mind. Just because you don't have time to work on them immediately doesn't mean that you shouldn't honour

these ideas. In this ritual, you will create a sacred space in which to keep each idea as it comes up. First cleanse the jar, inside and out, using the smoke from the incense stick. Hold the jar in your hands and say:

May this jar keep safe and bless all my
ideas until I am ready to work on them

When a new idea comes to you, write it down, tear off and fold the note and drop it into the jar. This will ensure that you always have plenty of ideas to fall back on when you need them. Simply take one from the jar and begin.

Ritual for Starting a Creative Session
Items required: a white candle and holder, frankincense essential oil and an oil burner, a cup of your favourite tea, some snacks
Timing: whenever you're about to get creative

Sometimes, getting started can be the hardest part, so add a little magic to make it easier. Atmospheres are a kind of magic, and creating the right one is a ritual in itself. To make the atmosphere conducive to creativity, you need to make sure your space is warm and comfortable, as you might be working on a project for several hours at a time. To begin, burn a few drops of frankincense essential

oil in an oil burner, or sprinkle it onto a hanky and place this on a radiator near your workspace. Frankincense is good for aiding concentration and creativity. It has a lovely, warm scent that can be very comforting. Next, light the candle and place this close by so that it casts a glow over your work. Finally, ensure that you have your favourite snacks and a drink handy, so that you don't have to keep going to the kitchen. When all is ready, settle into your space and say:

Golden hours of creative time
Offer me a chance to shine
A project here before me lies
As I work hard the time flies
Beat by beat of a creative heart
The project grows, which now I start
So it begins...

Get your head down and start working! This ritual helps to get you into the right mind-set for creative work and is useful for academic essays as well as creative projects.

Silent Seven-Day Spell for Successful Creativity
Items required: a tall orange candle and holder, athame or carving tool, a citrine crystal
Timing: during the seven days leading to full moon

This spell can be used to help support a fantastic new project you want to work on, be this writing a book or painting a portrait. Take the orange candle and carve something which represents your creative goal, so you might carve the word 'author' or 'novelist' into the length of the wax. Put the candle in the holder and place the citrine crystal in front. Citrine is a crystal of communication, and all forms of creativity are essentially a way of communicating, both with ourselves and with others. Light the candle and hold your hands on either side, palms facing the candle. Imagine the success of your creative project and see yourself enjoying that success, for instance your book being published, your paintings being exhibited, your audition going well, being invited to join a dance company or modelling agency. Wherever your creativity is aimed, see yourself reaching that target. Visualize this for a while, then let the candle burn a seventh of the way down. Extinguish the candle and repeat the process for the next six days. On the final day, let the candle burn all the way out. Keep the citrine crystal with you as you work on your project.

Dandelion Spell for Creative Growth

Items required: six dandelion flowers, a tea-light and holder, something to represent your creative interest
Timing: during a full moon

The humble dandelion flower has been much maligned by gardeners, often viewed as nothing more than a weed and treated accordingly. Yet try as they might, this little flower always makes a comeback. It is resilient, growing abundantly in most places. What is more, it has many, many magical properties and is frequently used medicinally in herbal remedies and healing spells. The dandelion also has planetary associations because it represents both the sun and the moon, first with its bright golden head, then later with its downy white orb. Thus it became known as a plant of abundant growth and self-transformation. For this spell you will need six golden dandelion flowers. Place them in a circle around the tea-light. Light the candle, focus on the item you have chosen to represent your creative goal and imagine living that life. Now say:

Precious bloom of golden hue
I seek out my golden days
To find transformation in what I do
When I am at play
Let my talent grow and yield
Brighter days ahead
Transforming the dream that I wield
Into reality instead.

Let the tea-light burn as you work, then press the flowers and use them to decorate your creative space, keeping the magic they hold linked to your creativity.

Spell to Manifest a Large Creative Goal

Items required: a sheet of paper, a golden ribbon, frankincense essential oil, a lodestone crystal
Timing: on the new moon

If there is a large creative project you are planning, such as writing a book, this spell can help to keep you on track. It is a type of scribe spell, so you will need to write down what your project is and why you want to do it. What are your motivations? Do you plan to share it with an audience or is it something private that you are doing for your own enjoyment? Get clear about why you want to make time for this hobby and what you hope to gain from it. Once you have it all written down, read through it to make sure it encapsulates your intentions clearly. Anoint the ribbon with a couple of drops of frankincense oil, then roll the paper up into a scroll and tie it with the ribbon. Kiss the scroll and say:

Here where my intention lies
A charm is made for dreams to thrive
A kiss to send them on their way
To manifest some future day
From this day forth I will go on
Working until the job is done

Place the scroll somewhere that you will see it every day and put the lodestone next to it to magnetize the completion of the project. Make time for your hobby each day and watch the project grow to completion.

Spell to Invoke Your Muse

Items required: *a bell or wind chimes, sandalwood incense*
Timing: *whenever you need a bit of extra help with your creativity*

Go to your creative space and take three deep breaths. Light the incense and waft it around the area to cleanse, then place it on your desk and say: *I offer this incense to my muse.* Next take the bell or chimes and ring them in all four directions: north, south, east and west. After each ring, say:

Angel of creativity I call you here to
*   assist me*
Light of inspiration, burning bright
Wings of genius taking flight

Sacred Muse I summon you from far or
*   near*
Come to me now and settle here.

Begin your work and know that your muse guides your hand and thoughts, bringing your dreams into being.

Ritual to Grow Your Own Creative Dream

Items required: *a shallow pan or seed tray, potting soil, water, watercress seeds, athame*
Timing: *when the moon is new*

To nurture the seeds of your dreams, transport them out of your mind and into reality. Hold a packet of watercress seeds in your hands and imagine your creative goal. Visualize that goal being absorbed by the seeds and think of a single word which sums it up. Put a layer of potting soil in the tray and level it out. Next use the athame to trace the word in the soil, then carefully sow the seeds along the channel of the word. Cover with another layer of potting soil, taking care not to destroy the word you have just written. Water the seeds and place them on a sunny windowsill to grow. Once grown, you can eat the watercress to take the success of the magic into yourself. Make sure that you are living intentionally and taking positive steps towards your creative dream.

Genius Burns Spell

Items required: a lantern, tea-lights
Timing: whenever you are inspired to work creatively

A perpetual flame is a way of keeping magic flowing and of honouring something. In reality, keeping a flame alight at all times is difficult, to say the least, not to mention a fire hazard! In this spell, we honour the idea of a perpetual flame but use it in a safe way to help ideas flow. You will need some kind of lantern that is designed to hold tea-lights and a good supply of this type of candle. Keep the lantern on your desk as you work,

lighting a candle in it each time you settle down to your project and saying:

If genius burns within me
Let me feels its flame
If a work of art shall shape me
Help me embrace the fame
This light that burns within
Now shines for all to see
Let the flow begin
As bright ideas burn through me

Dreaming Spell to Find Your Creative Passion

Items required: lavender pillow spray, nine stems of lavender, a purple ribbon
Timing: anytime from new to full moon

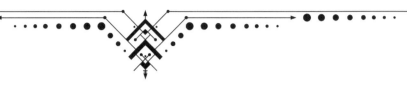

Your dreams are meant to guide you and to highlight your potential. They can show you all that you can be if only you trust the process and listen to your intuition. This dream spell is designed to help you to uncover where your creative talents lie. If you think that you have no talent, then think again, for everyone has a gift of some kind and you just need to figure out what yours might be. Lavender is well known for its power to induce sleep and relaxation. It can also help you to get in touch with your intuition through the power of your dreams. Just before you go to bed, use the pillow spray generously to fragrance your pillow. Now make a posy of the lavender stems by picking them up one at a time and saying the appropriate line of the charm below:

> *By stem of one the dream is begun*
> *By stem of two the dream comes true*
> *By stem of three so shall it be*
> *By stem of four the dream shows me*
>   *more*
> *By stem of five the dream comes alive*
> *By stem of six the dream is not fixed*
> *By stem of seven and all stars in heaven*
> *By stem of eight the dream holds*
>   *weight*
> *By stem of nine, the dream comes*
>   *tonight*

Tie the dream posy with the ribbon and hang it, upside down, from your bed post, or place it on the bedside table with the flowers pointing towards you. Pay attention to your dreams over the next few nights to gain insight into where your talent lies and which ambition you should follow.

Wax Talisman to Open Doors to Your Chosen Creative Industry

Items required: gold sealing wax, greaseproof paper, a fresh three- or four-leaf clover
Timing: cast on the full moon for greatest power

Carrying a talisman with you can ensure that you find yourself in the right place at the right time. It can open doors for you and lead you to the right people. This talisman is created to steer you ever closer to your chosen creative industry, be this publishing, dance, dramatics, music or whatever. Sometimes all you need is a lucky break, and a talisman is a simple way to give yourself the best chance of a breakthrough. Lay out a square of greaseproof paper. Light the stick of gold sealing wax and allow it to drip into a large pool on the paper. You need a pool of molten wax about the size of the base of a tealight, then take the clover leaf and press it gently into the centre of the pool of wax. Leave the wax to dry thoroughly, then gently peel it off the greaseproof paper. Carry the wax talisman with you at all times to bring about the best results.

Silent Spell to Publish a Book

Items required: a quill pen and ink or a fountain pen, a large A4 envelope, your pentacle, a silver ribbon
Timing: on the first full moon after your book is finished

For many people, writing and publishing a book is a long-held ambition. It could be a memoir, a novel, a children's book or a work of non-fiction. Once you have finished writing your book, print it out and place it in a large envelope. Next, use the fountain pen and address the envelope to your preferred publisher or literary agent. Tie the silver ribbon for success around the envelope. Leave this in place on your pentacle for a full lunar month, then remove the ribbon and post your submission, or email the digital version, following the publisher's guidelines on their website. Good luck!

Mirror Spell to Pass an Audition

Items required: a small compact mirror, a white pouch, clear quartz, carnelian and rose quartz crystals, the fragrance you intend to wear for the audition
Timing: one week before the audition

Auditions are an important aspect of many creative industries, so if your ambition is to act, sing, dance or model, you will have to learn to be comfortable attending them. They can be very nerve-wracking events because you can usually see exactly who the competition is and rejection could well take place face to face. To give yourself the very best chance, make sure that you are well prepared, in both appearance and performance. Then boost your chances with this spell. Look into a compact mirror and say *This is what a successful ballerina (or whatever) looks like. I am a successful ballerina and great opportunities just come to me.*

Next, spray a little of your chosen fragrance on the pouch then put in the following crystals: clear quartz to amplify your performance, carnelian for success and rose quartz to make those in power look on you with favour. Leave these items to soak up the light of the sun and moon for one week, then take them with you to the audition. Be sure to wear the same fragrance and, just before you go in, look into the compact mirror and mentally repeat the success charm above. While you might not always get the part you want, this spell will ensure that you will be given a chance to show what you can do, so don't waste it.

Honey Potion to Find Your Singing Voice

Items required: a slice of lemon, a teaspoon of honey, a mug of camomile tea
Timing: use each time you rehearse

Training a voice can be hard work, leading to strained vocal chords and hoarseness, but you can use this soothing potion to help you rediscover your singing voice. Add a slice of lemon and a teaspoon of honey to a cup of warm camomile tea. All these ingredients are known for their power to soothe and improve vocal performance, so it is good for singers and speakers alike. Hold the mug in your hands and empower it by visualizing your voice soaring to the rafters and charming your audience, then sip away.

Spell to Break Through Creative Blocks

Items required: a black candle and holder, a carving tool, a strand of your hair, a lighter
Timing: from full to dark moon

Creative blocks happen to the best of us at times, leaving us fresh out of ideas and with little motivation to create. Often people become blocked just after a project has been going particularly well; it can feel as if you have used up all your creative juices and have nothing left to give. This can be frustrating and annoying, particularly if you have a deadline to meet. All is not lost, however – it could just be that you need to sweep away the block with a touch of magic. Carve your name and the nature of the blocked project into the candle, then heat the side of the wax using the lighter and wind your strand of hair around it while the wax is warm enough for it to stick in place. Put the candle in the holder and light the wick as you say:

Creative blocks are cleared away
Let talent thrive another day
In peace and calm I find my way
Back to productivity

Allow the candle to burn for one hour each day and by the time it has burnt away, the creative block should have passed.

How to Recover from Creative Burnout

While the odd block is a normal aspect of a creative life, burnout is something more serious. All creative people experience occasions when they feel unmotivated or lack new ideas, but with burnout this is a long-term state of mind. Symptoms of burnout include lack of motivation, procrastination, depression, exhaustion, sadness and worry that you will never be creative again. It can be very debilitating and is usually caused by working too hard for too long, without enough clear breaks between projects. If you dread going to your desk or you feel tired just at the thought of returning to a specific project, it could be that you need to step back and give your mind space to recover.

Creativity is something you must feed with new experiences and adventures. You cannot use your creative juices without doing things to replenish them, because once the well runs dry, it can take time to fill. The trick is to be mindful and ensure that you keep pumping new sources of inspiration into the creative well. This involves getting out and about, away from your creative space. It means doing enjoyable things that are totally unrelated to your projects, finding inspiration in unusual places and storing them up in your mind, until you feel strong enough to start work once more.

Tips for Recovering from Burnout

• Take regular breaks, both short ones and longer ones such as a weekend away.

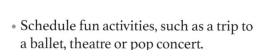

- Schedule fun activities, such as a trip to a ballet, theatre or pop concert.
- Listen to music, but don't play, sing, compose or compare – simply listen.
- Learn to appreciate your past work and know that your future work will come to you in good time, when you are ready to receive it.
- Remember your past successes and feel pride in them.
- Visit an art gallery, a museum, a stately home or an ancient castle.
- Go to the seaside.
- Book a holiday.

Take a Magical Meditative Walk

Walking is an acknowledged way to move through creative blocks and burnout. Many of the great writers were also great ramblers, including Thomas Hardy, Virginia Woolf, Jane Austen and the Brontë sisters. Communing with nature in this way is a fantastic way to refill the creative well, at the same time giving your mind the break

it needs. A meditative walk is a slow-paced wander as you appreciate your environment. You could take pictures of anything that catches your eye, or pick up leaves or other items of nature's discarded bounty from a forest floor. Let your thoughts wander, listen to the birds sing, and enjoy the time and space to yourself. Allow yourself to be refreshed, reinvigorated and inspired by the magic of Mother Nature, who is the best creator of all. Know that your own creativity will return, given time.

CHAPTER TEN

CASTING FOR PROTECTION

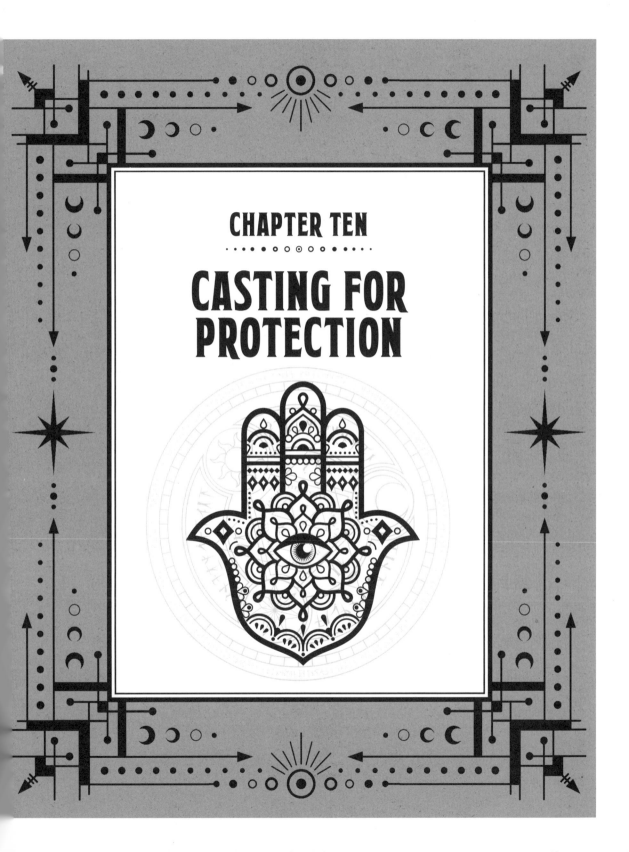

In an ideal world we would have no need of protection magic. You could walk down the street after dark without fear, or leave your handbag on the car seat beside you without worry. However, we do not live in an ideal world and day-to-day life can be quite scary at times. From news of local crime rates to areas of global conflict, it can seem as if there is much to fear, but if you think about it too much you might never leave the house!

Witches use protection magic to deal with the darker aspects of life. We cast spells regularly to help keep ourselves, loved ones and property safe. Protection magic is a preventative measure and such spells are cast regularly to ensure that the negative factions of society keep well away. Witches don't wait until their home is burgled to cast spells to protect it – we cast daily spells to ensure that we are less likely to be burgled. The magic always comes first. The result is that you should be able to move through the world relatively untouched by crime. This doesn't mean that you will never find yourself in the wrong place at the wrong time, but if you do, you should emerge unscathed, providing your protection magic is in place.

Protection spells tend to be layered up over time. Prevention is better than cure, so don't wait until something bad happens. Start to cast protection magic now to surround yourself and your property with positive magic. In this chapter you will find all kinds of protection spells, so that you can begin to weave a web of good magic around all that you hold dear.

BE YOUR OWN BACK-UP

Conflict is a fact of life. There may be occasions when you find yourself in the wrong place at the wrong time; perhaps you are caught up as a witness in a crime, or you are drawn into an altercation of some kind. Difficult neighbours, a bullying boss, relationships that become abusive and back-stabbing friends are all situations that absolutely anyone can suddenly find themselves embroiled in.

In some forms of employment, conflict comes with the territory, and not just in the most obvious sectors such as the armed and emergency services. Minor conflict can be a daily event for people who work in customer services dealing with client complaints, or for those who work in the justice and probation system, or in the welfare system. In short, if you work in an arena where people are experiencing strong emotions or the stakes are high, then you are likely to run into conflict every now and then. In general, people are more likely to become confrontational when one of the following areas of their life seems threatened in some way: territory, finances, family, personal values, religion, freedom.

Avoiding all forms of conflict is simply not possible, but you can learn to mitigate it as much as possible. Protection magic helps to safeguard you from the negative energies which might eventually escalate into areas of conflict, but there will still be occasions when you need to make a stand. Interestingly, being perceived as being too nice can actually attract *more* conflict, because people may think that you're a pushover, so they break agreements, trespass on your territory, become abusive and try to diminish your boundaries, knowing that you probably won't say anything and will turn a blind eye to their behaviour. So there comes a time when you have to stand up for yourself and your boundaries.

Making a stand isn't the same thing as picking a fight. It isn't about running around causing chaos or stirring up trouble. It is about being assertive in your own life and letting people know, quite clearly and firmly, where your boundaries are and what you expect. Laying your cards on the table in this way means that everyone knows where they stand and a state of peace and harmony can flourish.

It is vital that you learn to be your own back-up. If you wait around for someone else to fight your battles for you, then you will start to believe that you are incapable of standing up for yourself – and this simply isn't true. Furthermore, you are the *only* person who is always guaranteed to be right there whenever conflict presents itself to you, so it makes sense to rely mostly on yourself to resolve any areas of conflict in your life.

ENGAGE YOUR WARRIOR SPIRIT

The warrior spirit is something which we all have inside us. It isn't the preserve of men alone. Women have it too. It is the ability to stand firm in the face of adversity and conflict, to take a well-calculated risk and to develop a plan of action to see a hostile situation through to a more peaceful conclusion. It

is the power to safeguard loved ones and those who are vulnerable, such as children and animals.

Often conflict can be avoided simply by engaging the warrior-spirit aspect of your character, by making a stand and stating your boundaries. Throw a touch of magic into the mix and most enemies will walk away or find an easier target. Witches know how to make a stand when they need to. They are in tune with their warrior aspect and have the skills of spell-craft at their fingertips with which to defend themselves and their loved ones. There are not many people who will go up against a warrior-witch twice over! I must stress again that this isn't about looking for trouble. It is about knowing that you have the capability to deal with trouble if and when it presents itself to you. Use the blessing below to evoke your own warrior spirit.

Blessing to Evoke Your Warrior Spirit

Items required: a black candle, an essential oil of your choice
Timing: whenever there is conflict in your life

Anoint the candle with the oil. As you do so, imagine yourself standing your ground, stating your case firmly and with conviction. See the battleground of conflict before you in your mind's eye. Know that you have what it takes to achieve peace and/or victory. Now light the candle and say the following evocation to call out your warrior spirit.

> *As conflict now presents itself, so I will*
>   *engage*
> *I stand upon a battle ground and feel the*
>   *battle rage*
> *I evoke my warrior spirit side to*
>   *vanquish every foe*
> *To show my wrath till peace be gained,*
>   *for victory is all I know*

Let the candle burn as you come up with a plan of action to settle the conflict. Then blow out the candle and keep it safe for next time. Embrace your warrior spirit side and live your life with courage, confidence, wisdom and compassion.

Silent Spell to Protect Yourself
Items required: a good-luck charm or magical necklace such as a pentacle or triquetra, altar pentacle
Timing: on the full moon

Wearing a protective charm is a traditional way to ward off bad vibes and negative energy. On the night of the full moon, put the pendant or charm in the middle of the altar pentacle and place this where it can absorb the light of the moon. Leave it in place overnight, then begin to wear it as your everyday necklace, or carry the charm in your wallet or purse so that you always have it with you. The charm can help to ward away bad vibes in general, but if you feel that you are under threat, move on to the next step below.

Cast a Circle of Personal Protection
Items required: none
Timing: whenever you are feeling vulnerable

We looked at casting a magical circle earlier in the book, but while that was for the purposes of performing spells, you can also cast a circle around yourself for personal protection. Think of it as a magical force field that nothing harmful can penetrate. This is a visualization exercise, so you can use it at any time, in any situation. Your circle of protection can be visualized any way you like. Simply envision a circle of light all around you. The light then expands up over your head and beneath your feet, creating a sphere of magical protection, with you at the centre. This circle moves with you. It goes where you go and encompasses all your movements. You can imagine it being any colour you choose. Some people might see themselves in a bubble; others might picture a snow globe. What is important is that it makes you feel safe and comforted, so if you want your magic circle to be a pink bubble lined in swan's down, that's okay. Cast this spell regularly, because practice makes it stronger and more effective. You will also notice that people tend to walk around your circle – they can't see it, but they can feel its energy and they will often adjust their steps to avoid crossing the line you have created with your magical boundary. Take this as proof of its power to protect you.

Charm to Protect Your Car

Items required: *tiger's eye, haematite and smoky quartz crystals, a small pouch, bergamot essential oil*
Timing: *at midnight, the witching hour, when the moon is dark*

Take the pouch and scent it with the bergamot oil, which is known for its protective powers. Next add the protection crystals. Hold the pouch of crystals in your hands and say:

> *Protect this vehicle and all within*
> *By the power of this charm herein*

Leave the pouch and oil on your altar overnight. The next day place the pouch in the glove compartment of your car and use a little of the oil to anoint each of the tyres, both bumpers and the roof. This will seal and complete the spell.

Blessing for Protection When Driving

Items required: *Bach Rescue Remedy spray*
Timing: *use whenever you feel anxious while driving*

Driving on congested roads can lead to driver anxiety and nervousness, so it is a good idea to keep a Rescue Remedy spray in your car. This is a herbal remedy for anxiety, stress and nervous disorders. If you are starting to feel a little overwhelmed while driving, or even at the thought of driving, then spray a little Rescue Remedy on your tongue and repeat this blessing.

> *Sharpen mind and restore wit*
> *To anxiety I'll not submit*
> *East, south, west, north*
> *Angels protect me as I drive back and*
> *   forth*

This spell can also be used if you are about to embark on a long journey via public transport.

Spell to Protect Your Property Boundary

Items required: four black stones or pebbles, black pepper, a compass
Timing: at dusk on a waning moon

This spell is designed to create a magical boundary around the perimeter of your property. As dusk falls, go out into your garden and use the compass to determine where north lies. Head in that direction to the perimeter of your garden and put down one of the black stones. Now move to the east, sprinkling a little black pepper as you go, and place another stone at the eastern border. Repeat in the directions of south and west, sprinkling the black pepper to create a circle, all joined up with the boundary stones at each compass point. Continue back to the north and the point where you started, and say:

The boundary lines have now been cast
With protection magic built to last

Check your stones remain in place every month. If not, repeat the spell with new stones. If you live in an apartment building, adjust this spell by placing the stones at the compass points inside your flat, but don't use the pepper.

Silent Spell to Protect a Loved One

Items required: a small spell jar and stopper, a lock of your loved one's hair, protective dried herbs of basil, sage and rosemary, a small slip of paper and a pen, black sealing wax, a holly leaf, red thread
Timing: on the full moon for strongest protection

Cast this spell to keep your loved one safe from harm. Write their full name and date of birth on the slip of paper, roll it up and drop it into the jar. Add the lock of hair. Now fill the jar with the dried herbs, put the stopper in and seal it with black wax. Once the wax has hardened, tie the holly leaf around the neck using the red thread and place the jar in the light of the moon for a full lunar cycle. After this time, place the jar in a dark corner where it will remain undisturbed.

Rowan Spell to Guard Against Prowlers

Items required: two twigs of rowan, red thread, red ribbon to hang
Timing: at the time of the dark moon

Rowan is one of the most magical trees and is revered in many cultures, including Celtic and Norse. It was said to offer protection against witches, which is ironic as it is frequently used by witches in their spells! In this ritual, you are going to make a traditional charm which is said to guard against human prowlers and unwelcome visitors from the spirit realms. Fashion the two rowan twigs into an equal-armed cross and secure with the red thread. Use the red ribbon to hang the charm within or close to your property, to protect the area.

Spell to Protect Against Envious People

Items required: dried rowan berries, black thread, a needle
Timing: cast at midnight during the full moon

Envy is a poison that can have a very harmful effect. If someone is showing signs of envy towards you, then you have every right to guard yourself against any spitefulness that might be coming your way. While we all feel the odd pang of envy every now and then, there are some individuals who live in a permanent state of jealousy. Remember that this has more to do with their own unresolved issues than with you, so try not to take it personally. That said, if you have done everything you can to resolve the issue and nothing is working, then you should cast this spell to limit the impact such envy can have on you. Sit for a while and contemplate the envy that has been directed at you. Thread the needle with a long length of black cotton and knot the end. Now begin to thread the rowan berries onto the cotton to create a strand. As you put the needle through each one say:

> I prick the conscience of those who act
>   and speak against me
> For envy touches me not

Keep going until the length of cotton is full of berries, then tie off the strand. The next day, bury this strand of berries in the earth to help neutralize the envy directed at you. Rowan berries are harmful to pets and can have an adverse effect on people too, so be sure to bury the strand deep in the earth, keep any leftover berries locked away out of harm's reach and wash your hands thoroughly after working with them.

Blessing to Protect Against Storms and Bad Weather Conditions

Items required: a white candle or tea-light and holder
Timing: perform as the storm starts to come in

Global warming means that we are experiencing more adverse weather conditions than we have been used to in the past. Floods, heavy snowfalls and thunderstorms can all be a danger to life and property, so they are not to be taken lightly. When a storm is forecast, wait until you notice the first signs of it drawing in, then light the candle in the holder and say:

> Elemental spirits of this storm, I light
>   this candle to honour and respect you
> I ask that you pass swiftly over the
>   homes and property of myself and my
>   loved ones
> Leaving me and my family unscathed in
>   your wake
> So mote it be

If you are at work or out and about when the storm comes in, you can use a lighter to the same effect, letting the flame burn for a few moments as you speak the words of blessing above.

the middle of the paper and fold each corner of the paper into the middle, then secure it with sealing wax. Keep the protection charm in a safe place.

THE EVIL EYE

Many cultures still believe in the Evil Eye, which is the belief that some people can cause harm and chaos simply by glaring at their chosen victim. While this might seem a little far-fetched, most myths and legends have a basis in fact and it could be that the Evil Eye legend was a way of explaining extreme spitefulness or vindictive behaviour. In certain parts of Europe and in Mediterranean regions, special charms are still sold which are thought to ward off the

Spell to Protect a Pet

Items required: *some of your pet's naturally shed fur, a square of paper, a pen, sealing wax*

Timing: *from new to full moon*

Our pets are members of our family and they deserve just as much protection as any of our loved ones. One of the best things you can do for your pet is get it microchipped, so that if the worst happens, you will be more likely to be reunited. In addition, cast this spell to add a little magical protection around your four-legged friend. On the square of paper write your pet's name in the centre, then write the words *Protected Be* on all four sides, surrounding the name. Place your pet's fur in

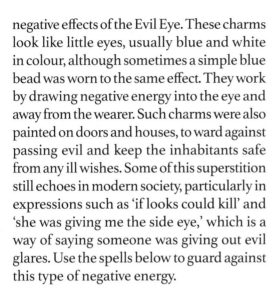

negative effects of the Evil Eye. These charms look like little eyes, usually blue and white in colour, although sometimes a simple blue bead was worn to the same effect. They work by drawing negative energy into the eye and away from the wearer. Such charms were also painted on doors and houses, to ward against passing evil and keep the inhabitants safe from any ill wishes. Some of this superstition still echoes in modern society, particularly in expressions such as 'if looks could kill' and 'she was giving me the side eye,' which is a way of saying someone was giving out evil glares. Use the spells below to guard against this type of negative energy.

Spell to Guard Against the Evil Eye

Items required: a lapis lazuli crystal necklace, a pebble, black, blue and white paint, clear varnish
Timing: during the waning moon to draw the negativity away from you

First draw or paint the image of a blue eye on the pebble. Use images of traditional evil-eye charms on the internet to inspire you. You don't need to be an artist as this charm is very simple in design. Once the paint has dried, add a coat of clear varnish to protect it. Leave the evil eye and the lapis lazuli in the light of the moon for a full lunar phase, then wear the necklace and carry the charmed pebble with you, to draw away all negative energies heading your way. This spell is particularly useful for people who work in customer service or anywhere there is likely to be conflict.

Spell to Deflect Ill Wishes

Items required: a mirror, or your dominant hand
Timing: use whenever someone is sending spitefulness or ill wishes your way

If you feel that someone is being spiteful towards you, here is a magical trick you can use to send their bad energy straight back to them. Ideally you would use a small compact mirror, but this isn't always possible and so you can also use your dominant hand instead. The next time someone throws spite in your direction or verbally attacks you, wait until they walk away then simply reject their bad energy by holding up the mirror or your hand towards their back and saying:

> *Deflected, rejected, returned times three,*
> *times three, times three again*
> *May your negativity surround only you*

Fire and Brimstone Spell to See Off Your Enemies

Items required: a box of matches, a cauldron or ashtray
Timing: on a waning moon

If you have a known enemy who is working against you, this simple spell can help to diminish their vendetta. Sulphur has been used in protection spells for centuries. Also known as brimstone, it is a staple in the witch's magical cabinet, usually in the form of matches. Matches are an easy and accessible way to use sulphur in your spells, so it's a good idea to always keep a box handy. Place your empty cauldron in front of you and the box of matches on your lap. Take out a match and name it for the *actions* of your enemy, for example:

I name this match for those who try to sabotage my career
Let their vendetta against me burn out with it

Strike the match and watch it burn, then drop it into the cauldron just before the flame reaches your fingers and say:

Ashes to ashes and dust to dust

Repeat with as many matches as it takes until you feel the magic *pop*. This is usually a feeling of energy released from the solar plexus area of your body, followed by a feeling of euphoria. Know that the magic is in play and your enemy should move on within the month.

Spell to Protect Your Own Interests

Items required: a small cardboard box such as a matchbox, the issue that is under threat written on a slip of paper, dried herbs of rosemary and basil for protection, a length of bramble, a thistle, gardening gloves
Timing: at the time of the waning moon

This is a great spell to defend against a covert foe who is working against you in some way, though not openly. It is a spell to protect yourself against the underhand back-stabbers of the world. They might be trying to sabotage your business, undermine you at work, steal your job or your partner, tarnish your reputation etc. You are entitled to defend your own interests and hard-won achievements, so whatever the nature of this covert attack is, write it down on a slip of paper as soon as you become aware of it. Sign and date the paper, then put it in the box and add the herbs until the box is full. Put on the gardening gloves and wind the bramble around the box, twisting the stem so that it is securely in place. Weave a thistle into the bramble on top of the box. Place it in the light of the waning moon and say:

> *You cannot touch me, you cannot*
> *harm me*
> *You cannot take what's mine*
> *You cannot scare me, you cannot*
> *diminish me*
> *You cannot destroy what's mine*
> *You cannot stop me, you cannot*
> *beat me*
> *For if you even try*
> *By sharpest thorn and vengeful thistle*
> *This magic will reply!*

Keep the spell box in a safe place, maybe near your altar. Know that if someone moves against you and your success, they will only bring upon themselves the retribution of your spell, via the threefold law.

GLOBAL THREATS

War zones, areas of conflict, terrorist attacks… the headlines can be scary at times and we should not underestimate global threats and their potential to impact on our own way of life. Although we are extremely well protected thanks to our armed and police forces, we ourselves are far from helpless and there are magical things that you can do to help those people who put themselves at risk to protect us.

Take a tip from the World War II years and the witches of that time who were very active in casting spells to aid the war effort. Among these witches was Doreen Valiente, widely regarded as the mother of modern witchcraft, who in interviews has spoken of standing with other witches on the coast

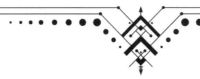

of Britain throwing 'go-away' powder (a blend of herbs with banishing properties) into an ebbing tide and chanting *Go away!* at the Nazis. This is proactive witchery at its best and Nazi boots never landed on UK soil, partly because their attempts floundered due to inclement weather conditions.

Modern witches can make a similar stand for their country by fighting the darkness of terrorism with the love and light of positive magic. We can join together to help magically protect our nations and all those who choose to live in peace. I live in the United Kingdom, which is a country where women are empowered. Our nation is ruled by a queen as head of state and is symbolized on the 50p coin by the powerful warrior goddess Britannia, dressed for battle. In standing together, we can project the light of peace and love across Britain with this magical ritual of protection.

A Blessing for the United Kingdom (you can modify this blessing for your own country)

Items required: a map of the UK and a 50-pence coin (or similar items to denote your own country), a lighter and a sage smudge bundle
Timing: on a waning moon to push back hatred and strife

Take the items to a quiet place and spend a few moments thinking about the love and peace you want to create. Open the map so you have a clear image of the UK, or your country, before you. Place the coin, tails side up, to represent Britannia, the goddess of these islands, in the middle of the map and then light the smudge stick. Blow it out when the end glows red and gently waft the smoke all around the map of the UK as you say the following incantation, or words of your own that reflect the values of your country.

By Andrew, Patrick, David and George
Our spell of love and light is forged
By Britannia's shield, helm and spear
We choose to live in peace, not fear
Four great countries united stand
A patron strong for every land
And with the strength of Wiccan school
We stand against hatred by Britannia's
 rule

Continue to smudge the map for a few minutes more, then end the spell by saying:

This blessing shines upon the UK
 this night; in love and trust, in peace
 and light.
Blessed be

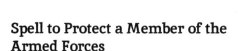

Spell to Protect a Member of the Armed Forces

Items required: a photo of your soldier and suitable frame, five pressed calendula flowers, a black pen and ruler, glue, a tea-light and holder
Timing: on the full moon for strongest power

Take all the items to a quiet place where you will not be disturbed. Spend some time thinking of your serviceman or woman and envisioning a sphere of white light all around them, guarding them and keeping them safe. Now draw a pentagram star on the back of the photo and glue a pressed calendula flower to each point. Calendula is associated with protection against harm, especially from unknown dangers. Let the photo sit undisturbed as the glue dries, then light a tea-light and say:

Guarded, guided and protected be
Everywhere you go
From all enemies that you face
From all the dangers you do not know
Protected be through time and space
Safe and sound from every foe
Come back safe, and well and whole
To those who love you best

Once the glue has dried, put the photo in the frame and keep it where you will see it every day. On a daily basis, light a tea-light before it and repeat the incantation to keep the protection magic strong. If you do not have a photo, you can use the soldier's name written down and glue the flowers to that. This spell can be used to protect all those who work in the armed forces and the emergency services too. Use it in conjunction with the *Spell to Protect a Loved One* for added power.

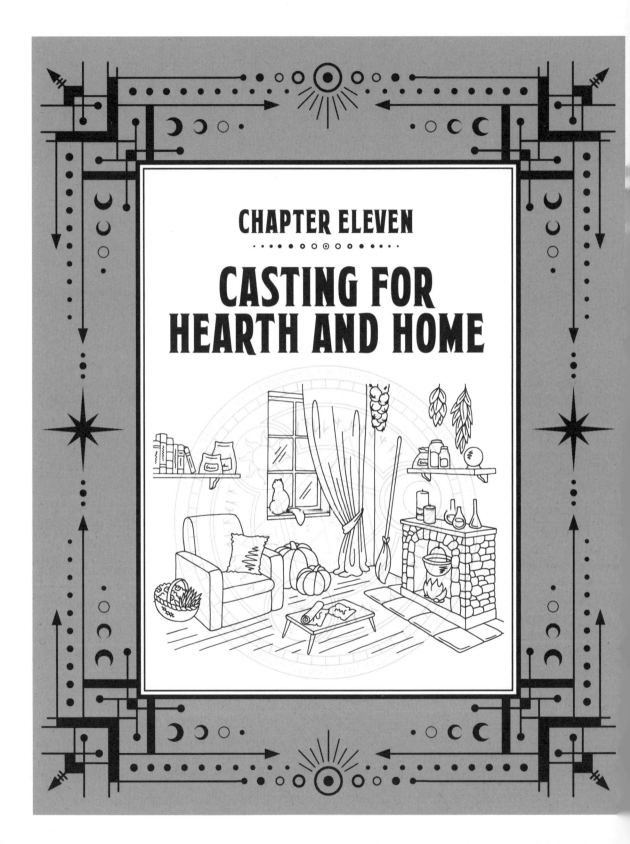

CHAPTER ELEVEN

· · · · · · ◦ ⊙ ◦ · · · · · ·

CASTING FOR HEARTH AND HOME

Your home should feel like the safest place in the world to you. Whether it is a student bedsit or a palatial mansion, it is your space and it should serve as a welcome retreat from the everyday world. A home is a place of cosy comfort and restoration, somewhere you can relax, recharge and close out the rest of society if you choose. It should be a place of freedom of expression, where you can speak your mind and display your personality in the decor and the things you have around you. It could also be somewhere that you throw open the doors to welcome friends and neighbours, in the spirit of congeniality. For some people, home will be a minimalist place, for others it will be full of things that hold memories and sentimental value. After all, no two homes are ever the same. They are as unique as the people living in them.

While few people are fortunate enough to live in a fairy-tale cottage on the edge of a forest or by the sea, you can still bring an element of witchy enchantment into your home, regardless of where you live. Witches have always placed charms upon their homes. These charms could be for protection, relaxation, harmony, hospitality and many other things, but a witch's house is always imbued with magical energy. Visitors often pick up on this energy, commenting on how relaxed they feel and how the house has a lovely atmosphere. Often, they can't wait to come back for another visit and might even try to evoke the same atmosphere in their own homes. You can create this kind of magical atmosphere too, using the spells in this chapter to cast an air of charm and enchantment around your place, however grand or humble your abode might be.

THE HEARTH WITCH

A hearth witch is a magical practitioner who works in solitude from the comfort of her own home. They are usually concerned with local issues and concentrate mainly on creating a safe and magical home for themselves and their families. Hearth witches tend to cast simple spells, using easily accessible ingredients that can be found around the house or purchased easily. Hearth witchery is a type of folk magic and the spells throughout this book fall into that category, in that they do not involve high-ritual magic. The spells in this chapter will help you to turn your home into a magical haven and a refuge from all the stresses and strains of everyday life. In using them, you can begin to turn your own home into a modern version of the fabled witch's cottage.

THE MAGICAL HEARTH

The hearth is the heart of the home. In the past it was where huge fires blazed to keep out the winter cold and where a great cauldron hung, cooking food for the family and their guests. These days not every home has a hearth, many being heated with central or underfloor heating systems. This has robbed some modern homes of the magical hearth, so it is always nice to recreate one if you can, using an electric stove or a collection of candles. If you do still have a hearth and mantelpiece, then try to make this the focal point of the room, arranging crystals, candles and ornaments here to represent your magical life and personal interests. The hearth is associated with the goddess Bride or Bridget and as such it should be swept clean, with a fresh candle lit here every day to honour her and encourage her blessings to fall upon the house. Tea-lights work best for this, as you can easily burn one each evening. If you have a real fire, you should not let the ashes mount up as that will draw poverty and hardship to the home. Keep your hearthside clean and the use the blessing below.

Bride's Blessing of the Hearth and Home

Items required: a stick of your favourite incense and holder, two white candles and holders
Timing: each new moon, and on the festival of Imbolc (St Brigid's Day), February 2nd

When you have cleaned your hearth and dusted the mantelpiece, arrange your candles on either side of the hearth or mantel. Light them and then light the incense stick. Wave

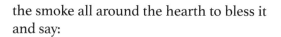

the smoke all around the hearth to bless it and say:

I call Bride's blessings here this day
To guard this place and keep ill at bay

Place the stick in an incense holder and allow it to burn in dedication to Bride and her powers of hearth and home.

Spell to Protect the Hearth
Items required: five small elder or rowan twigs, about 4–5cm (1½–2 inches) long, string or red thread and ribbon
Timing: when the moon is full

The traditional hearth and chimney was long considered to be a portal to the house through which negative energies could enter. Therefore, it was always protected with magic. Go to a place where elder grows and look on the ground for a fallen twig. If there are none, ask the tree's permission before you cut a small length of thin twig, ensuring that it is long enough to cut into the five pieces needed for the spell. Take the twigs home and let them dry out, then on the full moon use the twigs to create a pentacle or five-pointed star. Tie the twigs securely at each point with the string or thread, then loop the ribbon through the top point and hang it from the mantelpiece. The elder is a

sacred tree of protection and the elder star will protect your hearthside from bad vibes coming in and disrupting the harmony of your household.

Blessing to Ward Doors and Windows
Items required: a stick of your chosen incense
Timing: daily, ideally each evening before you go to bed

Windows and doors are also portals into your home through which negative energies can enter from the street. They are the usual way in which intruders get into your home too, so make sure that you have sturdy locks in place and never leave windows open when you are not at home. Use this daily

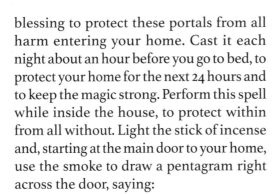

blessing to protect these portals from all harm entering your home. Cast it each night about an hour before you go to bed, to protect your home for the next 24 hours and to keep the magic strong. Perform this spell while inside the house, to protect within from all without. Light the stick of incense and, starting at the main door to your home, use the smoke to draw a pentagram right across the door, saying:

Keep safe this house, protected be
None shall cross this boundary
Keep safe this house, a welcome place
To those invited to this space

Move around the house in a clockwise direction, repeating the process at every external door and window, on all floors, then place the incense in a holder to burn out. Repeat daily.

Silent Triple-Goddess Blessing for a Harmonious Home

Items required: a small paint brush, silver paint or moonflower oil
Timing: new to full moon

Lots of witches' homes have hand-painted artwork, sigils and symbols on the walls and doors, and for this spell you are going to invoke the blessings of the Triple Goddess by decorating your home with her symbol. Don't worry if you don't have permission to paint, or if you need to keep your interest in magic a secret – you can substitute the silver paint for moonflower oil instead, which should dry without showing any sign. Decide where you want to paint the sigil. You could draw it at the top of the front door, over the mantelpiece, on a headboard, along beams or banisters and kitchen cupboards etc. Once you have decided on the area you wish to charm, use the silver paint or oil to paint the shape of the Triple Goddess symbol, imagining a silver-white light surrounding your home and blessing it with love, joy and harmony. Allow the paint to dry or the oil to fade and know that you have used the creative arts to imbue some magic into your house. You can repeat this spell in any room, or use other symbols too, such as power animals or runes, to give your home a very magical ambience. Be prepared to explain the symbols to visitors! As an alternative, you can purchase magical symbols as window decals that easily stick on and peel off, which would work just as well and can quickly be removed and reused.

A Magical House-Cleansing Ritual

Items required: a besom or broomstick, a mop and bucket, cleaning cloths, three lemons (sliced), hot water, eucalyptus essential oil
Timing: twice a year at spring and autumn equinoxes, or whenever your home feels a little heavy and stagnant

Magical cleansings are performed to imbue the home with fresh and vibrant energies. In this instance we are using lemon and eucalyptus as they can help to rid the house of any stagnant energy or bad vibes. Performing a cleansing like this one can be useful after a period of unrest or disagreement between residents. First clean the entire house from top to bottom as you normally would. Open all the windows to let fresh air circulate. Then ritually sweep your house throughout using the besom or broomstick – don't actually touch the floor, just sweep up all that negative energy, moving around the home in an anticlockwise direction and keeping the broom about 2.5cm (1 inch) or so above the floor. Take all that bad energy to the door and then sweep it right out of the house, saying: *Begone and don't return!* Next fill the mop bucket with hot water and add the three sliced lemons and ten drops of eucalyptus oil. Go around the home and use the cleansing water to wash down all doors, windows and touch points, again moving in an anticlockwise direction to banish the bad vibes, then finally mop the floors. Use what is left of the water to sprinkle along garden paths, or make up a new batch and wash the doors and windows on the outside too. Drain the water away and place the lemons to compost. Now have a cup of tea and a rest, because you've earned it!

A Quick Cleansing Ritual

Items required: a sage smudge stick, an ashtray or small heat-proof bowl, a feather or your hand
Timing: use to dispel a negative atmosphere after an argument, illness, bereavement or bad news

way, extinguish the sage and allow it to cool before you put it away for next time.

Apple Spell to Ward Off Nasty Nearby Residents

Items required: two apples, an athame, honey (optional)
Timing: use as needed, but this spell is more powerful when cast during a waning moon

If you have troublesome neighbours then this spell should nip their behaviour in the bud, or at least prevent it from reaching you and your property. First use the athame to cut the two apples in half across the equator line and straight through the apple core. This will reveal the five-pointed star at the heart of the fruit, which is made up of apple seeds. This spell works in two ways. The pentacle at the centre of the fruit acts as a ward to keep your neighbour's negative energy from encroaching on your life. At the same time, the apple is regarded as a fruit of love, so you are also sending positive energy in their direction, which should help to neutralize and diffuse any unpleasantness between you. If you like, you can add a coat of honey to the flat half of the apple to further sweeten the situation. After dark, place the four apple halves along the boundary line between their property and yours. Alternatively, place two apple halves by your front gate and two

Sometimes you might just need a quick boost to the energy of your home. If you don't have time to perform a full cleansing ritual like the one above, then sage is your best friend. It is renowned for its power to fill an area with positive energy and has been used by Native Americans in their rituals for centuries. Sage is a natural cleanser, the smoke is quite pleasant and smudge bundles are inexpensive to buy, or you can make your own by drying a bundle of sage that you have grown yourself. To clear your space of bad vibes, light the smudge stick and go all around your home, ensuring that you waft the cleansing smoke into every corner of every room. Keep going until each room feels lighter, then move on to the next. Once you have smudged the whole house in this along the boundary line of the gardens or by your front door, to keep trouble away from your home. If you don't have a garden, then substitute the apples for dark crystals which soak up negative energy such as smoky quartz or haematite, and place these on the inside of your apartment by the door and along the wall closest to the troublesome neighbours.

Spell to Live Safely in a Bad Area
Items required: a crystal sun catcher, bergamot oil
Timing: during the full moon

If you find yourself living in a difficult neighbourhood, guard your home with crystal magic. A crystal sun catcher is just the thing to keep your home full of positive energy as it will reflect the light of both sun and moon into it. In addition, its reflective surface will bounce away any bad vibes that come towards your house from the neighbourhood. Anoint the crystal with protective bergamot oil to further enhance its magic and re-anoint it every full moon for the best results.

Lilac Blessing for a Happy Home and Family
Items required: a stem of lilac or lilac essential oil, spring water, sea salt, a chalice
Timing: on the new moon

To bring good blessings on your home and family, call on the powers of lilac. Lilac is associated with fun, joy, happiness and the energies of late spring and early summer when it blooms. It is a very cheery bloom filled with positive energies. Pour the spring water into your chalice and add a pinch of sea salt. Swirl the chalice to help the salt dissolve, then add the essential oil if you choose to use it. Dip the lilac flower into the water and flick it around the house as you say:

Lilac bloom of springtime power
Fill this house with joy
Bring peace and happiness through this
  flower
And a harmony we all enjoy

Kitchen Witch Household Guardian

Items required: a small statue or picture of a witch that you find pleasing, salt, dried sage
Timing: best performed around Halloween/Samhain, October 31st

Most magical homes have some kind of household guardian within them. In this instance we are using a statue of a witch, but you can use something else if you prefer. Traditionally a small witch was kept in the kitchen to oversee all the domesticity that went on there. These little statues came to be known as kitchen witches and they were said to bring good luck. You can still find kitchen witches for sale online and in some New Age shops. Samhain, otherwise known as Halloween, is an excellent time to find one. Once you have found your witch, take her into the kitchen and put her on a plate, then surround her with a circle of salt and sage. Hold your hands over her and say:

A kitchen witch here resides
Her magic strong, no need to hide
All who come here feel her power
For she guards and protects us from this
hour

Leave the witch in place for 24 hours, then find a home for her somewhere in the kitchen where she can oversee everything. Scatter the salt and sage to the four winds, giving thanks.

Aloe Vera to Heal Minor Burns

Items required: a potted aloe vera plant
Timing: keep this plant in the kitchen at all times

Aloe vera is a natural remedy for minor burns so it is a good idea to keep such a plant in your kitchen, just in case. It is sometimes referred to as the burn plant for this very reason. To use, cut away two or three of the thickest leaves which tend to grow on the outer edge of the plant. Peel away the outside of the leaf to expose the soft gel inside. Apply this gel to the burn and gently rub into the skin. It

has a cooling effect which offers immediate relief and the medicinal properties of the plant make the burn heal faster. It is not to be used on severe burns, however, so if the burn site is deep or if it covers an area larger than 7.5cm (3 inches) across, seek immediate hospital treatment. You should never, ever put butter or oil on any kind of burn!

Silent Eucalyptus Ritual for a Sacred Shower

Items required: a stem of fresh eucalyptus
Timing: new to full moon

The bathroom is where you begin and end the day, so it needs to be a welcoming place. Showering off the day before bed is a sacred time of self-care. It helps your mind to move from work time into home and family time and it can aid in a restful night's sleep. To give your bathroom a more magical spa-like atmosphere, hang a branch of fresh eucalyptus inside the shower, where the steam will release its calming scent. As you shower, imagine all the psychic grime of the day washing away from you and going down the drain. Breathe in the rejuvenating scent of eucalyptus and know that you are safe at home and it is time to switch off and relax. You can enhance this spell by using lavender- or eucalyptus-scented toiletries.

And So to Bed Blessing

Items required: a small blue pouch, amethyst, blue lace agate and sodalite crystals, a teaspoon of dried lavender flowers, an altar pentacle
Timing: on the full moon

Your bed should be a welcome retreat at the end of a long day and this little pouch of crystals and lavender will help to ensure that you get a restful night's sleep. Place all the items to charge on the pentacle for a full lunar phase, then place the crystals and the lavender in the pouch. Hang it from the bedpost or place it beneath the mattress to bring about restful sleep.

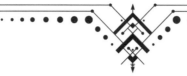

Blessing for Sweet Dreams

Items required: lavender sleep spray
Timing: perform each time you change the bed sheets

If you or your child has been having a run of bad dreams, then start to include this blessing as part of your household chores. First of all, change the bed sheets, and as you put on the clean bedding, spray it generously with the lavender sleep spray, inside and out. Give every part of the bedding a spray, so that the fragrance envelops the sleeper when they get into bed. You can also use lavender-scented ironing water to the same effect. As you spritz the bed say the following incantation:

> *Lavender let the dreams be sweet*
> *For all who lie within these sheets*
> *I cast this spell with love and charm*
> *To keep the sleeper safe from harm*
> *So mote it be*

As you finish making the bed, pat the pillow three times saying, *Rest, Recharge, Restore.* Hang a dream catcher close by for additional protection against nightmares.

Pins and Needles Spell to Keep Away Unwanted Visitors

Items required: an external doormat, two sewing pins or needles
Timing: on the night of the dark moon

It can be so annoying when your precious time at home is disturbed by salesmen, canvassers and nuisance neighbours, so try this little spell to keep all unwanted visitors away from your door. Take an extra-thick external door mat and on the underside of it weave two sewing pins or needles through the fabric so that they form the shape of a St Andrew's cross and remain in place. Ensure that the sharp points of the pins or needles are facing away from your home and out into the street or the corridor of the apartment block. Put the mat in front of the main door to your home and, as you place it down, say,

> *Those I do not wish to see, banished,*
> *banished, banished be!*

piece of paper, light the end and drop it in the cauldron to burn. Finally add a pinch of dried basil to the flames and say:

I wish to move, I will not stay
A new home comes to me this day
A dream now burns for which I long
Basil moves all things along
It brings to me that which I desire
As I move on to a new hearth fire

Angel of the House Blessing

Items required: incense and candle of your choice, but these are optional
Timing: *on a Sunday*

The Victorians believed in the angel of the house. There were two ways they looked at this concept. The first was that every home had a celestial being watching over it and protecting the family that lived there. The second was that the lady of the house was the human embodiment of this angel and should be honoured and respected as such. It was the Victorian way of saying *Happy Wife, Happy Life!* Pagans also believe that buildings have guardian spirits watching over them, so with this little blessing you are going to invoke the angel of your home and ask for their blessing. You don't need any

Fire Spell to Move to a New Home

Items required: a notepad and pen, an idea or image of where you want to move to, your cauldron, lighter, dried basil

If you are wanting to move house but don't seem to be getting anywhere, try this spell to get things moving. Fire spells are a great way to remove any blocks that are in your way. First, write down all the reasons you wish to move and what you are looking for in your new home. Picture the area or house you want to move to clearly in your mind. Hold that visualization and see yourself there, unpacking boxes and directing the movers with your furniture. Once you can see this plainly in your mind, roll up the

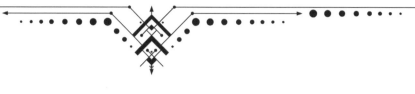

tools for the spell, but you can light candles and incense if you wish. Stand in the main hub of your home – perhaps the kitchen or by the hearthside, wherever you feel the heart of your home is. Close your eyes and visualize the angel of your home. What does it look like, how does it act? How would you know that this angel is connected to your home and family and not to anyone else's? When you feel ready, introduce yourself and then say the following prayer.

Angel of this home I call you near
To guard this sacred space
Bless this abode and settle here
Fill this house with grace
Watch over all who live within
The safety of these walls
Guard and guide all herein
Angel heed this sacred call

Magical Tips for an Enchanted Home

- Plant lavender for good luck.
- Plant rosemary by the gate or near your front door for protection.
- Stick dried bay leaves inside the letterbox to bring prosperity to your door.
- Nurture a money tree to keep poverty at bay.
- Place a broomstick by the door to keep away unwelcome guests.
- Always keep salt in the home to ensure a life of plenty.

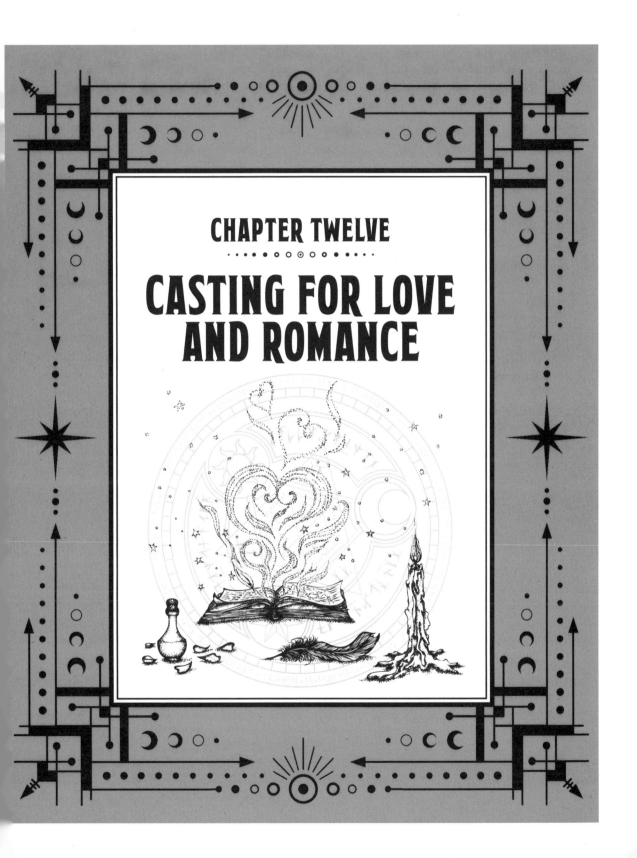

CHAPTER TWELVE

CASTING FOR LOVE AND ROMANCE

Witches are often asked to perform magic on behalf of other people, with prosperity magic and love spells being the most frequently requested. While it is possible for a witch to cast a spell for you, it will never be as effective as the spells that you cast for yourself. This is because the witch simply does not have the same emotional investment in the outcome that you do and we mentioned earlier how crucial your emotions are to effective casting. This is especially true when it comes to love spells.

Love magic is particularly dependent upon emotions, for there is no greater feeling than that of love. There is no drug or adrenalin-junkie experience that can compare to the feeling of falling in love with someone you think is wonderful. They don't call it *falling* in love for no reason. Love frequently takes us completely by surprise, coming along when we least expect it and leading us into a headlong stumble into a relationship. The fall can be amazing – providing that the object of your desires is there to catch you. Unrequited love is a painful experience, yet the love itself is real enough – it just isn't being reciprocated. And then of course there is heartbreak, brought about by betrayal, loss or a lover who simply changed their mind, as people are wont to do.

Love is amazing, exhilarating, confusing, infuriating and frustrating. At times, it can be a lonely experience too. It is nevertheless a road that we must all navigate in our lives, often more than once, so having magic on your side to help smooth out the bumps in the road towards romance can only be a good thing!

The image of a witch casting spells to *make* someone love them, however, is exaggerated to say the least. You cannot force someone to love you. Either they do or they don't. Maybe they did once, but not any more. They have the free will to choose to love you or to pass you by and that is their prerogative. Love is a gift that must be offered freely and unconditionally. It is not something that can be bartered for.

The feeling of falling in love is so intense and joyful that it should come as no surprise that people want to experience it more than once. If a relationship becomes stale or entrapping, it makes sense that they might want to break free so that they can have another chance at that wonderful free-fall into romantic bliss. In any long-term relationship, both parties come to a stage where they either agree to tolerate one another's foibles, or they go their separate ways. The most damaging relationships are the ones where there is no tolerance, but no possibility of escape either, meaning that the couple are stuck in a cycle of mutual loathing and resentment. This toxic situation is extremely damaging to both parties and to any children they might have. While not everyone is lucky enough to spend their lives billing and cooing at their ideal partner like a pair of doves, there are ways to keep the romance alive for the long term. It all begins, however, with love for yourself.

SELF-LOVE IS KEY

We live in a world where comparison is rife in society. Social media means that we are constantly bombarded with images of other people, their lifestyle, their clothes, even the food they eat and the places they go. All of this can have a negative impact on your self-esteem if you let it. Remember that social media is a highlight reel and the people you follow will have dark days and low moods, just as you do. After all, nobody's life is perfect.

The impact of all this comparison, however, is that people often find it challenging to love themselves or to think of themselves as worthy human beings. Instead they fall into the trap of feeling as if they aren't good enough, rich enough, pretty enough or *anything* enough for the modern world. But for someone else to love you, you have to love yourself first. Why is this? Well, it's because bolstering someone else's self-esteem can be exhausting and it is quite a turn-off. People are reluctant to attach themselves to someone who is extremely needy, clingy and dependent on them for feelings of worthiness. They are more likely to be charmed by someone who is in a good place mentally and who is okay with being alone from time to time. So your best chance at a love match is to learn to love yourself first and foremost and to know that you are a worthy human being.

Continue for as long as you feel comfortable, then blow out the candle. Repeat each night until the moon is full or the candle has burnt away.

Silent Ritual Charm for Self-Love

Items required: a small spell jar and stopper, rose incense stick and holder, a small slip of paper and a pen, a lock of your hair, three rose quartz shards, three dried rose petals, pink Himalayan salt, a pink candle or sealing wax, a pentacle
Timing: at the time of the full moon

To begin with, cleanse the spell jar using the smoke from the rose incense stick, then place the incense in a holder to burn throughout the ritual. Write your name and date of birth on the slip of paper, roll it around the lock of hair and put it into the spell jar. Add the three rose petals and rose quartz shards. Fill the jar with the pink salt, put on the stopper and seal it with pink wax. Leave the spell jar in place on the pentacle until the following full moon, then place it by your bed or on your dressing table to exude its magic.

Blessing for Self-Love

Items required: a pink candle and holder, a pink ribbon, a ring that is special to you
Timing: at the time of the new moon to bring out your self-worth

When the first sliver of a new moon is visible in the sky, go to a quiet place, taking the necessary items with you. Light the pink candle and focus on the flame. Then thread the ring onto the pink ribbon and begin to twirl it around the candle flame in a clockwise direction, following the path of the sun. As you do so, chant the words

I am worthy of love, from myself and others

ROMANCING YOUR LIFE

Dating yourself is one of the most positive things that you can do, not only when you are single but when you are in a relationship too. It simply isn't healthy to *not* go out alone from time to time. You need to experience and maintain your independence, even if you are deeply in love. Romancing your life is the art of turning everyday events into moments of magic. It is about using the best china if you want to, or wearing your best outfit to go shopping. It is about going to see a movie on your own, stopping for coffee at a nice café on the way back.

Saving things *for best* is the antithesis of romancing your life and dating yourself. Don't keep your best candles just for when people come over! I'm not suggesting that you swan down the supermarket aisle in a ball gown and tiara, but I am saying that life is too short to keep loveliness at bay, which is what we do when we save things for best. So make sure that you do light the posh scented candle, wear the expensive perfume, use the *good* coffee and enjoy it! Life is meant to be lived one day at a time, with the things we have at our disposal in the moment. You never know what is around the corner, so make sure that you are enjoying the things you own now and in the moment. Not only will this make you happier in the short term, that daily joy will compound over time, leading to a sense of deep contentment in your own life – which can be very attractive. Make time to date and romance yourself and your own life, without a partner, and then when love shows up, not only will you already be living a lovely life, but you will probably be wearing one of your best outfits too!

Tips for Romancing and Dating Yourself

- Buy yourself fresh flowers.
- Treat yourself to a box of chocolates.
- Write a love letter to yourself, expressing admiration for all your charms and gifts.
- Take yourself to see a film or theatre

production alone.

- Visit a nice café or restaurant alone and order something delicious.
- Buy a pastry from a patisserie, have it boxed up and take it home to eat as you choose.
- Set the table and make a delicious breakfast or brunch to start the day.
- Go on holiday alone and explore new places.
- Try something new.
- Book a lesson in something you have always wanted to learn such as horse riding or piano playing.
- Have a spa day, either at home or at your favourite spa.
- Find a love poem which sums up your personality and quote it like a mantra.
- Wear diamonds and pearls, or your best adornments.
- Wear your finest fragrance just because you can.
- Burn scented candles or essential oils daily, to create a romantic atmosphere.

Pink Self-Love Bath Potion

Items required: pink candles, pink Himalayan salt, a few rose petals
Timing: whenever you are feeling frazzled

There will be days when you feel that you cannot do anything right, when you've been running late since the beginning and one mishap led straight into another, leaving you feeling stressed and decidedly frazzled. On those days, show yourself some love with this bath potion. Mix together equal parts pink Himalayan salt and rose petals, then stir this mixture into a hot bath. The salt is known to reduce fatigue, replacing tiredness with feelings of contentment and emotional balance, while the rose petals will soften the skin as the fragrance uplifts you. Wallow in the water for as long as you comfortably can, then dry off and allow your troubles to go down the drain, ensuring that you dispose of the rose petals on the compost heap. Enhance this ritual by using rose-scented toiletries.

ATTRACTING LOVE

Self-love also involves making the best of your appearance, which in turn helps you to attract a mate. There is no use complaining that you never get invited on a date if you go about your day looking as if you have just been dragged through a hedge! In order to attract love, you need to make sure that you are looking as attractive as possible and making the most of your charms. You don't need film-star looks, you just need to make sure that you look your best at all times, as you never know who you might meet. You don't want to have to jump *back* into the hedge because your Mx Wonderful is across the street and you look a mess – what a wasted opportunity for romance that would be! In movies they sometimes call lovers' first meeting the *meet-cute*. While this doesn't mean to look cute when you meet someone, you can use the phrase to remind you to look attractive as you go about your daily life.

There are some things in life that you cannot control, but your appearance and how you present yourself to the world *isn't* one of them. If you want to attract love, prepare for each day as if you are going to meet it head on. Then cast the following spells to enhance your allure and attract love.

Three-Moons Spell to Attract Love

Items required: three red candles, half a teaspoon of blessing seeds, mortar and pestle, kitchen roll, rose or lavender oil, an athame or carving tool, a cauldron or heat-proof bowl, a lighter
Timing: on the full moon, three months in a row

Take one of the candles and carve what you are hoping to attract into the length of the wax; you could carve Love, Romance, New Boyfriend/Girlfriend etc. Put half a teaspoon of blessing seeds, also known as nigella seeds, into the mortar and grind to a powder with the pestle. Empty the powder onto a sheet of kitchen roll, anoint the candle in the oil then roll it through the blessing-seed powder, pulling the candle towards you to draw love into your life as you say:

> *A lover comes by candle's glow*
> *From where or when I do not know*
> *They come to me, true love to share*
> *As the smoke curls through the air*
> *As this wax melts, so do our hearts*
> *Together a new life we start*
> *And by the burning of this flame*
> *Within three/two/one moons I will*
>   *know their name*
> *So mote it be*

Melt the bottom of the candle and set it in the cauldron. Light the wick and allow it to burn down completely. Repeat with the next candle on the next full moon, adapting the final line of the incantation so that you are counting down the moons until your lover appears.

Love Witch Spell

Items required: a king or queen of hearts playing card, rose oil or water, a magnet
Timing: on the new moon

If you want to draw more love into your life, then use this spell to become a love magnet! On the night of the new moon, take the items to a quiet place where you will not be disturbed. Take the playing card and anoint the four corners, back and front, with rose oil or rose water, then gently brush the magnet across the image of the king or queen, beginning at the crown and moving down towards the chest of the image. As you do so, chant the words:

Like the king/queen of hearts, I am a magnet to love

Continue until you feel the magic *pop*, then place the playing card in your purse or wallet and carry it with you at all times. You should notice that you attract more romantic attention in the coming weeks and months.

Silent Charm for Luck in Love

Items required: red or pink sealing wax, greaseproof paper, ground cinnamon powder, a seal which represents love – a heart, rose or cupid design – or a carving tool

Heat the sealing wax and pour or drip it into a large pool on the greaseproof paper, add a sprinkling of cinnamon to draw good luck and blessings towards you, then apply the seal to the cooling wax to create an image. If you do not have a romantic seal, then use your carving tool once the wax has cooled and carve a love heart into the wax. Once the wax has hardened, peel off the greaseproof paper and carry the charm with you to attract lucky love prospects.

White Rose Spell to Determine Someone's True Intentions

Items required: a single white rose, a white ribbon, a bud vase and water, a slip of paper, a red pen
Timing: at the new moon

Not everyone who flirts with you will have positive or good intentions. The white rose is a symbol of purity and can be used to determine if your lover's intentions towards you are honourable or not. To begin with, write their name on the slip of paper in red ink. Use the ribbon to tie the name tag on to the stem of the rose. Hold your hands over the rose and say:

> *A nagging doubt is in my mind so I must test their will*
> *Their true intentions I would find, be they good or ill*
> *Rose of love and purity, now tell all with your charm*
> *Is this lover true to me, or do they mean me harm?*

Place the rose in a bud vase of water and care for it well. If it blooms and opens wide, your lover's intentions towards you are pure and kind. If, however, the rose fails to open

fully, then wilts and dies, they are holding secrets from you and their intentions are questionable. Let the rose be your guide.

Spell to Bring Love to Your Door

Items required: three red or pink roses
Timing: best performed at sunset, during a waxing moon

Pull the petals from three red or pink roses and put them in a pocket, pouch or bowl. Go outside and walk away from your house, enjoying the sunset and imagining sharing the view with a lover. Once you are some way from your home, turn around and begin to walk back. Chant the following words, out loud or in your head:

Love will come knocking and I will answer

As you walk, scatter the rose petals so that they form a trail right up to your door, but do not use them all up. Keep a few back and place these in a pouch or trinket dish by your bed. Love should come knocking within a full lunar phase.

Apple Spell to Deepen Bonds of Love

Items required: at least one apple (more if you choose the pie option), a sharp knife, cinnamon and nutmeg
Timing: best performed during a waxing moon, or on a special anniversary
Tradition states that to share an apple with your partner will help to deepen the bonds of love between you, and there are two ways that you can use this magic. For a simple charm, cut an apple in half horizontally through the core to expose the seed pentacle in the middle, sprinkle it with cinnamon and nutmeg for a fruitful union, then give one half to your lover and eat the other half yourself. Alternatively, you can choose to bake the magic into an apple pie, by following a basic recipe and adding a generous sprinkling of the spices to the apples just before you cover them in pastry. For added magic, top the pie with the initials of you and your lover in pastry, then share the pie as part of a romantic dinner.

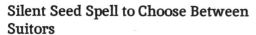

Silent Seed Spell to Choose Between Suitors

Items required: a pink, white or cream pillar candle, three (or however many suitors you have) pumpkin seeds, a black felt-tip pen, a lighter

Timing: on the full to waning moon to whittle down the competition

If you are a flower to bees (lucky you!) and you are having difficulty in choosing between suitors, then use this simple spell. First write the initial of each suitor on one of the pumpkin seeds with black pen. Next heat up the side of the candle with the lighter so that you can stick the seeds to the candle. Make sure that all the seeds are in a row, at the same height. Each suitor is now represented with a seed that bears his or her initial. Finally, light the wick of the candle. As the candle burns, the seeds should fall, but the seed which sticks the longest is the suitor you should choose, as they are the type to stick around.

Spell to Heal a Rift Between Lovers

Items required: an empty jar and lid, a jar of runny honey, pink paper, scissors, a pen, pink or red sealing wax

Timing: during the waning moon to remove the discord between you

Relationships can be hard work at times and you won't always see eye to eye with your partner. If an argument has left a lingering atmosphere of discord between you, cast this spell to help heal the rift. Cut two love hearts from the pink paper. Write your name on one heart and your lover's name on the other. Hold your hands over the hearts and visualize the rift healing. Imagine enjoying happy, romantic times with your partner again. Drop both hearts into the empty jar, then add enough runny honey to cover them, surrounding the couple in sweetness as you say:

I am sweet to you, you are sweet to me
Together we restore harmony
Heart to heart our spirits lift
By sweetest spell we heal this rift

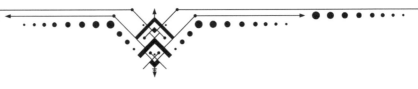

Seal the spell jar with the sealing wax and keep it in the bedroom. Remember to let bygones be bygones and know that to move forward, you must let go of the past.

Two-Hearts Spell for Long-Distance Love

Items required: two heart-shaped pebbles, stones or crystals, a pentacle, a chalice of wine or juice
Timing: each full moon to keep the bond strong while apart

There are many reasons why you could suddenly find yourself in a long-distance relationship, but the most common one is work commitments. If you or your partner have to work away from home for a while, it can be tough to keep the bond strong. This is especially true if your partner is in the armed forces and cannot contact you regularly due to deployment. Different time zones might mean that you are living your lives on completely different days. I remember a friend who was going to the other side of the world telling me that he would live the day first, to make sure there were no nasty surprises for me when I woke up to start living the same day! It is that kind of sweet sentiment that helps to keep the bond alive during times of distance.

So how do you ensure that your love survives such a situation? Well, you need to find things that forge a bond across the distance, things that you can both appreciate and which remind you of one another, no matter where you are. The moon is an obvious choice, for its light is reflected the world over. Make a pact with your partner that you will think of each other whenever you see a full moon, and send blessings their way. Then enhance this sentiment by placing the two heart pebbles on the pentacle in the moonlight, toast the moon with the chalice and say:

I drink to you, my lover true
No matter where thou be
I drink to the moon and ask this boon
To send my lover safe home to me

Send your love to your partner, using the moon as your messenger, and finish the wine or juice. Leave the two hearts side by side until the moon begins to wane, then repeat the spell each full moon.

WHEN LOVE TURNS BAD

Occasionally a relationship will fade and deteriorate over time. When this happens the pain can be acute as you are forced to say goodbye, not only to your partner but also to the life you lived and the future that you planned together. Like many things in life, love can have a shelf life. People come into our lives for a reason, a season or, if we are very lucky, a lifetime, but there are no guarantees. Even the sweetest love can fade over time, leading to loss and heartbreak. If you are nursing a heartache, use these spells to help you cope.

Fly-by-Night Spell

Items required: a notepad and pen, sage essential oil, a cauldron, twigs to make a small fire
Timing: on the waning moon, outdoors

If you have discovered that your lover has deceived you or let you down badly, use this spell to clear them from your life. We think of a *fly-by-night* as someone who is only around for what they can get and has no real intentions of sticking around for a committed relationship. Perhaps you have learned that they are already married, they are moving away, or something else. Whatever their transgression might be, this spell will help you to clear their energies from your life so that you can move on without them.

First write a letter to your ex-partner explaining how they have made you feel. Tell them of your confusion, resentment and upset. Don't worry, you are never going to send this letter! Just get all your feelings, hurt and anger down on paper. Next make a small fire in the cauldron using the twigs. Anoint the letter with the sage oil to cleanse this fly-by-night individual from your life, then fold the letter into the shape of a paper aeroplane. Hold the plane to your heart and say:

Fly-by-night, leave my sight
Never to return
You had your chance, but by
  happenstance
The truth I had to learn
The love I felt now must wither
It fades within my heart

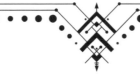

You let me down so go from hither
I am glad that you depart!

As you say the last line of the incantation, throw the paper aeroplane into the fire and watch it crash and burn.

Spell to Heal a Broken Heart

Items required: a heart-shaped stone or crystal, tissues
Timing: from full to dark moon

If you have had your heart broken, try this little spell to kick-start the healing process. Hold the pebble to your heart as you think about the circumstances of the heartbreak. If tears bubble up, wipe them with a tissue. When you are ready, kiss the stone and wrap

it in the tissue as you say:

I wrap my heart in tears so that I can
release the sorrow it holds

Next go for a walk, taking the stone with you. Try to find a crossroads where three or four paths meet and bury the stone in the earth there. Next say:

Earth heals my heart which is heavy
and sore
Let healing begin, that it bleeds no more
Take all my heart's trouble deep into
your glen
Lighten my load, that I might love
again.

When the heart is safely buried, walk away from the site and do not look back.

CHAPTER THIRTEEN

· · · · · ◦ ◉ ◎ ◉ ◦ · · · ·

CASTING FOR FAMILY AND FRIENDSHIP

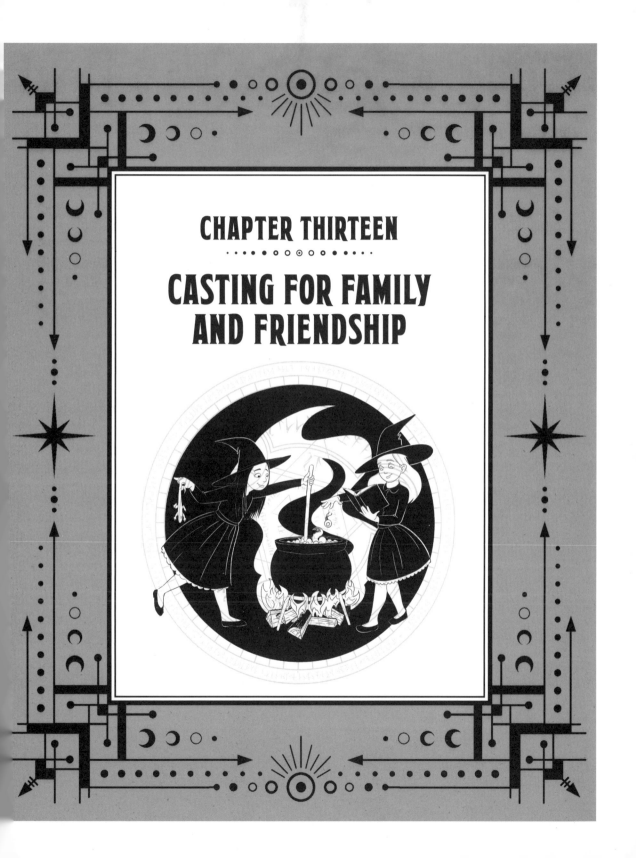

The relationships we have with friends and family members can often be some of the most challenging. While you can choose your friends and the kind of company you keep, family is a different matter. It is a unit made up of several individual personalities, so there are bound to be clashes every now and then. Family dynamics also change over the years, as siblings grow up, leave home, get married and have kids, as parents age and grandparents pass away. A family is an ever-changing entity with a neuroplasticity of its own, growing and expanding with new generations but shrinking and adapting with the losses too.

The family is also our very first experience of society, with the world around us initially being viewed through the prism of family values and beliefs, which tend to be passed down through the generations. Yet in any family there are often universal issues that come up time and again, such as sibling rivalry and jealousy, the black sheep who turns away from the flock and strikes out alone, the covert competitiveness, the needy/naughty sibling who takes up all the attention, or the controlling parent who just won't let go, and so on.

Sometimes members of our own family can be the hardest people to try and understand, while at other times it can feel just like looking in a mirror. Is it any wonder that family issues are one of the leading causes of people seeking therapy? Add into this mix changing dynamics that come with divorce, step-relations, extended family and so on and it is not surprising that people seek help and guidance to navigate their way through the challenges of being part of a family unit, yet for the most part we just wouldn't want to be without them! It's a minefield to say the least. Fortunately, this chapter has lots of spells and rituals that you can use to help make your interactions with family and friends run as smoothly as possible.

DEFINING FAMILY

The people you feel closest to and spend the most time with are your family. These people might not be blood relations, but could be step-relatives, work colleagues you get on especially well with, or a circle of friends. Some magical people who take part in a coven might also consider the coven to be their magical family. So the word *family* has a different meaning to different people. How you define your family is up to you, and if you'll pardon the pun, it's all relative. You might feel closer to an urban family of friends and colleagues than you do to your birth family, or it could be that you could not imagine going a week without

seeing your parents and siblings. Whatever works for you is okay, so don't feel that this chapter is irrelevant to you if you don't have a traditionally defined family. Simply adapt the spells to suit the kind of family you do have and go from there.

DINNER'S ON THE TABLE!

Have you ever wondered why your parents may have insisted that you all gather round the table at dinner time, or why the traditional Sunday roast took place at your grandparents' house every week? It is because sharing food is a primal form of bonding. From as far back as the Palaeolithic period, people would come together to share the food that had been hunted and gathered. It was a way to

ensure everyone was fed and made the bonds between groups of people much stronger. That still holds true today and, while many people are unaware of the bonding origins of having a meal together, it is something that we are innately drawn to do. It is in our DNA. Sharing mealtimes as a family creates a stronger bond between family members, whether that is dinner on a tray in front of the TV while watching a favourite programme or sitting around a beautifully laid table – the act of sharing food creates a stronger bond between individuals and that cannot be understated when it comes to family. So why wait until Christmas?!

Blessing for a Family Meal
Items required: prepare a lovely meal for your family
Timing: as often as possible

Arrange a lovely home-cooked meal with your family members. It need not be anything elaborate, something simple will suffice, so if you prefer a barbecue, a curry or an afternoon tea to a Sunday roast with all the trimmings, then go with that. As you prepare the meal, think back on all the times you have enjoyed good food with your family and express gratitude that they are in your life. Then say:

The food we share shows that we care
And that our bond is true
As we eat this meal, the love we feel
Is strengthened and renewed
So mote it be

Enjoy the meal with your family and friends and know that you have partaken in an ancient form of magical bonding. If you don't enjoy cooking, book a table at a nice restaurant and say the incantation just before you leave the house.

COMFORTING CRAFTS
Another form of familial bonding was craft work. In the past, when people had to make virtually everything they used, handcrafts were a necessary aspect of daily life. Making

rag rugs, tapestries, clothes, candles, soaps, baskets etc. was something that had to be done, so making these things together in groups helped to make the chores more fun. During such times secrets would have been shared, advice given from elders and problems solved collectively for the good of the whole clan. There are many ways in which you can use craft work to share a special bond with members of your family. Obviously cooking together is one of them, but think about incorporating some of the following hobbies into your family leisure time too.

Tips for Comforting Crafting with the Family

- Candle making.
- Soap making.
- Needlecrafts.
- Brewing beer or ale, or making wine.
- Woodcrafting.
- Model building.
- Gardening.
- Flower arranging and drying.
- Board games.
- Jigsaw puzzles.
- Baking.
- Storytelling.
- Discovering your ancestry and family tree.

- Enjoying a music night/family disco.
- Creating a family bucket list and starting to tick things off together.

SIBLING RIVALRY AND FRENEMIES

The people you grew up with will always have the ability to push your buttons because they probably know you inside out. They have been privy to your past moments of embarrassment, and may know who your first kiss was with or how you got that scar on your left knee. That is a lot of ammunition! For many people this amounts to no more than a bit of teasing in adulthood, but for some it becomes a source of bitter divide, leading to arguments and disharmony, possibly even a rift. It can also be indicative of covert jealousy or competitiveness.

While a certain amount of competition is healthy between siblings, if this goes too far it can become damaging to the relationship. The same is true when it comes to your best friends, especially if they are the same people you went to school with. There may be times when your best friend can seem more like an enemy and you might wonder just whose side they are on. You can also experience a challenging relationship with siblings. If you are dealing with a friend who has demonstrated enmity towards you on several occasions, it might be best to leave that particular friend behind, especially if you have confronted them over their spitefulness before and their behaviour towards you still has not improved or they deny any wrongdoing and continue as before. In this case, it is probably better to end the friendship than to come to resent it. With a sibling, however, it is not that easy and regardless of how strained the relationship might be, you will probably still need to interact with them. Use this spell to try and restore a sense of peace between you.

Spell for Easing Sibling Rivalry

Items required: your toothbrush, your sibling's toothbrush, a pink ribbon
Timing: on the full moon

At the time of the full moon, gather the items together and go where you will not be disturbed. The toothbrushes act as a tag lock because they are something that you use every day so they are imbued with your energies. Take up your toothbrush and name it for yourself, then do the same with the other toothbrush, naming it for your sibling. Lay the toothbrushes side by side on top of the ribbon. Hold your hands over them and say:

This sibling bond now turned sour
Will begin to repair from this hour
I am here for you, you are there for me
Together we are a family
From this day forth and by this spell
We learn to wish each other well

Finish the spell by tying the ribbon in a bow and securing the two toothbrushes together. Keep them hidden and do not untie them until the sibling bond has strengthened between you.

Spell to End a Toxic Friendship

Items required: one lemon, salt, two pins, an athame or sharp knife
Timing: on the waning moon

If a friendship has turned irretrievably sour, it is in your own interests to end it. If it cannot be mended, then it needs to be broken. There is no point wasting your time and energy on someone who is working or speaking against you, or who has otherwise proven that they don't deserve to be in your life. Allowing the friendship to fade by simply drifting apart is one option, but if they show signs of trying to reel you in just so that they can continue their toxic behaviour, it's time to nip it in the bud with a bit of magic. Lemon and salt are both natural cleansers and this spell uses both to cleanse the toxic friend from your life.

Hold the lemon as you think of your ex-friend. Think of all the things that have gone wrong in the friendship and the reason why you want to end it. Next cut partway through the lemon in an X shape. Gently pull the lemon open to reveal the citrus flesh inside and pour salt into the fruit as you say:

I cleanse toxic friendships from my life
I do not need the trouble and strife
Go from me and get thee gone
By this magic be it done!

Push the lemon together and secure with the two pins, crossing them in an X shape, like crossed swords. Leave the lemon in place on your altar for three days, then remove the pins and put the salted lemon in the compost. As the fruit rots away, so will the friendship fade too.

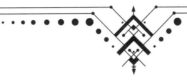

Spell for Communication

Items required: the family toothpaste
Timing: charge and empower at the time of the new moon

Empowering an everyday object with magical intent is one of the easiest ways to create positive magic. Family harmony depends largely on how well you communicate with one another and you should all be able to express your feelings in a kind and considerate manner. As practically everyone uses toothpaste each day, this little charm will help to ensure that the communications between family members are positive in nature. Hold the tube of toothpaste in your hands and say:

> *I turn to you, you turn to me*
> *We unburden our hearts freely*
> *We speak our minds, get things off our*
>   *chest*
> *In love and trust we are blessed*
> *This paste keeps communication clear*
> *For within this house there is nought to*
>   *fear*
> *Blessed be*

You can repeat this charm with each new tube of toothpaste. If communication has been especially difficult, or you come from a family where toxic interactions are a regular occurrence, you might need to cast this spell several times before you begin to see the positive effects. Don't give up! Remember that all magic has an effect, but it isn't instantaneous. For extra power, work this spell in combination with the one below for harmony.

Lavender Scones Spell for Family Harmony

Items required: ingredients to bake scones, half a teaspoon of lavender, clotted cream, jam or honey, a pentacle
Timing: whenever your family get together

For this simple kitchen-witch spell you will need to bake scones. Use a recipe of your choice and as you mix the dough, imbue it with your magical intention by saying:

> *Lavender's blue, lavender's sweet*
> *Harmony comes through this treat*

Stir in the lavender as you mix the dough, then bake according to the recipe. Serve the scones with cream and honey or jam, using the altar pentacle as a serving platter and offering the scones to each member of the family. This will help to keep the dynamics harmonious.

Screw on the top and shake well to disperse the oils, then spray liberally throughout the room you spend most time in as a family, to fill the air with love and harmony. Use this potion whenever your family needs an extra boost of love.

Spell to Call in a Black Sheep

Items required: a spool of black cotton, an empty loo-roll tube, scissors, a small picture of the relative you want to connect with, glue
Timing: begin at dark moon

Occasionally family dynamics can be so stifling to some people that they feel the need to break free and go off alone. They might cut themselves off from some relatives altogether. This autonomy and free will should be respected, but there may also be times when you need to contact and reconnect with them, and that is where this spell comes in. Bear in mind, however, that it may not lead to a lasting reconciliation, although it should at least bring about a temporary reunion. The final decision as to whether they re-join the family permanently has to be down to that family member.

Begin this spell when the moon is dark. It will take several days to complete and must be worked on daily. First glue the picture of

Silent Spell to Spread a Little Loving Energy

Items required: an empty spray bottle, spring water, rose and lavender essential oil
Timing: make the potion on a new moon

Scents are one of the quickest ways to create an atmosphere of comfort and safety. Some fragrances take us straight back to our childhood home – the smell of baking or Christmas spices, for example – such is the power of scent memory. With this simple potion you can create an atmosphere of loving energies, using the natural properties of essential oils. First fill the spray bottle with pure spring water, then add ten drops of lavender and ten drops of rose essential oils.

the black sheep onto the cardboard tube. Next cut a small nick in one end of the tube and use this to secure the end of the black cotton. To perform the spell, turn the tube three times, using it to reel in the cotton from the bobbin. As you do so, say:

> _____(Name) Come out from the
> cold, back into the fold and I will
> welcome thee
> Come out from the cold, back into the
> fold and complete our family

Do this each day, reeling in the cotton by three turns a day until the bobbin is empty and the tube is full. Seal the end of the cotton in place with a little wax. You should hear news of the black sheep within three moons.

Silent Spell to Hear from an Old Friend

Items required: a piece of pink paper and a red pen, a pink birthday candle, a citrine crystal
Timing: on the new moon

If there is an old friend whom you have lost touch with and you would like to hear from, then cast this spell. Write their name seven times in a column on the pink paper, using the red pen. Then, from the top, fold the paper towards you seven times, folding in each name as you go. Think of your friend as you do this. Light the pink birthday candle and seal the folded paper with the wax, then blow out the candle with a wish to hear from your friend. Place the paper and the citrine crystal, which represents communication, by the phone. Repeat the wish every day until the birthday candle has burnt down. You should hear news of your friend within one lunar cycle.

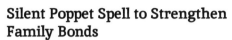

Silent Poppet Spell to Strengthen Family Bonds

Items required: paper, a pen, glue or tape
Timing: new to full moon

Use poppet magic to strengthen the bonds of the family unit. Simply make a chain of paper dolls, ensuring that there are as many dolls as family members. Lay the dolls out in row before you and name each one for a relative by writing their name on a doll. Finally draw the dolls into a circle, with the names facing inwards and secure together the hands of the two end dolls with the glue or tape. These poppets now represent the family circle, so keep the poppets somewhere safe. This is a lovely spell to do with small children as you can get them to paint the poppets to represent each member of the family.

ONE OF THE FAMILY

Families change over time and they often expand to include new members. Usually this is due to a marriage or engagement, or the birth of a new baby. Families also expand when two families are united by marriage or a romantic relationship, leading to step-families, or reconstructed families as they are also known. It isn't always easy to adjust and it can take time for someone new to feel like part of the family. Such changes involve a period of transition, as everyone gets acquainted and eventually settles down together. A simple ritual to welcome a new member of the family can help to smooth things along.

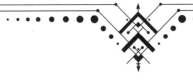

Ritual to Welcome a New Family Member

Items required: tea-lights, a wax taper
Timing: on the first full moon following the introduction to the new member

You can cast this spell with your family or alone. Take as many tea-lights as you have relatives, including yourself and the new member. Keeping back one of the tea-lights, place the rest in a circle and name them for yourself and your relatives as you light them with the taper. Allow them to burn for a short time, then carefully widen the circle of flames to leave a gap. Light the final tea-light, naming it for the new member, and place this in the gap to complete the family circle. Then say:

> *A kindred spirit comes our way*
> *We welcome him/her in kind*
> *We hope they choose to join and stay*
> *As a welcome place with us they find*
> *Blessed be*

Allow the candles to burn out naturally and do all you can to make the new relative feel welcome and accepted.

BABY BLESSINGS

It is customary in many traditions, including magical ones, to bless a newborn baby soon after birth in order to protect it until its official naming ceremony. Keys have long been used in magical protection. In the past it was said that placing an iron key beneath the baby's pillow would prevent it from being stolen away by fairies and a changeling left in its place. Here in Yorkshire it is customary to offer keys as post-birth gifts and also to give the baby a piece of jet to ward away bad omens and energies. This little ritual honours both these customs and should ensure that the baby comes home to a safe and protected space.

Key Blessing for a Newborn

Items required: a baby toy shaped like a key, a piece of jet, a silver coin, a dried rosebud, a pouch
Timing: soon after the baby is born

When you see the baby for the first time, take with you the key toy and the pouch into which you have placed the piece of jet crystal, the silver coin and the dried rosebud, thus offering protection, prosperity and love to the babe. Place the pouch into the folds of the baby blanket for a few minutes, then replace it with the key toy. Once you have offered both these things to the newborn, take them to the baby's nursery at home, placing the key into the empty crib to guard its void and hanging the pouch close by. This will ensure a safe space ready for when the protected child comes home from the hospital.

SAYING GOODBYE

Just as new people come into a clan, so too do people leave it. This is usually due to a death in the family or may be a result of divorce or relocation. Saying goodbye to someone you love is never easy, but families have a remarkable way of adapting and coming together in such difficult times. It is not

unusual for a bereavement to be the catalyst which heals a rift, for example, or for some relatives to maintain friendship connections with a sibling's or child's ex-partner, once officially divorced from the family. Whatever the circumstances, saying goodbye to a loved one is always hard. Use this spell to make the adjustment a little easier.

Ritual to Say Goodbye
Items required: tea-lights, a wax taper
Timing: on the first dark moon following the loss

You can cast this spell with your family or alone. Take as many tea-lights as you have relatives, including yourself and the person who is no longer around. Keeping back one of the tea-lights, place the rest in a circle and name them for yourself and your relatives as you light them. Allow them to burn for a short time, then carefully place the final tea-light in the centre of the circle and light it. This candle represents the person who is gone. Allow the candles to burn for a while, then extinguish the tea-light in the centre, leaving the others alight as you say:

A soul is gone from us this day
We bid a fond farewell to them

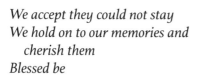

We accept they could not stay
We hold on to our memories and
 cherish them
Blessed be

Allow the candles to burn out naturally and know that it will take time to process the loss you have suffered, so be kind to yourself and each other.

A Spell for Understanding

Items required: a small pouch, citrine and rose quartz crystals, a pentacle
Timing: new to full moon

If there is something that you want to discuss with a family member and you are nervous about their reaction, cast this simple spell for greater understanding between the two of you. Place the crystals to charge on the pentacle from new to full moon. When the moon is full, put them in a pouch, hold them and say:

A secret I would share with you
Please try to see my point of view
I will empathize with you
And a new understanding bonds us two

Keep the pouch with you as you speak to your relative. Remember that people need time to process new information, so allow them space if they need it.

Ritual to Draw New Friends

Items required: none
Timing: whenever you see a fallen penny

To draw new friends into your life, say this charm whenever you see a fallen penny on the ground:

See a penny, pick it up
With new friends I soon will sup
As I walk down every street
Each shining penny is a pal I'll meet!

To Make a Blessing Charm for a Loved One

Items required: silver or gold sealing wax, greaseproof paper, blessing seeds
Timing: during a waxing moon

To make a magical good-luck charm for a loved one, heat the sealing wax and pour it onto the greaseproof paper to form a pool of molten wax. Add a pinch of blessings seeds while the wax is hot and say:

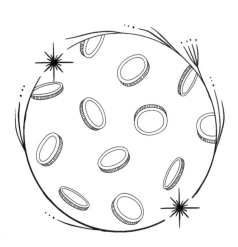

I cast this blessing from me to thee
That good fortune finds you wherever
      you may be

Wait for the wax to cool and once it has
hardened, peel off the greaseproof paper
and give the talisman to your loved one,
explaining that it is a charm for good luck
and they need to carry it with them.

CHAPTER FOURTEEN

CASTING FOR FAMILIARS AND POWER ANIMALS

When people think of magic, they invariably think of the witch whispering secrets into the ears of her feline familiar. This image is iconic and it is displayed every October in the form of Halloween decorations. Witches and magical practitioners have always had a place in folklore and the familiar is an aspect of that, yet – as with most myths and legends – there is a grain of truth in the tale, for witches *do* have a very special connection to the animal kingdom.

To begin with, we see animals as being our equals, rather than our inferiors. Some witches live a vegan or vegetarian lifestyle, while others choose to consume only ethically reared meat and fish. More than this, magical practitioners believe in the sacred spirit of animals as tutors, protectors, companions and conversationalists. Animals will communicate with us very clearly if we are open to listening to them and, while they do not have language in the way that humans do, they get their feelings across quite well with body language and non-verbal communication.

There is much to be learned from the birds and beasts of the world and from the pets we choose to share our lives with. Having a deep connection with a pet is one of the most rewarding and sacred relationships that you will have, because pets love unconditionally. They don't mind how you look or behave, just so long as you look after them and treat them well. They will lie at your feet for the rest of their days, for while they are an all-too-brief element of your life, you are their *whole* life.

Working magically with familiars and power animals can be very satisfying, as you come to understand your animal friends better and a deeper bond of love and trust develops between you and your pets. But familiar magic isn't just for those people who have pets. It can be used by anyone, especially in the form of power animals, which is a way of connecting with the spirit of an animal through visualization. This means that you can work magically with the kind of animals that it would be dangerous or impossible to connect with in reality, opening up the realms of large predatory animals such as lions, tigers, wolves, bears, alligators or aquatic creatures. It is up to you what type of power animal you work with in your magic.

spells in this chapter therefore use few tools, relying mostly on your ability to create strong visualizations and to connect with that which you cannot see in the real world.

THE ANTLERED GOD – LORD OF ANIMALS

In pagan belief the Antlered God or Horned One is considered to be the lord of all animals. He is depicted as a man, wearing animal skins and with a magnificent pair of antlers growing from his brow, which represents his overlordship of and connection with the animal kingdom. He is neither a man nor a beast, but something between the two, protecting the creatures

IT'S ALL IN THE MIND

Working with familiars and power animals is a visionary exercise. You need to be able to picture the creature in your mind's eye. You can use photos, statues, feathers and so on to help you with this, but for the most part, familiar magic takes place in the mind as you connect with your chosen animal, spirit to spirit and heart to heart. Even when you are working with pets, the interactions and responses from your pet might be something that you dismiss as your imagination, but given time and practice you will come to trust that you are building a very special bond with a sacred creature that has a spark of magic within them, just as you do. The

of earth, air and sea, while ensuring the patterns of fertility, birth, life and death are maintained. As you might suppose, the stag is the animal that is most closely linked with this pagan god, and is considered to be his earthly representative, so visiting places where there are herds of deer is a good way to connect with him. That said, all animals come under his protection and the entire animal kingdom is his dominion.

Working with animals is a dream for many people, but spending your days in service of the Horned God and the animal kingdom isn't always easy. Often it involves very long hours, seven days a week, giving your time to look after the creatures in your care, usually for low pay. Nonetheless, there are lots of ways that you can serve the Horned God. You could get a job working in a zoo, wildlife park or veterinary practice. You could volunteer at a rescue centre, or give your time to an animal charity, or raise funds for them. Bear in mind, however, that when you work in service of the animal kingdom you are likely to see sick and injured animals, euthanasia and so on, as well as happy, healthy creatures, so it's not a job for the faint-hearted.

Ritual to Offer Your Services to the Antlered God and His Animal Kingdom

Items required: a picture or statue of the Horned God, a tea-light and holder
Timing: at the new moon

Go to a quiet place and take the image of the Horned God with you. Light candles and incense if you want to. Spend a few minutes contemplating the pagan god and your wish to work with animals, or to serve them in some way. When you feel ready, light the tea-light in the holder and say:

I offer my service to our animal friends
To care for and protect them

To guard and defend them
To heal and hearten them
To feed and nurture them
To love, honour and respect them
In the Horned God's name
I make this pledge
Blessed be

Allow the tea-light to burn out naturally and follow your intuition to discover where your skills are most needed.

Spell to Deepen Your Connection with a Pet

Items required: a spell jar and stopper, some of your pet's naturally shed fur, a lock of your hair, an incense stick of your choice

Timing: during the waxing moon

First cleanse the jar using the smoke from the incense stick. Next, twine together the lock of your hair with your pet's fur and put it into the jar. Put on the lid, hold the jar to your heart and say:

Two friends come together on four legs
    and two
The bond growing stronger between me
    and you
This vial now encases the love that we
    share
Entwined evermore, your fur and my
    hair
Two hearts with one rhythm, beating in
    tune
My pet, my familiar, my magical boon
Blessed be

Ritual to Call Your Familiar or Power Animal

Items required: a brown candle and holder, a carving tool, lavender pillow spray
Timing: at new moon, at the witching hour of midnight

If you are thinking of getting a pet but you're not sure what kind to go for, or if you want to discover your power animal or totem, then cast this spell to encourage the animal to reveal itself to you. Carve the word Familiar into the length of the brown candle and set it in the holder. Light the wick and hold your hands on either side, palms facing up to receive the inspiration you need. Now say:

I offer up my home and mind
A magical familiar soon to find
Be it in life or be it in spirit
I come here to find it, I come here to
  greet it
A pet or a totem creature of power
Reveal yourself to me, by the next
  witching hour

Spray your pillow with the lavender mist before you go to sleep. Your new familiar should reveal itself in your dreams.

THE MAGICAL MOON HARE

Some animals seem to be more magical than others, and the hare has been associated with witches and spell-craft for centuries. In the past it was believed that witches could transform themselves into hares in order to escape their persecutors. In most cultures, however, the hare is considered sacred and is widely regarded as being a creature of good fortune. To see a hare at any time is considered lucky, but to see one at night gazing up at the moon is especially fortunate. As a highly fertile creature, the hare is associated with prosperity, abundance, fertility and rebirth, being most active during the spring and early summer months. To see one during the day is rare as they are quite elusive, but if you do, make a wish as it is sure to come true. The hare is a popular power animal and totem. Its image is sold widely in the form of paintings and statues and wall-plaques, so they are a lovely addition to an altar space or to any magical home. To call in the moon hare's energies, cast the spell below.

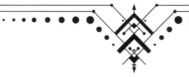

Spell to Attune with the Spirit of the Moon Hare

Items required: something that represents the moon hare such as a picture or statue, a gold or yellow candle and holder
Timing: at the full moon

Light the gold candle and place it next to the item representing the moon hare. Attune with this creature in your mind and consider all the folklore that we attribute to it: the boxing matches during mating season and the strange 'madness' that goes with it, the habit of gazing upwards at the night sky seemingly mesmerized by the moon, the elusive behaviour and erratic speed with which it evades its enemies and predators. When you feel that you have connected with the hare in your mind, say:

> *Come into my life, spirit of the hare*
> *Help me avoid those who ensnare*
> *Let your magic and wisdom fill up my*
> *   days*
> *As the silvery moon sends down her rays*
> *I call you in closer, bring your moon-*
> *   stricken gaze*
> *And look on me kindly, bringing luck to*
> *   my days*

In the coming weeks you should see hares popping up everywhere – as images on merchandise, on TV and, if you're lucky, in real life too. Take these as signs that your spell has been heard and the moon hare now shines her light upon you.

WHEN THE WOLF IS AT THE DOOR

Wolves have been much maligned down the ages, to the point where they were hunted to near extinction, disappearing from the UK during the 1700s. Fortunately, these resilient animals managed to survive in other parts of Europe, but the negative propaganda surrounding them still echoes today. 'The wolf is at the door' is a common saying meaning that a time of hardship has to be endured, as it was thought that wolves would come closer to populated areas during a hard winter when food was scarce. We still use this phrase today, often with a shiver of dread at the difficulties that lie ahead when times are hard. But the spirit of the wolf can be called upon to help you endure a less prosperous period in your life, for they are nothing if not survivalists!

Spell to Keep the Wolf from Your Door

Items required: a picture of a wolf that you can frame and hang
Timing: during the dark moon

In times of hardship it can be difficult to remain positive or to maintain hope that there are brighter, easier days ahead. When the wolf is at the door, do not fear him but invite him in to share the warmth of your hearthside in return for his protection during a period of hardship. Learn to see him as more of a pet than a threat and if he starts to turn up in your dreams, heed his warning and begin to save for leaner days ahead. Concentrate on the image of the wolf and think of how protected you would be

by having such a magnificent creature as your power animal. Invoke his energies with these words:

> *When the wolf is at the door, I'll fear no more*
> *I choose to invite him in*
> *To share my hearthside on this darkest tide*
> *Until better times begin*
> *His protection is strong; he knows where he belongs*
> *As we wait to see the lean times out*
> *I share what I have, I know this won't last*
> *For all seasons turn and turnabout*

Put the picture of the wolf into a frame and hang it near the main door to your home, asking the wolf to guard you from lasting hardship.

Ritual to Build a New Pack

Items required: none
Timing: at the full moon

Wolves become increasingly active as the moon waxes from new to full. By the time the lunar cycle is at its peak, they are frequently heard howling throughout the night. They do this to find a mate, to communicate with other packs and to coordinate movements

Blessing for the Spirit of Feline Independence

Items required: an image of a feline, or your pet cat, a stick of Night Queen incense and holder
Timing: whenever you need a boost of independence and autonomy

Felines can teach you all you need to know about maintaining an independent spirit, and if you have cats as pets you will know that they will never be fully tamed! A cat does just as it likes, whenever it likes, and it doesn't care what anyone thinks. You can draw on this autonomy by attuning with cats to become more independent yourself, whether that means leaving home for the first time or setting stronger boundaries within your relationships. Sometimes you just need to do things on your own, to go wherever the mood takes you. To borrow some feline independence, sit with your cat on your knee or focus on the image and imagine how the world looks through a cat's eyes. How must it feel to stay out all night or to sleep all day in the sunshine, without judgement? How would it be if you didn't care what others thought of you? Once you feel attuned to the feline spirit, light the incense in offering and say the following blessing, then make plans to have

and hunting expeditions within their own pack. There may be times in your life when you need to build a pack of your own, whether this be by starting a family or creating a team for work or sport. Channel the spirit of the wolf to help you. Go outside on the night of the full moon and spend some time gazing at the bright orb which lights up the night sky. Know that in certain parts of the world, wolves are howling at this very moon. Make your intention to the moon, by telling it why you want to build a pack and what its purpose will be, then say:

By light of moon I ask this boon, please help me in my quest
To find the team who lives the dream and works together best

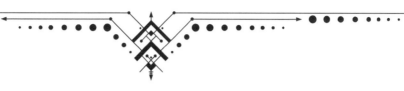

an independent adventure of your own:

I move through the world with feline
grace
I go where I choose and set my own pace
I do as I please, take my rest as I need
I do not follow, nor do I lead
I live a good life in comfort and bliss
My days now unfold with a feline's kiss

Black-Cat Spell for Indifference

Items required: a black-cat candle, a notepad
and pen, a cauldron or heat-proof dish
Timing: on a waning moon

If someone is trying to rile you in some way, the best defence is always indifference. Show them that you are above their petty games by not rising to the bait. In fact, don't

acknowledge that they are baiting you at all, just treat them with indifference. Use this spell to help you to maintain an attitude of indifference towards them. Write on the slip of paper the nature of their baiting behaviour – are they flirting with your partner or undermining you in meetings at work? Whatever it is, write it down and add the words *It stops today*. Next, light the black-cat candle, then hold the note in the flame before dropping it into the cauldron to burn away as you say:

A problem burns within this flame
I call you out, yet name no names
Your baiting antics now must cease
As the flame burns out this spell is
released

Allow the candle to burn out naturally.

A Chameleon Spell to Help You Fit In

Items required: seven small spell candles, one
for each colour of the rainbow, a lighter, a
tray or large plate
Timing: perform at the full moon for
strongest power

The chameleon is a fascinating reptile which changes its colouring to match whatever background and environment it

In all environments I find my place
I am true to myself, exuding grace
I get along with all people, find my voice
*   in a crowd*
I show all my true colours with which
*   I'm endowed*
Blessed be

finds itself in. This means that not only is it camouflaged from any predators but it can also use its vibrant array of colours to attract a mate and intimidate rivals. The colour-changing nature of this animal is crucial to its survival. Take a tip from the chameleon by learning how to adapt your appearance and presentation in order to fit in with different groups of people in different situations. This will improve your social skills, by widening your circle of friends and acquaintances. Melt the bottom of each candle and set it on the tray, then light them all one by one in a spectrum of colours. As they burn, say:

It is a chameleon that I would be
To adapt to any company

A Swan Blessing to Reveal Your Inner Beauty

Items required: a photograph of yourself, three white swan feathers
Timing: on a new moon

Swans are renowned for their beauty and have long been considered sacred birds, said to represent innocence, trust, fidelity

and self-esteem. In some cultures, they are held to be the souls of poets and bards, in others they are reincarnations of women who died in childbirth. No one can deny that they are very beautiful birds, who move across the water with seemingly effortless grace. For this blessing you will need to collect three swan feathers, so go to a place which swans inhabit and look on the ground for discarded white feathers. Gather three feathers and take them home, then place them in a triangle shape around your face in the photograph as you say:

Through the swan prism I see my face
That I come to know the beauty within
Through the swan feathers my charms
*   I embrace*
That the world will see my beauty
*   within*

Keep the feathers and photo in place until the moon begins to wane, then put one feather in the bathroom, one by your bed and one in your purse or wallet, as reminders to trust in your inner beauty and to let it shine its light on the world.

Peacock Blessing for Greater Confidence

Items required: a piece of card, blue, green and gold paints or crayons
Timing: on the new moon

To bring about greater self-confidence, imagine that you are a stunning peacock, showing off your colourful tail with its many eyes. This display is meant to charm the peahens, but it is also designed to protect the bird from predators, as the eyes of the tail could be confused for many more animals rather than just one. To attune with this powerful display, paint the eye of a peacock's feather onto the card and allow it to dry. Then imagine the way a peacock struts around, completely confident in its own power to attract mates and defend itself as you say:

A fair peacock of blue and green
Draws many, many eyes
It is not afraid to be seen
With attention it primps and thrives
As I focus on this peacock's eye
All eyes are drawn to me
I do not flee, I do not hide
Now I have confidence for all to see!

Keep the painting somewhere close to where you get ready every morning, perhaps in the

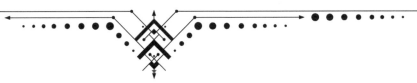

bathroom or on the dressing table, to be reminded of your inner peacock.

Silent Spell to Live in the Moment
Items required: a tea-light and holder, a picture of your pet or your favourite animal
Timing: during a waning moon

Animals are far less concerned with the past and the future than humans are. Some schools of thought claim that animals have no concept of linear time at all, though this is disputed. What we do know is that all animals are very good at living in the moment. Their instincts lead them to getting their needs met and they seem to have little care for anything else other than their current objective. We can all learn from this. Living in the moment and learning to be more spontaneous is good for you, because it means that you are not tied to the past or fearful of the future. It isn't about being selfish. It simply means that you are ready to go with the flow and are open to opportunities as they come along. Animals know the thrill of an unexpected lucky find, the adventure of following their nose and seeing where they end up and the excitement of meeting new acquaintances. Use this meditation to help you live in the moment more often.

Place the tea-light next to the picture and light it. Focus on the flame and imagine yourself being more spontaneous, saying yes to invitations, challenging yourself to try new things and meet new people. Visualize that you are enjoying this greater sense of freedom, to live in the here and now and let go of all thoughts of past and future. When you feel ready, blow out the tea-light and be prepared to go with the flow from now on.

A Charm of Three Horseshoes
Items required: three used horseshoes, salt water
Timing: at the full moon

Three horseshoes interlocked are frequently seen in pubs and inns up and down the UK. This is an old charm to ward away evil and to protect the premises with the powers of the Triple Goddess, for the interlocked shoes represent the waxing, full and waning moons. For this spell you will need three horseshoes that have been worn by horses. Cleanse them by sprinkling them with salt water. Interlock them so that one faces north, one east and one west, then nail this charm to the outside of your home or business, to ward away negativity and bless the premises with equine magic and goddess power.

A Workhorse Spell for Industry

Items required: an item that has once been worn by a horse such as a horseshoe, ribbon, rosette, bridle charm etc., a pentacle
Timing: on the new moon

We owe a huge debt to the workhorse. Not only was he once a vital mode of transport, he also helped to farm the fields and fight wars. In modern life, he is still a respected service member of the police force and the military, as well as a much-loved companion. His loyalty and service to humankind is unparalleled and you can call on this level of industry to help you in your own productivity. Take the item that was worn by a horse and place it on the pentacle in the light of the new moon. Hold

your hands over it and say:

> *Gracious steed of endurance*
> *Your spirit strong in resilience*
> *As you plod on and on each day*
> *Help to make my way*
> *To give my all in what I do*
> *To keep going until dreams come true*
> *Spirit to spirit carry me forth*
> *I summon you, my spirit horse*

Leave the item in place on the pentacle for a full lunar cycle, then keep it with you as you work or use it to decorate your desk or office space.

Crow Spell for Magical Guidance

Items required: a black feather
Timing: on the waning moon

Crows are birds of magic. They are linked with Celts, Druids and Saxons, who saw them as birds of augury or fortune-telling. In magic, the crow is linked to the Morrighan, the Celtic battle-goddess of war, who decided which side won and which warriors fell in battle. Crows are part of the corvid family and they thrive in most regions. Known for their raucous calls and their ability to fight well on the wing, they are formidable opponents, especially for their cousin the magpie. Crows are said to

your garden. They are the messengers of the Morrighan and this spell will invoke their magical guidance. Find a black feather and hold it to your heart as you say:

Black as night is Morrighan's bird
Its call throughout the world is heard
I summon the crow and call it here
To make my magical path both smooth
    and clear
Guide my steps and show the way
Help my magic thrive each day
So mote it be

be drawn to magical practitioners, so don't be surprised if they take up residence in

Keep the feather on your altar or tucked into your Book of Shadows.

CHAPTER FIFTEEN

· · · · ∘ ⊙ ∘ · · · ·

CASTING ELEMENTAL FAERIE SPELLS

Elementals are the spirits of the natural world and the four elements are governed by them. They are known by many names, such as faeries, the fey, the sidhe, the seelie court and elfenfolk, and appear all over the world in various folkloric traditions. These are the guardians of nature and wild places, helping plants, trees, woodlands, moors and glens to thrive. Wherever there is nature, there are faeries and elementals, from the smallest potted plant to the largest forest.

Magical practitioners work with four main elemental groups. These groups of fey were named by the sixteenth-century doctor and astrologer Paracelsus, who believed that each element had its own fey spirit which could be called upon for magical assistance. He named these spirits gnomes for earth, sylphs for air, salamanders for fire and undines for water. Modern practitioners still work in this way today and as the world shows signs of suffering due to global warming, more and more witches are turning to faerie magic and green witchcraft to try and find a gentler way to coexist with the natural world.

DO YOU BELIEVE IN FAERIES?

Working with the faeries or elemental spirits is not childish or immature. It is a way to connect with nature on a deep spiritual level. If you have ever walked through a woodland and felt a sense of sacred peace, you have felt their presence enchanting the environment around you. They are playful beings and communing with them can help you to live with a sense of wonder. All you need is an open mind and heart, and a willingness to call their magic into your life. They can help you to create a lovely garden, enjoy a meditative walk in the woods, work with siren energy while soaking in the bath or provide inspiration for creativity. Faerie beings are not to be taken lightly, however,

WILD JACK AND JACK FROST

Wild Jack, or Jack in the Green as he is also known, is one of the spirits of earth. He is a foliage-faced pagan nature deity and he was the original sacrificial god, being cut down each autumn to leap back up again come springtime. He is the masculine, untamed spirit of nature and, like all aspects of nature, he has a shadow side.

As the deity of the verdant forest, Wild Jack can be raw, brutal, cruel and poisonous. Left unchecked, his green fingers will trace around buildings, prise through concrete and steal the sunlight for himself. He spreads his seeds prolifically and indiscriminately, his rogue saplings popping up just about anywhere. His trailing, climbing tresses have the power to both strengthen and strangle trees and to smother roots. He demands a regular sacrifice of blood and tears as his spikes, prickles, thorns and brambles cut through flesh, his stinging nettles chafing skin. His prettiest, brightest berries administer the strongest poisons of deadly nightshade, monkshood and hemlock.

In autumn he brings the sickly-sweet odour of decay as fallen leaves rot back into the soil and the earthy scent of mushrooms is carried on the wind. Old bark and branches are stripped away and the once-lush forest becomes a tangle of bare branches, twisted roots and the odd hollow tree.

In winter Wild Jack takes on a new guise – that of Jack Frost, the icy spirit of the winter woods and the cold season. Now his trees beckon enticingly as he silvers the cobwebs, displaying a glimmering world of winter white. Beneath the pretty blanket of snow, life sleeps on as Jack Frost paints the trees silver. The darker aspects of Jack do not make him an evil entity, for he is simply weaving out the three threads which form the tapestry of life – birth, death and rebirth.

As the sunlight strengthens, Jack's frosty edges thaw. His snowflake beard turns into a growth of fresh leaves, his icebound hands shake off their shimmer-season gloves and his long twiggy fingers begin to scatter the seeds of new growth. Spring is here and Wild Jack is roaming the forests once more, ensuring that the cycle continues evermore.

A Wild Jack Libation Ritual

Items required: a can of cider or ale, suet balls for the birds, a picnic
Timing: on a full moon, or on summer or winter solstice

You can honour Wild Jack and his counterpart, Jack Frost, by offering a libation. Ideally you would do this at least twice a year on the summer and winter solstice, but you can also perform this ritual on a full moon. Go out into your garden or to a wild place, and take the cider and suet balls with you. Find a spot that you think Jack would be drawn to – a beautiful tree in a wild area would be ideal. Pour the cider around the roots of the tree as you say:

I come here to honour the spirit of trees,
Wild Jack in the Green
I offer this libation in love and trust, to
guard and protect this tree

Once you have poured out all the cider, hang the suet balls from the branches of the tree with these words:

I offer this food for the birds of the forest,
to sustain them in times of need
I offer my thanks for the food that I have
and for each abundant seed

Sit close by the tree and enjoy your picnic. You might like to complete this magical excursion with a meditation or card reading as you spend time in the company of Wild Jack.

GNOMES OF EARTH

The gnomes are also spirits of earth, associated with growth, abundance,

prosperity and wealth. They are said to have the power to grant happiness to those who respect nature and punishment to those who do not. As elementals of Earth, gnomes are the guardians and protectors of all plants, gardens, trees and shrubs. They are drawn to parks, woodlands, meadows, hedgerows, glens and groves. You can work with the gnomes to help you create a beautiful garden of your own, be this a large outdoor garden or a collection of indoor plants and herbs.

Gnome Ritual to Create a Lovely Garden
Items required: a new plant, a collection of crystal tumble stones of your choice
Timing: best performed during the new moon

Go to a garden centre and find a lovely plant that you would like to add to your garden, or ask a friend for a cutting from their garden. Take the plant home and feed it with water and a little plant food to give it a good start. Next, go to your garden and sit with the plant on your knee. Close your eyes and picture the gnomes in your mind industriously helping plants and trees to thrive. Now call this energy to your own garden by saying:

Spirits of earth I call to you
I ask that you help my garden to thrive

and grow in abundance
I dedicate this plant to you, I welcome you with exuberance
Accept this invitation and make my garden grow
And when each flower blooms, your magic I will know

Put the plant into your garden and surround it with the crystals, dedicating it to the gnomes and the spirits of earth.

Silent Spell to Request a Wand
Items required: an offering of seeds or nuts for the birds to eat
Timing: during the waning moon, or on the autumnal equinox

Ask the gnomes to help you to find a magical wand. Go out to a woodland, find a quiet spot and close your eyes. Try to connect with the spirit of the woods and the surrounding area. When you are ready, make a silent request for the spirits of earth to send you a small branch that you can use as your magical wand. Open your eyes and scatter some of the seeds for the birds. Continue walking through the woods, scattering the seeds as you go, until they are all gone. As you walk, keep your eyes peeled for any fallen twig or branch that might make a good magical wand. Don't be surprised if you hear one snap from a tree and drop at your feet! Accept the wand with thanks, take it home, and once it has dried you can decorate it however you choose.

A Gonk Ritual for Peace and Plenty

Items required: a gonk ornament of some kind, salt water

Timing: on a new moon, or on the winter solstice

Gonks are the gnomes and hobgoblins of Norse mythology. Originally they were said to reside in agricultural buildings, working their magic at night to ensure a good yield for the farmer. Over time they came to represent general prosperity and the peace of mind that comes with knowing that you have more than you need. Invite their magic into your home with this spell. First find a gonk ornament that you like. Cleanse it by sprinkling a little salt water on it. Next, carry the gonk all around your home, taking it to every room and introducing it to the family. Find a place for it, which traditionally would be either near the stove in the kitchen or by the hearth. As you set the gonk in its place, empower it by saying:

Spirit of earth and northern light
Your glow is welcome here
Bring peace and plenty through each
    night
That want we need not fear
Blessed be

SYLPHS OF AIR

The sylphs are the spirits of air. They are the power behind every gale and strong wind, every gentle breeze, every turn of the windmill and tinkle of wind chimes. They are linked with all birds and flying insects. Their song can be heard as the wind rushes through a field of wheat or rustles the leaves on the trees. They carry autumn leaves to the ground and spread seeds far and wide in a puff of wind. Magically the sylphs are associated with communication, inspiration, creativity, music and the arts, new beginnings and fresh starts. They can stir up stagnant energy and get your life moving forwards again.

A Spell to Ring in the Changes

Items required: wind chimes, a pentacle
Timing: on the new moon or on the spring equinox

There may be times when you feel the need for change. Change doesn't have to be a negative experience, and when you welcome it into your life every so often you may be able to prevent the kind of catalytic changes that come about when you don't heed the warning signs that a change is needed and it is therefore forced upon you. Take control with this spell to bring about a positive change for the better. First open all the windows and allow the sylphs of air to circulate their power. Then take the wind chimes around your home and ring them softly in each room as you say:

I ring in the changes, it's time for
*   renewal*
Sylphs of air provide the fuel

A happy new start now comes to pass
As a wind of change comes in with a
*   blast*

Lay the chimes on the pentacle until the full moon, then hang them where they can catch the breeze from an open window, allowing positive change to manifest in your life and your home.

A Sylph Spell for Inspiration

Items required: five feathers that you have found on the ground
Timing: perform during the waxing moon

To begin with you will need to collect five feathers, which should be ones that you find shed naturally on the ground. Once you have the feathers, take them to a breezy hilltop or an open window and hold them to your heart as you say:

In love and trust I call upon the sylphs
*   of air*
Guide and inspire me from this moment
*   on*

Throw one feather at a time out into the wind and say one line of the incantation with the release of each feather.
This feather of flight inspires my might

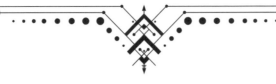

This feather of grace shows in my face
This feather of wind inspires my mind
This feather of love brings ideas from
  above
This feather of creativity always
  inspires me
So mote it be

Give thanks to the sylphs and birds of the air and be sure to act upon any inspired ideas you have in the next few days.

Silent Elf-Bolt Charm
Items required: an elf-bolt stone, black cord or ribbon
Timing: on the night of the full moon

For this charm you will need to find an elf-bolt or elf-arrow, which is a small arrow-shaped flint or stone. You can find them on beaches in most parts of the UK, but failing that, you can also purchase them from New Age stores and online. Elf-bolts were said to be arrow heads used by the fey. They could be directed for love or harm. To find one is especially lucky, but to have one in your possession is said to bring good fortune and the blessings of the fey. You should never give one away, as that would anger the faerie beings and show ingratitude for their magic. Once you have your elf-bolt, wrap the length of cord around it so that you can wear it as a talisman. Glue the cord in place if you need to. Wear the talisman for luck, to ward away danger and to connect with the fey.

Should You Go or Should You Stay?
Items required: a large leaf
Timing: on a breezy day

If you are in a quandary about whether to leave a situation or not, this simple spell asks the sylphs of air to help you come to a decision. Go outside on a breezy day, taking the leaf with you. Close your eyes and concentrate on your question or dilemma. Ask the question *Should I stay or should I go?*

Let go of the leaf to determine your answer. If the sylphs blow it back in your direction they are suggesting that you should remain where you are and stay grounded, but if the leaf blows away from you they are encouraging you to be bold and head in a new direction.

SPIRITS OF FIRE

The spirits of fire, called salamanders, are often depicted as tiny dragons dancing in the heart of every flame. Their power is strong but, due to the nature of fire, it can also be unpredictable. They are present in every flame, from a birthday candle to a large bonfire. At their most destructive they are the wildfires that rage in summertime and the flash of lightning striking the earth. Magically

they can help you to purge anything that no longer serves you. Their power is also associated with love and passion, and its projective energy can get you noticed for all the right reasons.

Silent Ritual to Consume the Need to Consume

Items required: a cauldron or fire-proof bowl, something to represent your consumer habits (shopping receipts, gambling stubs, labels from bottle of alcohol etc.), a notepad or paper and pen, matches, dried basil
Timing: perform outside during a waning moon

We live in a very consumerist society and, while it might be convenient to have whatever you want at the click of a mouse, excessive consumerism can be damaging to your finances and your mental health. Too much shopping, smoking, eating, gambling and drinking can all become destructive habits that need to be broken. Use this spell to help you purge the habit. Write down the nature of your consumerism on a piece of paper, then write the words *I end this pattern, it is no more*, and sign and date it. Fold the paper around the items you have that represent excessive consumerism, place in the cauldron and light with a match. Throw on a pinch of basil, which is the herb most closely associated with salamanders. As the smoke rises, ask for the salamanders' help to purge this bad habit from your life. Keep an eye on the fire to make sure it burns safely.

Salamander Worry Spell

Items required: *a candle, a cauldron or heat-proof dish, a notepad and pen, scissors*
Timing: *at dusk each day*

If you are in the habit of going to bed in a state of stress, then cast this simple spell which is designed to purge away your worries at the end of each day. First light a candle or tea-light. Then spend a few minutes making a list of all the things that you are stressed about. Cut the list into slips of paper so that each slip represents one worry. Read each worry, then light it in the candle flame and drop it in the cauldron to burn as you say:

> *Spirits of fire, take my worries and fears*
> *Please take it from me or make the*
> *solution clear*

Continue until you have burnt away all your worries for the day. If the same worries come up day after day, then cast them into the fire daily, knowing that either you will find a way to deal with it or the responsibility that causes it will be lifted from your shoulders
.

Spell for Passion

Items required: *a red candle, a red carnelian crystal, a red pouch, a pentacle*
Timing: *at noon during the time of the full moon*

A life without passion would be very stale, but passion doesn't only come from love and romance, it can be experienced through sport, hobbies, debate, the arts and so on. There will be something which stirs up your own passion and gets you excited. You might already know what it is, or you might need to discover it. Either way, this spell can help you to draw more passion into your life. Light the red candle and say:

> *I will not stand in passion's way*
> *I will embrace it from this day*
> *Passion comes in every pulse*
> *I seek it out with the craft of the wise*

Place the crystal on the pentacle to charge in the light of the fiery midday sun and leave it there. Allow the candle to burn for one hour a day until it has burnt out, at which point you can put the crystal in the pouch and keep it close to pull in more passionate experiences.

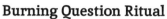

Burning Question Ritual
Items required: a white candle
Timing: best performed on a full moon

If you have a burning question that you cannot find the answer to in a mundane way, ask the salamanders help you to uncover the truth. Light the candle and make sure it is away from any drafts. Allow it to burn for a while and focus on the flame. Ask your question out loud. The answer will be determined by the dancing of the flame. If it suddenly burns low, the answer is no; if the flame leaps high, the answer is yes. If the candle starts to gutter, the situation is still unclear and you should ask again at a later date. If the wax starts to drip down the candle, outside forces are in play and all will soon be revealed.

UNDINES OF WATER

Undines, meaning *waves*, are the elemental spirits of water, and this is the collective name for sirens, mermaids, merrow-maids and nixies. Their energies are found in all bodies of water, from the ocean to the bathtub, from rivers to rainfall. They are in every drop of dew and snowflake and they preside over the hydration of the planet. Undines are associated with emotions, sexual allure, beauty,

captivation, infatuation, harmony and dreams. Magically they can be invoked for seduction and matters of the heart, psychic ability, beauty rituals and prophetic dreams and visions. They are also associated with healing and restoring energy.

Siren Spell to Calm an Infatuation
Items required: a small photo of the person you are infatuated with, a spiral seashell that has a cavity within it
Timing: on the waning moon

Infatuation can happen to anyone of any age. It isn't something that only teenagers experience. It is usually a result of unrequited love and it can be a painful experience. Social media has an impact too, as it has never been easier to keep up with what someone is doing and you might find yourself constantly checking their status for updates. This only feeds the infatuation. It can be tough to let go of a love you have poured your heart into, but if the relationship is purely one-sided, it is better to let it go. First of all, unfollow the person in question, or at the very least, mute them on all your social media platforms. Try not to look at their feed at all and wean yourself away from them. Then take the picture and roll it up as small as you can. Place it into the spiral cavity of the seashell and say:

I loved you long, I loved you well
You loved me not and my heart fell
I loved you well, I loved you long
I let you go, I must move on
Siren take this loss from me
As I live my life with dignity

Release the seashell in some way, either by burying it in the earth or sand or by throwing it into a river or the sea. Know that there is someone else out there for you who will return your affections and give as much as you do.

Siren Spell to Ward Off Unwelcome Attention

Items required: a black candle, clove oil, an item of seashell jewellery
Timing: at the dark moon

Not all romantic attention is welcome, and sometimes it can be downright creepy! If you are the object of someone else's desires but you don't feel the same way then you need to tell them this, kindly but firmly. If their attention shows no signs of abating, cast this spell to ward them off. On the evening of the dark moon, anoint a black candle with

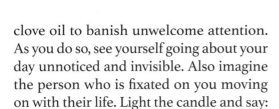

clove oil to banish unwelcome attention. As you do so, see yourself going about your day unnoticed and invisible. Also imagine the person who is fixated on you moving on with their life. Light the candle and say:

> Do not see me, do not seek me, leave me
>   well alone
> Do not call me, do not text me, leave me
>   well alone
> Do not visit me, do not look for me, leave
>   me well alone
> Do not want me, do not hunt me, leave
>   me well alone
> Do not contact me, do not check up on
>   me, leave me well alone
> Do find yourself another love and make
>   a happy home
> Blessed be

Anoint the seashell jewellery with the clove oil and wear this to ward off any more attention. Remember that while an innocent crush is one thing, stalking and sexual harassment are crimes, and you should report them and seek advice from the correct authorities.

River-Stone Spell for Healing

Items required: a stone or pebble
Timing: on the full moon

Take a walk by a river and silently invoke the blessings of the water spirits there. Pick up a pebble from the shore and hold it as you walk. Focus on the issue that you require healing magic with as you hold the pebble, then when you feel ready throw it back into the depths of the river, imagining that you are casting away the illness as you do so. Walk away from the river and do not look back.

CHAPTER SIXTEEN

· · · · · ∘ ◦ ⊙ ◦ ∘ · · · ·

CASTING SEA SPELLS

As the name suggests, sea magic is the art of using the power of the sea in your spells. Ideally they should be cast on the beach, but there are ways that you can bring the power of the sea inland too, by creating a special place in your home or garden that is dedicated to the ocean. You will find ideas for both practices in this chapter. It is always worth planning a spell or two in advance if you know that you will be spending time at the coast, so that you can make the most of these extremely powerful energies.

The ocean has always been revered, and ancient cultures would worship gods and goddesses of the sea. The power of the sea has a very beneficial impact on health and well-being, so it was frequently prescribed as a curative environment. Most people have experienced the euphoria of a trip to the coast and that first glimpse of the sea in the distance. It heals us on every level, with the sounds of the waves soothing the mind and the fresh air filling the lungs. Being near the ocean has a positive impact on the mind, body and spirit.

LAND-LOCKED!

What do you do if you love the sea but the area where you live is inland, miles away from the coast? In that case you need to find ways to bring the sea to you and to your home. You could collect seashells or pebbles, you could hang seascapes on the walls or work with power animals such as dolphins and whales. You should also make time to visit the coast as often as you can, to reconnect with the ocean and experience working sea magic in the most natural environment – on the beach. The most powerful sea spells you can cast are the ones you perform directly with the sea. However, there are ways that you can maintain your spiritual connection with the ocean when you are inland.

Tips to Connect with the Ocean When Inland

- Have the gifts of the sea around your home: seashells, driftwood etc.
- Pick a spot on the coast and keep up to date with the tidal times for that area.
- Use a sea clock.
- Hang a witch ball in your magical space.
- Wear seashell jewellery.
- Work with aquatic power animals.
- Work magic with the elemental undines.
- Remember that all rivers connect to the sea, so get to know your local rivers too.

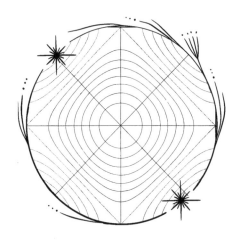

THE FOUR TIDES

As the sea rolls in and out each day, it creates four different tides in every 24-hour period,

meaning that we have two high and two low tides a day. It takes approximately six hours for the sea to go from high to low tide and vice versa, so if the tide is in at noon, it will be out for 6pm, back in again at midnight and out again for 6am, giving two high tides and two low tides to work with. Between high and low tide are the ebb and flow tides, when the sea is either receding from the coast or coming back in to land again. Magically speaking, you can use all these tidal patterns, but they each have their own specific energies.

- Flow tide, when the sea is coming in, is good for calling things in towards you.
- Ebb tide can take things away and is good for banishing.
- High tide is good for spells of completion and fulfilment.
- Low tide is great for gentle workings such as meditation, altar building or calming magic.

SEA CLOCKS

A sea clock is one of the most useful tools in sea magic for those who do not live on the coast. Such a device will tell you exactly what stage the tides are at in your preferred coastal spot. You can purchase these clocks quite inexpensively and they make an unusual addition to any sacred space. Once you have your sea clock you simply need to choose a location and set the clock to the next high tide in that area. So if you were to choose Oban in the Scottish Highlands as your location and you know the next high tide there is at noon (you can find this out by looking up the tide times), you would set your sea clock to high tide at exactly 12 o'clock midday. The clock will then show you all the tides as they occur in Oban. Choose a location that has a special meaning to you or the one that is closest to where you live. Remember that some rivers and lochs are also tidal, so you can channel these tides into your magic as well.

WITCH BALLS

Witch balls are spheres of coloured glass, typically used by fishermen to ward off bad luck and to protect their boats. These balls came to be used more widely within fishing communities and were often seen hung in windows and doorways, over hearths and in chimneys of fishing cottages. They were said to protect against evil and were used by witches as magical wards and as scrying (see page 280) devices. Many coastal-area gift shops have witch balls on sale, particularly in touristy areas, as they can often be very decorative as well as magical. Some are painted, others are filled with dried herbs and flowers or twine, adding to the protective powers of the ball.

Charm to Make and Bless a Witch Ball

Items required: an empty glass sphere (available from craft shops) or traditional witch ball, a piece of black netting, black cord or ribbon, dried camomile, lavender and mugwort, an incense stick of your choice
Timing: at the full moon, preferably at high tide

Take the items to your sacred space and begin by cleansing the witch ball using the smoke from the incense stick. Be sure to cleanse it both inside and out. Next fill the ball with equal amounts of the protective dried herbs lavender, camomile and mugwort. Place the ball in the netting, gather the net around the neck of the ball and secure it in place using the cord, leaving enough cord to make a loop for hanging. Snip off any excess net with scissors. Leave in the light of the full moon overnight and, if possible, dip the ball into the waters of the high tide to bless it, then hang it in your home where it can work its magic.

To bless your ritual space, sprinkle the whole area with sea water, moving in a clockwise direction. As you do so, say these words to dedicate the space to the ocean.

I dedicate this space to the ocean
Where the sea is in constant motion
Its power here within resides
As I work in tune with ocean tides
So mote it be

Sea Spell to Bless a Pendulum
Items required: *a pendulum*
Timing: *at full moon and high tide*

All divination tools should be blessed and consecrated before use, and this simple ritual uses the power of the sea to add a little ocean magic to your future divinations. On a full moon, when the tide is high, take your pendulum to the water's edge. Wrap the chain or cord around your fingers so as not to lose it, then dip the pendulum into the water and allow the water to tug and pull it in play. Now say:

Spirits of the water, goddess of the sea
Show me the way and help me to see
The pendulum that I offer here
Bless it to make my way forward
*   clear*
So be it

HOW TO CREATE A SACRED SEA SPACE

Having a space in your home that is dedicated to the sea is a lovely way to connect with the ocean. All you need to do is pick a spot and decorate it with seashells, driftwood, seascape pictures, a bowl of sand, statues of aquatic animals and sea deities you feel drawn to and so on. Hang your witch ball above to protect the space and keep a sea clock close by so that you can attune with the tides. Then use the flowing blessing to consecrate the area and dedicate it to the sea.

Blessing for a Sacred Sea Space
Items required: *a little sea water or spring water with a pinch of sea salt mixed in*
Timing: *at new moon and during a flow tide*

Let the pendulum dangle in the water for a little while then when you feel ready, dry it off and take it home with you. This spell can attract inquisitive creatures, so don't be surprised if a friendly seal or seagull pops up to see what you are doing!

Silent Sea Spell for Serenity

Items required: the sound of the sea
Timing: use whenever you need to

There is nothing more tranquil than a calm sea, as the waves gently lap in and out, whispering to the sands and chattering over rocks. Spending time actively listening to the ocean can help you to calm anxiety, stop the chatter of a whirring mind and generally feel more at peace. Ideally, you would be by the sea for this ritual, but if that isn't possible you can use a recording of sea sounds to the same effect. If this has been recorded by you in a quiet moment at the beach then so much the better, because then it will tap into your memories of that time.

- To begin, sit or lie in a comfortable position, limbs uncrossed and relaxed.
- Close your eyes.
- Breathe deeply three times, then breathe comfortably.
- Listen to the sound of the waves coming in to shore.

- As you hear them come in, imagine that they are bringing blessings to you.
- As you hear the waves swish out, picture them taking away your stress etc.
- Continue for as long as you need to, allowing the soothing sounds of the sea to ease your mind and carry you to a place of peace and tranquillity.
- When you feel ready, end the meditative exercise and go on with your day.

Driftwood Spell for Safe Travel

Items required: a small piece of driftwood, a black marker pen, clear varnish
Timing: at the time of the new moon and ebbing tide

If you or someone you know is about to go off travelling, use the power of an ebb tide to ward away harm. Find a small piece of driftwood, or cut a larger piece down to pocket size. On it write the name of the traveller on one side and draw the Algiz or Elhaz rune of protection on the other. Now say:

> As the ebbing tide takes you away
> So this rune keeps you from harm's way
> By ebb and flow of every sea
> So you return safely to me
> So shall it be

Coat the talisman with clear varnish and allow it to dry, then give it to the traveller as a good-luck charm.

SOUL ANCHORS

Soul anchors can be found up and down the coastline of the UK. They are old ships' anchors, cemented in place at certain points along the coast and made to look decorative. However, they do have a spiritual purpose as well, for they are meant to give those who were lost at sea a safe resting place. This is why they are often found near war memorials and Unknown Soldier statues. Soul anchors are usually placed on promenades or in coastal gardens, on the cusp between land and sea, and are frequently decorated with flowers and wreaths. They are a sacred space and should be respected in the same way as a stone circle or burial mound.

Soul-Anchor Charm for a Sailor

Items required: two small anchor charms, a haematite crystal, a small pouch, a pentacle
Timing: perform on the full moon and at high tide for greatest power

If you know a sailor, or someone who spends a lot of time on a boat of any kind, then use the power of a soul anchor to keep them safe while at sea. The anchor represents safety in a storm and a safe port. Leave all the items to

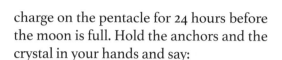

charge on the pentacle for 24 hours before the moon is full. Hold the anchors and the crystal in your hands and say:

May a safe port always be found
May all storms be weathered
May your vessel always be sound
Let your boat be strongly tethered
No matter where you choose to roam
Let this anchor draw you safely home

Put one of the anchor charms into the pouch, along with the haematite crystal for protection and give this to the sailor, keeping the other anchor in a safe place at home. This will help to ensure the sailor's safe return.

Braiding Charm to Leave Your Troubles by the Sea

Items required: seaweed found on the beach
Timing: during a waning moon and an ebbing tide

This is a simple charm that you can use to bind your troubles. Go for a walk along the beach as the tide is ebbing. Look along the shoreline for any seaweed that the sea has left behind. When you find a clump, do not remove it but take three strands and braid them together into a plait. As you do so, imagine that you are braiding your

troubles into the seaweed. When you have finished, walk away from the weed that you have braided. When the tide next comes in, it will pick up the energies of your spell and the following ebb tide will carry them far out to sea.

Three-Wave Spell to Banish a Troublesome Person

Items required: three pebbles or seashells
Timing: on a waning moon as the tide ebbs out

If there is a troublesome person interfering in your life and you have tried all mundane ways to reason with them, cast their difficult

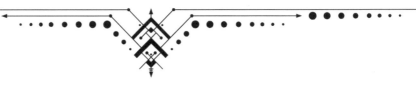

behaviour out to sea with this spell. As you walk along the beach, pick up three pebbles or seashells. Hold them in your hands and consider the situation you are faced with. It could be a difficult boss, an interfering in-law or a toxic neighbour. Think of the situation and head towards the sea. Stand at the edge of the ocean and start to count the waves, throwing a pebble into the sea as each wave comes in and saying the appropriate line:

Wave one takes the person
Wave two takes the issue
Wave three takes the misery
As I stand upon the shore
It troubles me no more

As the tide ebbs out, it will take with it the toxic energies of the situation and this person should soon move on.

Spell to Send Your Love to Someone Overseas
Items required: three red or pink roses
Timing: on the full moon at high tide

If someone you love is working or travelling overseas, use this charm to send your love to them across the waves of the ocean. Take the three roses down to the promenade when the tide is in. Look out to sea and think of your loved one. Feel your heart fill with love for them and kiss the roses, then cast them into the sea one by one, as you say:

I cast my love from me to thee
As you are far away from me
As the waters of the world unite
The undines hear and heed my plight
And so it comes from me to you
A love that is pure and true
May it fill you heart and soul
Until you hear a homecoming call

Have faith that your loved one will feel your magic, possibly dreaming of you and feeling the need to check in and make contact. You can also work this spell in conjunction with those to protect a traveller or sailor.

Sea Spell to Summon a Lover
Items required: a pebble from the beach
Timing: on an incoming or high tide

If you are looking for love, then a sea spell can help to bring a new lover your way. This spell calls on the ocean deities Galatea, Melusine and Aphrodite. To begin, spend some time by the sea, connecting with the oceanic energies. When you are ready, being to chant the incantation – you can do this in your head if there are other people around. The important thing is that you build up the internal desire for a lover and weave it into the spell.

> Galatea, Melusine, Aphrodite, Merrow
>   Maids all
> Nurture my desires and hear my call
> I summon a lover by the power of this tide
> I summon a lover to my side
> As I stir up my passions and awaken my
>   charms
> I summon a lover into my arms
> As I channel desire and tap into my glow
> A new lover comes to me by tide's ebb
>   and flow
> So mote it be

Keep chanting until you feel the power build inside you, then throw the pebble into the sea as far as you can, saying *What is yours I return to thee, what I've requested please send to me.*

High-Tide Chant for Completion
Items required: none
Timing: during a waxing moon, at high tide

If you are having trouble completing a project, or you keep running into obstacles that are holding you back from the finish line, spend some time repeating the sea chant for completion. The beauty of this chant is that you can use it inland as well as by the sea, so you can sit at your sea altar or relax in a warm bath. You just need to know when the high tide is in your preferred location. Concentrate on the energies of high tide and envision pulling these energies into the project you need to complete. Hold the visualization in your mind of the project being finished and celebrating the final results. Now chant:

> By time and tide, by ebb and flow
> The joy of completion I soon will know

As you chant you should begin to feel the motivation to work on the project well up, or to attend to administration connected to the project, say a mortgage or building application. Once you feel this you can stop chanting and crack on.

THE MAGICAL SEVENTH WAVE

In marine folklore the seventh wave is considered to be the most powerful and to hold stronger magical properties. There is some truth to this, as waves tend to move in sets, with the middle wave, the seventh, usually being the biggest and the strongest. In numerology, seven represents adventure, exploration, completion of goals and the quest for knowledge, so a seventh wave might lend itself to spells for all those things. In the following spell the seventh wave is used in conjunction with a traditional witch's-ladder chant to bring in a large goal or ambition, such as a career change, a new baby or a marriage.

Seven-Waves Life-Goal Spell

Items required: *a piece of driftwood, a black marker pen*
Timing: *between new and full moon, as the tide is coming in*

Go to the beach as the tide turns and begins to come back in. Find a piece of driftwood and write on it a symbol or word that represents your main goal or ambition. Carry this wood down to the sea with you. Begin to count the waves and identify the pattern – a much larger wave is usually the seventh, so when you see one, begin counting from one to make sure that you are in alignment with the wave sets. When you have identified the ocean's pattern, begin to say the correct line of the incantation below with each wave, throwing the wood back into the sea on the seventh incoming wave:

This wave of one means the spell is begun
This wave of two makes my dream
   come true
This wave of three, so may it be
This wave of four brings this blessing to
   shore
This wave of five makes my ambition
   thrive

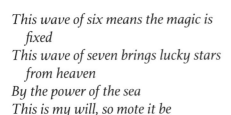

*This wave of six means the magic is
 fixed*
*This wave of seven brings lucky stars
 from heaven*
By the power of the sea
This is my will, so mote it be

Kisses from the Sea

Items required: none
*Timing: high tide, when the sea is in a
playful mood and the spray blows high*

On windy days the spray from the sea can
often be blown right over a promenade,
soaking many an unwary walker! I call this
kind of spray *kisses from the sea* and it is a
mark of the sea's often playful characteristics.
Children love to play with sea spray, often
running forward and back, trying to dodge
the spray. So long as the sea isn't angry, there
is usually no harm in this game, although
obviously heavy seas can be dangerous, so
use your common sense. When the sea is
gentle, however, you can use these 'sea kisses'
to help you practise directing energy. Wait
for the spray to rise and then flick your hand
in the direction you want the spray to go.
See how many times you can get the sea to
kiss your companions! This is good practice

because you will be able to see the results
instantly by watching where the sea spray
falls, so you will know if you have managed
to direct the energy or not. Remember to
ask the sea's permission before you start to
play with it in this way, to show respect for
the power you are working with.

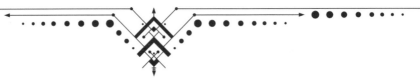

Quick Sea Spells

- Carve the appropriate runes into wet sand to manifest what you want.
- Carve an ex's name into sand on an ebb tide to diminish their effect on you.
- Dry some seaweed and add it to your witch ball or use it in witch bottles.
- Place seashells by your door or garden gate to protect against weather damage to your property.
- Place dried seaweed in the hearth to guard against house fires.
- Write a word in wet sand during a flow tide for manifestation.
- Women should carry a cowrie shell to enhance their sexual allure, while men should carry a whelk for virility.

CHAPTER SEVENTEEN

CASTING FOR HEALING AND BALANCE

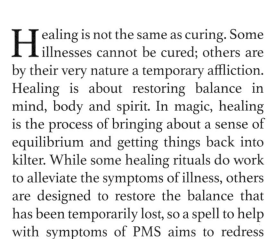

Healing is not the same as curing. Some illnesses cannot be cured; others are by their very nature a temporary affliction. Healing is about restoring balance in mind, body and spirit. In magic, healing is the process of bringing about a sense of equilibrium and getting things back into kilter. While some healing rituals do work to alleviate the symptoms of illness, others are designed to restore the balance that has been temporarily lost, so a spell to help with symptoms of PMS aims to redress the imbalance brought about through the monthly cycle of hormones – it doesn't *cure* the cycle, it just makes its symptoms easier to bear.

Witchcraft has always been a healing tradition; the wise women of old acted as local doctors and midwives to their neighbours. In the days before antibiotics and vaccinations, people relied heavily on herbal remedies which were their only source of medicine. Being a wise woman during this time was a dangerous business as many of the plants used medicinally could also have nasty side effects. Take digitalis, or the humble foxglove, as an example. This plant is widely known for its power to boost and regulate the heart and ease the symptoms of heart disease. It is still used

today in medicines for angina, albeit in a harmless synthetic form as actual digitalis is poisonous. The problem in the past was that there was no regulated dosage, so the wise woman had to make a rough guess as to how much digitalis to administer, depending on the age, height and approximate weight of her patient. Just enough digitalis eased the symptoms of heart disease, but too much would stop the heart altogether and kill the patient, which in turn could lead to a charge of witchcraft and a one-way trip to the scaffold!

Thankfully these days witches have no need to scour hedgerows trying to identify the correct plants for medicinal use. In fact, unless you are trained in plant identification, leave the woodland foraging to the experts and purchase your healing herbs from supermarkets and herbalists. Or grow them yourself. That way you know that you will not confuse something poisonous, such as water hemlock which is a lethal member of the carrot family, for something harmless like carrot plants!

In addition, you should never claim to be a medical practitioner or to have healed/cured someone. There are firm laws in place that regulate medicine and medical practice, which mean that unless you are a GP you are not qualified to offer a diagnosis or to claim that you can cure anyone. What you *can* do is cast spells to offer strength and positivity to someone who is going through a tough time and you can use simple alternative practices such as herbal blends, crystal therapy and aromatherapy potions to offer comfort to yourself and others when daily life gets hard. You can also offer the most traditional of healing rituals, tea and sympathy, because you should never underestimate the power of a listening ear to help someone to feel better.

The gentle healing rituals in this chapter make use of easily available herbs, essential oils and spell ingredients. There are potions for easing period cramps or for boosting the immune system, along with simple ways to ease a headache, calm a toothache and steam a congested chest. In addition, there are spells to send healing energies to someone who is ill or experiencing a trauma of some kind, plus rituals to cope with sorrow and grief if someone you love is diagnosed with a terminal illness. Use these spells responsibly and always do your own research into any herbs or oils before you use them, particularly if you are substituting ingredients or if you are pregnant or trying to conceive.

A WITCH WHO CANNOT HEX CANNOT HEAL

There is a saying in Wicca that a *witch who cannot hex cannot heal*. This saying has been much maligned and has been interpreted by some as proof that witches cast spells to hurt other people. The truth is that this saying is nothing to do with the spells as such, it is simply a way of reminding magical practitioners that if they cannot raise and direct enough power to harm someone, then they will never be able to heal someone, because it takes the same amount of magical energy to hurt as it does to heal. It is only the intention behind the spell that differs. We see echoes of this in the modern saying *kill* or *cure*, which amounts to the same thing – to kill or cure anything takes time and effort. To understand the power of helpful, healing magic, you must understand the power of harmful, baneful magic too. That is not to say that you must *use* baneful magic, you just need to have an understanding of how magic works, in respect of both healing and harming, because it is all the same energy. It's all magic. It is only the intention that determines whether a spell harms or heals. The spells in this chapter are positive in nature, yet they take as much effort as any baneful spell would. Just because magic is good doesn't mean that it is effortless. All magic takes time, effort and energy, and if you do not have the ability to direct magical energy, then you can neither hex *nor* heal.

TISANES, INFUSIONS AND SIMPLES

Many healing potions come in the form of infusions or tisanes. An infusion is made by steeping leaves in boiling water. When you make a cup of tea you are making an infusion. A tisane is made by steeping other plant ingredients – flowers, roots, shoots and spices – in hot water. Usually a tisane is a blend of more than one plant, while an infusion is made with a single plant such as tea leaves, and is also known as a *simple*. Most herbal tisanes do not contain caffeine

so they are best enjoyed before bed to aid relaxation. Some tisanes can also be used as restorative bath soaks, by adding them to the water as you draw a bath. Lavender and lemon balm, for example, is good for a calming bath, while rose geranium can help to ease menstrual pains.

Lemon and Ginger Potion to Strengthen Immunity
Items required: two lemons, ginger root, approx. two teaspoons honey, 2 litres (3½ pints) spring water
Timing: make during a new moon

This potion is great for strengthening the immune system and for easing or warding off colds, flus and bad coughs during the

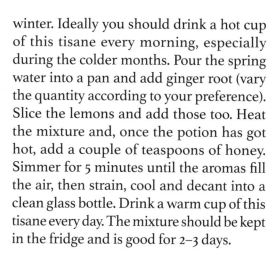

winter. Ideally you should drink a hot cup of this tisane every morning, especially during the colder months. Pour the spring water into a pan and add ginger root (vary the quantity according to your preference). Slice the lemons and add those too. Heat the mixture and, once the potion has got hot, add a couple of teaspoons of honey. Simmer for 5 minutes until the aromas fill the air, then strain, cool and decant into a clean glass bottle. Drink a warm cup of this tisane every day. The mixture should be kept in the fridge and is good for 2–3 days.

Coltsfoot and Eucalyptus Steam Bath
Items required: one teaspoon each of dried coltsfoot and eucalyptus leaves, a large bowl, hot water, a large towel
Timing: use whenever you have a bad head cold or chesty cough

Steaming the lungs is a traditional way to provide relief from congestion. It is an easy way to treat a bad head cold or a chesty cough, as the steam helps to clear the airways. The herbs in this steam bath are known to break up mucus and ease breathing difficulty. First put the dried leaves into the bottom of the bowl and pour on hot water from the kettle. Place the bowl on a table and sit down. Put the towel over your head and the bowl to create a tent, and inhale the herbal steam. Keep inhaling the steam for about 20 minutes, or until the water has cooled. Repeat twice a day, morning and evening, for the best results. As an alternative, you can add this potion to bath water instead. This is sometimes a better option for small children.

Clove Oil for Toothache
Items required: clove oil or half a clove, a cotton pad
Timing: use whenever you have a toothache

The nagging pain of a toothache can be most uncomfortable and, while this traditional remedy is no replacement for a visit to the dentist, it should help to make you more comfortable until you get to your dental appointment. Place a few drops of clove oil on a cotton pad and tuck this onto the affected tooth. Alternatively, cut a clove in half and place this by the tooth instead. Needless to say, due to the choking hazard, this remedy isn't suitable for children.

Feverfew to Ease a Headache
Items required: one teaspoon of dried peppermint or feverfew leaves, honey, lavender essential oil
Timing: use as soon as you feel the first niggle of a headache

Feverfew or peppermint tea is very good for soothing a headache or the beginning of a migraine. However, feverfew should not be used if pregnant or breastfeeding, nor should you use it if you are taking any medication for thinning blood or for blood pressure, so use peppermint instead. Steep the leaves in hot water for 3–4 minutes, strain and sip slowly. Rubbing a drop or two of lavender essential oil into your temples can also help to reduce the headache, as can lying in a darkened room. Try to avoid any kind of stimulant such as caffeine, tobacco or chocolate, which can all exacerbate a headache. Also avoid any screen time, so no TV, laptop, gaming or scrolling through your phone. Turn off all devices and allow the tea and oil time to work, without doing anything to counteract the beneficial effects.

Arnica to Bring Out Bruising

Items required: an empty dark glass bottle, arnica essential oil, 10ml (¼fl oz) almond oil
Timing: make up on a waxing moon if possible

Arnica is traditionally used to treat bumps, bruises, sprains and joint pain. It is a natural anti-inflammatory so it can ease lots of mild aches, pains and soreness. Due to its potency, you need to dilute it in a carrier oil first, so add 5 drops of arnica essential oil to 10ml (¼fl oz) of almond oil. Store it in a dark glass bottle, away from sunlight. To ease the pain of bumps and bruises, gently rub a little of the oil onto the affected area. This will help the bruise to bloom quickly and therefore heal more rapidly too. Apply daily until the bruise is gone or the soreness has eased. Do not use arnica on broken skin as it is too strong and can cause irritation.

Rose-Water Compress to Bring Down Swelling

Items required: a crepe bandage, rose water or rose essential oil, spring water, a bowl
Timing: use on sprains and swollen joints

Rose is a good all-round plant, which is why it is used in so many beauty products and natural remedies. It makes an excellent base for a cold compress, which can be applied to reduce swelling caused by sprains. Place an unrolled bandage into a large bowl, add cold spring water to completely cover and soak the bandage. Next add two tablespoons of rose water, or 6 drops of rose essential oil. Stir the bandage around in the rose water, then place the bowl and its contents into the fridge for about 10 minutes. Once the bandage has cooled and soaked up the rose water, wring it out and apply the damp bandage to the swollen area, being careful not to wrap the bandage too tightly. If the swelling hasn't reduced with an hour seek medical attention.

Calendula to Soothe Irritated Skin
Items required: two tablespoons of dried calendula flowers, 50ml (1½fl oz) almond or sunflower oil, an empty bottle
Timing: make at the time of the new moon

Calendula is a little golden marigold flower that is frequently added to beauty products. It is a mild astringent and has antifungal properties. It is a gentle way to treat mild skin irritation, mild sunburn, rashes and blemishes. It can also be used as an anti-aging treatment when applied to dark spots to make them appear less visible. To make calendula oil, drop two tablespoons of dried calendula flowers into a bottle and add 50ml (1½fl oz) of a carrier oil such as almond, olive or sunflower. Let the flowers steep in the oil, shaking the bottle each day. There is no need to strain, you can leave the flowers in the oil. Apply the potion to irritated skin to soothe and smooth. Do not use if pregnant as calendula can bring on menstruation.

Geranium Massage Oil for Menstrual Discomfort
Items required: an empty dark glass bottle, 30ml (1fl oz) almond oil, rose geranium essential oil
Timing: make on the full moon

This gentle message oil can help to alleviate the discomfort associated with painful periods, such as stomach cramps, lower back pain and breast tenderness. Pour 30ml (1fl oz) of almond oil into a clean dark glass bottle and add 6–10 drops of rose geranium oil. Gently massage the oil into the stomach,

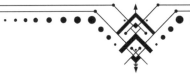

lower back and breasts to quickly ease the discomfort. Use every month as soon as you feel the first twinges of menstrual pain.

Raspberry and Sage for Sore Throats

Items required: half a teaspoon of dried raspberry leaves, half a teaspoon of dried sage leaves, honey
Timing: use whenever you have a sore throat

Steep the herbs in boiling water for around five minutes, then strain and add honey to taste. Use this infusion as a gargle to soothe sore throats and tonsillitis.

Quick Remedies

- Drink cranberry juice to heal or ward off urinary infections.
- Drink dandelion tea to cleanse the digestive system.
- Simmer lemongrass essential oil to uplift the spirits.
- Apply tea tree oil to spots and blemishes.
- Apply lemon balm oil to a cold sore.
- Drink raspberry tea to ease menstrual cramps.

Spell to Send Strength to a Sick Person

Items required: three pieces of narrow blue ribbon or cord, a lock of the sick person's hair
Timing: on a full moon

Willow trees are known as wishing trees, because it is said that a wish whispered beneath its boughs is sure to be granted. Trees of all kinds are also a great source of strength. This spell calls on the spirit of the willow tree to lend strength to the person who is ill. To begin with, you will need to ask the patient's permission to work a healing spell on their behalf. Once permission is granted, obtain a lock of their hair and begin to plait the three ribbons together, weaving the lock of hair into the plait about halfway down. Secure the braid and then take it with you to your chosen willow tree. Stand beneath the tree, tie the ribbon to a branch and say:

> Willow tree, wishing tree
> Send your strength to one dear to me
> I tie this braid with hair within
> I ask for strength and swift healing
> Send your blessing to the one
> Who needs it now, so be it done

Give thanks to the spirit of the tree and walk away when you feel ready, leaving the ribbon in place on the tree.

Charm to Make a Healing Poppet

Items required: blue felt, a needle and thread, a pen and piece of paper, dried herbs for healing – lavender, sage, calendula, camomile and feverfew, a pentacle
Timing: on the full moon

To begin with, write the name of the person you want to send healing energies to on the slip of paper, along with their date of birth. Next fashion a poppet from the felt, cutting two humanoid shapes and stitching them together, but leaving the head open. Place the name tag into the poppet first and say _____(name) I send healing energies your way this day. Fill the poppet with equal amounts of the dried herbs and stitch up the head, then say:

> Little poppet I fashioned you from love
> I name you for_____
> May their illness fade way, may their
>   recovery be swift
> May healing magic pass from you to
>   them, this charm is your gift
> When this work is complete and all is
>   said and done
> I'll cast your herbs onto the earth to once
>   more feel the sun

Keep the poppet in a safe place. Once the illness has passed, unstitch it and scatter the herbs on the earth. Burn the name tag and the felt poppet, giving thanks.

A Candle Ritual for Healing

Items required: a blue candle and holder, lavender oil, an athame or carving tool, a photograph of the person you have permission to cast for
Timing: waxing moon

To begin, place the photograph where you can see it as you work. This will be your focus as you cast the spell. Next carve the name of the person you are sending healing energies to, down the length of the candle. Anoint the candle with lavender oil, from the top

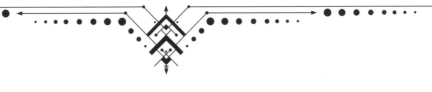

to the middle and then from the bottom to the middle. This will help to draw healing energies to them from all sides. Set the anointed candle in a holder and light it. Close your eyes and picture the sick person in your mind. Imagine that they are surrounded by a sphere of healing blue light. As you visualize this, begin to chant the following words:

Healed from above, healed from below
Healed from all sides, good health you
now know
Healed from without, healed from within
Healed in all ways, let the healing begin.

Continue this chant for as long as you can – you can chant in your head if you want to. Place the candle next to the photograph, so that its light shines on their face. Let the candle burn down naturally and know that you have sent good energies to your loved one in their hour of need.

Valley of the Shadow Ritual
Items required: small black candle, myrrh essential oil (or frankincense or sandalwood oils)
Timing: on a waning to dark moon

Sometimes all the healing spells in the world won't change the outcome, and if someone has been diagnosed with a terminal illness then it is cruel and irresponsible to offer false hope. It is one of the hardest things in the world to cope with when you know for a fact that someone you love is dying and there is nothing you can do to prevent it. Even medical science has its limits, so you should not feel bad that your magic cannot work miracles. You might not be able to offer a cure, but you can perform rituals to help smooth out the dark path you and your loved one must take, in order to make the journey as gentle as possible for both of you. This ritual is designed to be repeated whenever you have need of it, but is best performed on a waning moon. Take the black candle and anoint it with essential oil of myrrh. If you can't find myrrh you can use sandalwood or frankincense oil as a substitute. Anoint the whole candle from top to bottom, then place it in a holder and light the wick as you say:

I'll walk the shadow-way with you
I see all that you're going through
I'll hold your hand till it be time
I'm safe in your heart, you're safe in
mine
Through all the dark days and nights
ahead
My spirit is there, beside your bed
I'll walk with you till we must part
Spirit to spirit and heart to heart
Blessed be

Spell to Invoke a Healing Angel

Items required: *an angel lapel pin, a pentacle, a tea-light and holder*
Timing: *whenever you need a little extra healing power*

Angels are universally recognized as benevolent guardians and guides. They can assist with all manner of things, but you must ask for their help before they can intervene. If someone you know needs a little extra healing, then invoking an angel is a good way to ensure that they are comforted, supported and guided as they navigate their way through illness or trauma. For this ritual

you will need a little angel lapel pin, which you can purchase from most gift shops or online. You are going to give this pin to the person who needs extra healing, but first you need to empower it to its purpose and invoke angelic energies to go with it. Place the pin in the centre of the pentacle to charge. Light the tea-light and call on celestial help with the following invocation:

Angels of healing from far and wide
I invoke your assistance, be by my side
I cast forth this spell to help heal one I
*   love*
I ask for your aid, shine your light from
*   above*
Let your magic be felt through the
*   charm of this pin*
And as you hold _____ (name) in your
*   wings, let the healing begin*
So mote it be

Leave the pin in place to keep charging for 24 hours and allow the candle to burn out. The next time you see your loved one, give them the pin and tell them it is a reminder that they can call on their angels for help when they need to.

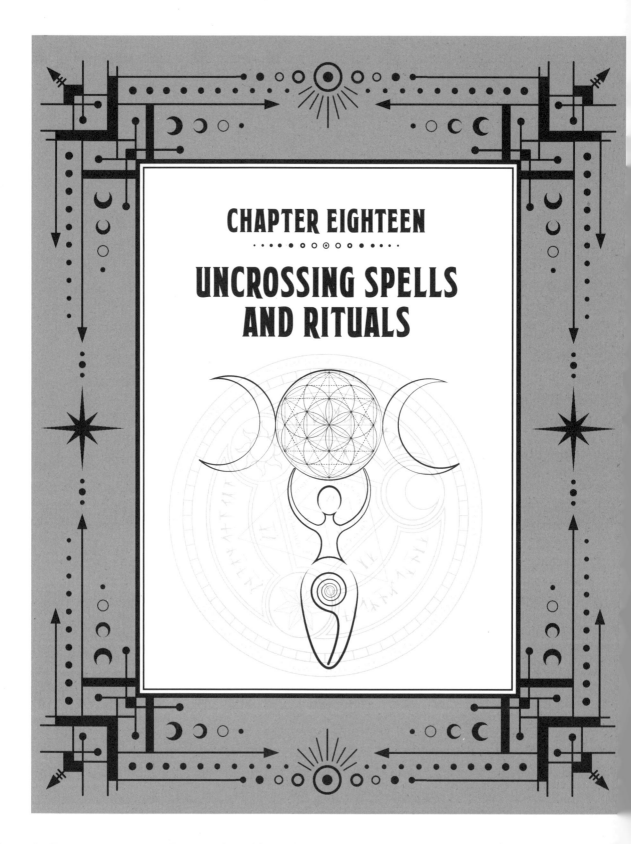

CHAPTER EIGHTEEN

UNCROSSING SPELLS AND RITUALS

Sometimes you might come into contact with negative and unsavoury situations. It doesn't matter if you live your own life from a place of kindness, sadly there are some people who take joy in causing trouble or living in a constant state of chaos and drama. From getting caught up in a crime, as a witness or innocent bystander in the wrong place at the wrong time, to being used as a sounding board by a garrulous colleague, such events can leave a negative imprint on the psyche if you allow them to. This build-up of darker energy can block more positive things from coming to you and it can have a negative impact on your mood and your ability to envision good things happening, so it is essential that you clear away any dark energy that is having a negative influence on you and your life.

Negative encounters can happen anywhere, but if you work in an environment such as a hospital or a funeral home, then you will naturally come into contact with more dark energy than someone who works in a children's nursery or child-care centre.

Not all encounters have to be aggressive to have a negative impact on you – working as a grief counsellor means regularly coming into contact with a lot of dark energy, but no one is to blame for that, as it is just the nature of the job. That said, if the dark energy is allowed to build up, it can soon have a negative impact on your mood and your life, so it needs to be cleansed away on a regular basis, using uncrossing magic. This makes space for more positive energy to come your way instead.

In a more deliberate way, there are lots of encounters that might make you feel uncomfortable – being approached in the street by a stranger, having an altercation with a boss or co-worker, fending off a nosy neighbour every time you leave the house and so on. Then there are also the aggressive interactions that you might occasionally experience, such as road rage and impatient drivers, spurned suitors and people with personality disorders like narcissism and psychopathy. Life can be fraught at times and it all adds up to a maelstrom of dark energy that needs to be cleared.

bad things have happened to *them*, so why should anyone else be happy and successful? That kind of behaviour is deliberate and you should be wary of such unpleasant characters and nip their behaviour in the bud. Learning how to recognize such individuals is half the battle, so read on.

THE DARK TRIAD

This is a term psychologists use to identify the three main personality traits proven to have a negative impact on other people: narcissism, Machiavellianism and psychopathy. Most people have some trace of each of these traits within their personality. In small doses they can be a good thing, but too much leads to negative and destructive patterns of behaviour. Getting to know the symptoms

THE BAD INFLUENCE OF DARK ENERGY

What do we mean by dark energy? Essentially dark energy is the vibe that is left behind after a negative event has occurred. Some people hold on to this dark energy for the rest of their lives, following a trauma of some kind. They carry it with them and will infect others with it too, either intentionally or unintentionally. The garrulous, chaotic individual probably has no idea that their constant chatter and endless drama drains other people, so their dark energy is spread quite unintentionally.

However, there are also those individuals who enjoy stirring up trouble for other people and who go out of their way to cause conflict. They might hold the opinion that

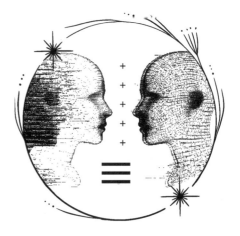

of these dark personalities can help you to identify them early on, thereby limiting their damaging effects on your own life.

Narcissism

Narcissism is much more than simply thinking too well of oneself – it is a tendency to grandiosity and an over-inflated idea of self-worth. The narcissistic personality lives for attention, adoration and worship. They love people who agree with them and will wage a brutal vindictive war against anyone who dares to find fault with them or who confronts them about their lies. Deep down, the narcissist feels inadequate and vulnerable, so they cover this up with an act of pretence and boasting, much like a tiny bird will fluff out its feathers to appear bigger to a predator. They are terrified that they will be seen as being just like everyone else. They want to appear superior to everyone else, at all times. They see themselves as being without fault.

Signs to look out for:
- *Boasting and hubris* – they like to brag about their achievements so you'll look up to them and admire them.
- *Lies* – they are happy to lie about what they have done and may invent an alternative past or fabricate qualifications, wealth and titles.

- *Centre stage* – they love to be the centre of attention; even if the attention is negative, they thrive on it. Narcissists are the drama queens of life, frequently being the ones to start up the rumour mill.

Machiavellianism

Put simply, Machiavellianism (named for the Renaissance thinker Niccolo Machiavelli) is the art of manipulation, covered by charm. These are the con-artists, the Casanovas and the powerful influencers of the world. Machiavellians always get exactly what they want and they are prepared to break the rules to get it. This might mean that they spike drinks for sex, make promises they don't keep, or attempt to undermine others. They are interested in power and control and are motivated by self-interest.

Signs to look out for:
- *Superficiality* – they are all charm. They say all the right things but there is never any real substance behind their words. They make empty gestures/promises just to get what they want.
- *Control* – they like to have as much control over things as possible, and that includes you! They can be pernickety and hard to please.
- *Brainwashing* – they undermine you by

telling you how useless you are and how you need them to get ahead in life.

Psychopaths

The 'psychopathic scale' suggests that most of us have at least a touch of this trait; it is what helps us to achieve and without it, we might never get out of bed in the morning! The higher up the scale you go, the less empathy and compassion for others is evident, which means that psychopaths can range from media moguls and skilled surgeons to cold-blooded killers. Used effectively, it can produce a successful individual; used destructively, it can ruin and take lives.

Signs to look out for:

- *Selfishness* – psychopaths really don't care what you want, they only know their own needs.
- *Obsession* – they can focus absolutely to the exclusion of everything else, similar to a horse wearing blinkers.
- *Lack of empathy/compassion* – they cannot feel for the sufferings of others and have no ability to put themselves in someone else's shoes.

Being able to recognize these personality types means that you will know when you are in the company of one and will be on

your guard. Forewarned is forearmed and you will be able to limit your interactions with these people and then cleanse their dark energy and bad influence from your life using the spells and rituals in this chapter.

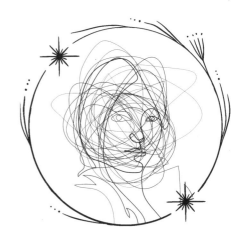

ENERGY VAMPIRES

In addition to the Dark Triad, there is one more personality type that you need to look out for and that is the 'energy vampire', so termed because they drain away the energy of other people in order to fill themselves up. Although not as deliberately destructive as the Dark Triad can be, energy vampires are still just as difficult to be around. They are known for being self-absorbed, and this can come across in two ways.

First there is the energy vampire who

just never stops talking! They are not looking for a conversation, just a sounding board and an audience. They are easily spotted because, having spent several minutes or hours telling you all their troubles, as soon as someone new comes into the group, they will immediately turn to that person and start to tell the whole story again, from the beginning. They continue in this manner on a daily basis and usually throughout their lives, often repeating the same narrative over and over. While being overly chatty isn't a crime, it is nonetheless an imposition on others. Being around this kind of person can leave you feeling drained, headachy and exhausted.

The second type of energy vampire is the one who runs a victim narrative in their mind, using this as an excuse as to why they cannot take full responsibility for themselves and their actions. They may also suffer from depression and possibly addiction. While it might be true that bad things have happened to them in the past, that is no reason to make everyone they come into contact with pay for their experiences! This kind of energy vampire not only drains you energetically, they are likely to drain you emotionally and financially too. They are masters of emotional abuse and manipulative mind games, and they tend to project their own fears and flaws onto you. As a result, they

can leave you feeling confused, gaslighted, drained, emotionally fragile and probably skint too!

HOW TO DIMINISH DARK ENERGY: UNCROSSING SPELLS

So how do you deal with the dark energy that comes from these kinds of bad influences? The short answer is: you need to clear it. Cleansing rituals are the initial step, then you can move on to shielding spells to diminish someone's influence over you. Cutting the energetic connection also helps. All these are forms of uncrossing magic, whereby you eliminate the dark energy that has built up and invite positive blessings instead.

Uncrossing spells and rituals are your first line of defence and the gentlest form of banishing magic. Like most other types of cleansing rituals, uncrossing spells need to be performed on a regular basis to keep your energy field as positive as possible. You should ideally cleanse dark energy immediately after a negative event or encounter, or as soon afterwards as possible. If you know that you have been in the company of someone with one of the negative personality traits described above, then as soon as you get home, take a shower and perform an uncrossing spell, to prevent their dark energy attaching to you. A monthly dark cleansing ritual is also a good way to start working this type of magic.

It is always a good idea to cast some simple manifestation spell shortly after an uncrossing ritual, as this will ensure that positive energies come to fill the space you have created. Protection spells are good for this purpose.

Dark Moon Cleansing Ritual

Items required: a black candle, patchouli oil, sea salt
Timing: on the dark moon

To begin with, take a bath or shower and use the sea salt as a body scrub. As you rub it onto your skin, visualize that you are rubbing away the bad energy that has accumulated around you over the month. Rinse off the sea salt and let it wash away down the drain. Once you are dried off, continue with the rest of the spell. Take a black candle and anoint it with patchouli oil, moving from the top to the bottom of the candle. Set the candle in a holder and light it as you say:

All dark energy is now cleansed away
I start afresh with each new day
No bad influence may linger here
All dark energy will disappear

Allow the candle to burn for one hour, then blow it out. Repeat this spell each dark moon.

Simple Aura Cleansing Ritual

Items required: none
Timing: whenever you feel bad vibes and stagnant energy surrounding you

Your aura is the energy field which protects you spiritually. It is made up of colours – the lighter and brighter the better. A dark aura is indicative of illness, addiction or the accumulation of bad energy. Although some people can see auras, for most people they are not noticeable. An aura is something that magical practitioners often visualize as a glow surrounding the entire body. If your aura is bright and healthy, you will feel happy and energetic. If it is dull and contaminated

least once or twice a week, or incorporate it into any stretching or exercise routine you do, as part of your cool-down process. This will help to ensure that your aura doesn't become too clogged up.

Cord Cutting Ritual

Items required: black thread or string, a cauldron or heat-proof bowl, scissors, matches
Timing: as the moon wanes

with dark energy, however, you will feel sluggish, tired and lethargic. It is therefore a good idea to get into the habit of cleansing the aura with a simple visualization exercise. Stand or sit in a comfortable position and visualize your aura all around you. Raise your arms high until your palms meet over your head, then slowly lower your arms, imagining that you are pushing any dark colours down and into the ground where they will be neutralized by the earth. When your arms are by your side, breathe deeply three times, then slowly raise your arms up again, this time imagining that you are pulling light, bright colours into your aura from the earth. When your palms meet, your aura has been cleansed. Try to do this at

Whenever you form a relationship, be it personal or professional, you create a psychic connection with that person. This is as true for someone whom you don't like as it for the relationships you have with loved ones. Our emotions, good and bad, create enmeshments with other people. In magic we refer to these links as psychic cords. In order to be free of someone's influence over you, you will need to cut the cords; whether that person is an ex-partner or you need to cut ties with an old workplace so that you can move forward in your life, the cords need to be cut so that your life can progress in a positive way. This is one of the oldest forms of uncrossing spell. To begin with, sit and think about the person who is influencing you. Anyone who makes you feel strong emotions such as love, hate, envy etc. has an influence

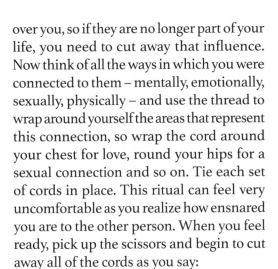

over you, so if they are no longer part of your life, you need to cut away that influence. Now think of all the ways in which you were connected to them – mentally, emotionally, sexually, physically – and use the thread to wrap around yourself the areas that represent this connection, so wrap the cord around your chest for love, round your hips for a sexual connection and so on. Tie each set of cords in place. This ritual can feel very uncomfortable as you realize how ensnared you are to the other person. When you feel ready, pick up the scissors and begin to cut away all of the cords as you say:

I sever the ties that bound us together
I free myself as these bonds I now sever

When you have cut away all the cords, drop them in the cauldron and light them with a match. As you watch the cords burn, know that they are freeing you from someone who is a part of your past, leaving you free to move on.

Shielding Visualization Ritual
Items required: a tea-light and holder, Night Queen incense and holder
Timing: on a waxing moon

Shielding spells are somewhere between a protection spell and an uncrossing spell, because they work to repel the negative influence of another. It is a type of visualization exercise, so once you get used to performing it at home as a ritual, you will quickly be able to visualize your shield as and when you need to. This is useful if you know that you are going to be meeting someone who has a negative impact on you, as you can quickly throw up your psychic shield to mitigate their influence. Light the incense and pull some of the smoke towards you as a personal cleansing, then light the tea light and focus on the flame for a time. Decide what your personal psychic shield will look like; it could be an actual shield like the ones carried by knights, a thick hedge of thorns all around you, a ring of flames or a wall of ice. Whatever kind of shield you choose is up to you, just make sure that you can visualize it clearly in your mind's eye. Imagine the shield in place all around you, protecting you on all sides from dark energy and bad influences. Negative people might even avoid you altogether! Once you have your psychic shield in place, blow out the candle and go about your day. Repeat this ritual until you can picture the shield at a moment's notice. You can then call it up whenever you find yourself in bad company!

Diminishing Spell for a Bad Influence

Items required: a notepad and pen, a cauldron or heat-proof bowl, a lighter
Timing: on a waning moon

If there is something or someone that you know has a bad influence on you, cast this spell to diminish their power. On a piece of paper, write down the nature of the influence as a complete sentence, for example, *social media influence on body image*. Next write out the sentence again, leaving out the last letter. Repeat this until you are down to a single letter:

Social Media Influence on body image
Social Media Influence on body imag
Social Media Influence on body ima
Social Media Influence on body im...

Once you have diminished the sentence, fold the paper into three and light the end with the lighter, then drop it into the cauldron to burn. When the ashes have cooled, scatter them to the winds. Monitor the amount of time you spend around any influences that make you feel bad about yourself.

Silent Spell to Free Yourself from a Bad Influence

Items required: a leaf
Timing: at full to dark moon

Go for a walk by a river or stream. As you walk, look for a fallen leaf or flower blossom. When you see one you like, pick it up and silently name it for the bad influence you are trying to escape from. When you feel ready, drop the leaf into the river and watch the water carry it away from you. Walk away from the river and don't look back – know that the leaf has gone and is no longer any part of your life. The bad influence will soon follow it.

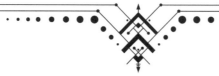

Spell to Stop Gossip

Items required: black pepper, an empty spell jar and lid, black sealing wax, paper and a black pen
Timing: on the full moon for strongest power

Being talked about is no fun, especially if people are deliberately telling lies about you. There will always be people who trade in rumours and most people have been guilty of gossiping every now and then, but if someone has set the rumour mill against you and it shows no signs of petering out on its own, cast this spell to stop the rumours from escalating any further. Write the nature of the rumour on a slip of paper in black pen, roll the paper up and put it in the jar. Fill the jar with black pepper and say:

Black pepper to banish, no grist to grind
Uncrossing you brings me peace of mind
Of your gossip and lies I've had my fill
May your own life be food for the
    rumour mill!

Put the lid on the jar and seal it with black wax, then bury the jar close to your front door or workplace, wherever the rumours are rife. This spell should turn the attention to the one who is pointing the finger within a moon phase.

Simple Incense Uncrossing Spell

Items required: two incense sticks in one of the following scents, cinnamon, frankincense, cedar or lavender, a plate or tray, Blu Tack or mounting putty
Timing: on the first night of the waning moon

This is a very simple uncrossing spell which is meant to cleanse away all negative energies that surround you. On the first night of a waning moon, take your two chosen incense sticks and lay them on the tray, so that the sticks are crossing one another. You can use Blu Tack or mounting putty to hold them in place, just make sure that the sticks cross over one another, like crossed swords. Next

light both incense sticks and say:

All negative vibes, all curses and crosses
I break and diminish, I suffer no losses
I break up the darkness, with magic and
*   light*
As this cleansing smoke curls into the night

Once the incense has burnt away, throw the ashes outside into the air to complete the uncrossing cleansing ritual.

Bay Leaf Uncrossing Spell

Items required: six dried bay leaves, a white candle and holder, a cauldron or heat-proof dish
Timing: on the full moon

Bay leaves have been used in protection and cleansing magic for hundreds of years. In the past it was thought that they could ward off the Great Plague and so bay was often added to posies and pomanders during the Plague years. In this ritual you are going to use the power of bay leaves to both uncross and protect your home. This is an especially good spell to use if you have been having issues with neighbours or your home has been targeted by crime. Such events can leave behind a lot of dark energy, which this uncrossing spell will help to clear. First light the candle and say:

I work in the light, for the good of all here
To dispel any darkness that lingers near

Next, take three of the bay leaves and hold them, one by one, in the flame of the candle, then drop them into the cauldron to burn, saying the appropriate line of the incantation below:

I name this leaf for the darkness –
*   I banish it from this place*
I name this leaf for the curses – I banish
*   them from this place*
I name this leaf for uncrossing all within
*   this space*
So mote it be

Finally, take the other three leaves and place them in strategic points around your home – one near your main door, one by the back door, chimney or stove, and the final one by your bed. As you place each leaf say:

Blessed and Protected Be!

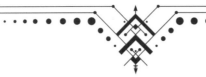

How to Make Uncrossing Oil

Items required: an empty dark glass bottle, 10ml (¼fl oz) carrier oil, rosemary and lemon balm essential oils
Timing: make on the night of the dark moon

Uncrossing oils are good for anointing candles that you are going to be using in banishing spells. They can also be added to bath water as a personal cleansing ritual, or to cleaning water when you are doing domestic chores around the house. Pour 10ml (¼fl oz) of carrier oil such as almond or olive oil into a dark glass bottle and to this add five drops each of rosemary and lemon balm essential oils. The lemon balm is a well-known cleanser and the rosemary attracts positive energy and blessings. Keep the bottle in a cool, dark place so that it is ready for when you need it

To End a Spell of Bad Luck

Items required: rose water in a spray bottle, rose quartz crystal
Timing: on a full moon

If you have been having a run of bad luck, try this simple spell to break the pattern and bring about good fortune instead. Seven has long been considered to be a very lucky number. It is a celestial number, linked to the angels. It is also a number related to the creation of the natural world and our concept of time – seven oceans of the world, seven days of the week etc. First cast a circle around yourself. Next say out loud all the instances of bad luck that you have had in the past six months, followed by the words:

My luck must change, bad luck be done
In seven days, bad luck be gone!

Turn anti-clockwise seven times and say:

By the power of lucky seven,
I am blessed with all good things under
*   heaven*

Spray the rose water into the air before you and walk into the mist. This will help to draw positive things your way. Carry a rose quartz crystal to add to the positive vibes.

Spell to Clear Blocks from Your Path

Items required: the shoes you wear most often, blessing seeds, a mortar and pestle
Timing: from full to dark moon

This spell will help to enchant your footsteps so that all blocks and obstacles will soon fade away. Take half a teaspoon of blessing seeds and grind them to a fine powder using the mortar and pestle, then

the contents of the egg out of the bottom hole and into the bowl. As you do so, imagine any dark energy is passing out of your breath and through the egg. Once the egg is completely empty, flush the contents down the toilet and smash the shell on a piece of kitchen roll, then add it to the compost heap.

Burn Juniper to Remove Stagnant Energies

Items required: a bowl of sand, a charcoal block, a lighter, dried juniper leaves
Timing: whenever the energy around you feels blocked and stagnant

You don't have to wait until something bad happens before you do an uncrossing ritual – in fact you shouldn't! Sometimes the energy around you can feel blocked and stagnant, not because of a negative experience, but simply because you haven't done regular cleansing rituals. To counteract this, burn a little juniper each week. Light a charcoal block and place it into a bowl of sand to safely absorb the heat. Then add about a teaspoon of dried juniper leaves to burn on the smouldering charcoal block. Juniper is great for freeing up old energy and giving it a fresh lift. It is one of the classic witch's herbs and has been used in purification rites since biblical times. You can also buy juniper smudge sticks, which are just as effective.

put a pinch of the powder into the shoes you wear most often and say:

Step by step, clear my way
All blocks crumble and fade away
All obstacles shall be surmounted
For now, I walk with steps enchanted!

Egg Uncrossing Spell

Items required: one egg, a needle or pin, a bowl, kitchen roll
Timing: on a waning moon

This spell is designed to cleanse your body of any dark energy that might have accumulated. Take the egg and prick the pin into the top to make a hole, then make a bigger hole in the bottom. Next gently blow

Juniper Spell for Good Fortune

Items required: *a small pouch, nine dried juniper berries, a pentacle*
Timing: *on the full moon*

Juniper berries are associated with luck and good fortune, so once all your uncrossing magic is done, make this simple charm to attract good fortune. Place the dried juniper berries on the pentacle and leave in the light of the full moon overnight, then put them in a pouch and carry them with you to bring you good luck. Replace and repeat every three months.

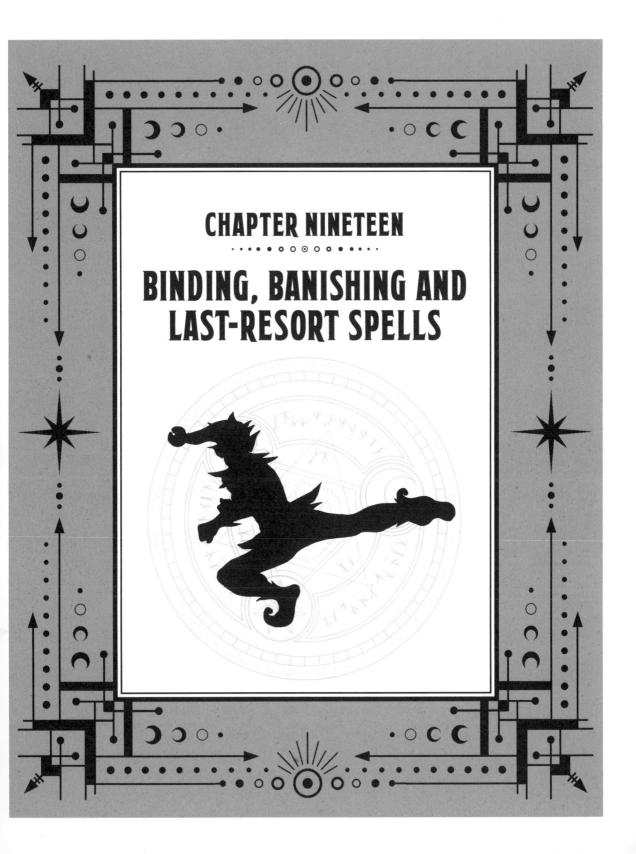

CHAPTER NINETEEN

BINDING, BANISHING AND LAST-RESORT SPELLS

It is a myth that witches are powerless in the face of aggression, or that we are so bound by the Wiccan Rede of *Harm None* that we cannot act when someone attacks us. The Wiccan Rede also states: *Lest in thy self-defence it be, ever mind the rule of three*, which basically means that the power of witchcraft can be used in self-defence if necessary. Witches often talk of binding and banishing spells, which are forms of self-defence magic. If protection and uncrossing magic hasn't had the desired effect, it could be that you need something stronger in the form of spells to bind or banish, or both.

HOW DO BINDING AND BANISHING SPELLS WORK?

These types of rituals are the strongest form of protection magic that you can cast. They should be used as a last resort, after you have used uncrossing magic, and they should not be taken lightly. They work by stopping someone from acting against you or by removing them from your life and environment. With a binding spell you would be preventing a person from doing harm to you and others using some form of binding agent, while a banishing spell basically makes them go away.

Neither binding nor banishing rituals are cast with the intention of causing harm to the subject. Instead they work to prevent harm being done by the subject, to you and to other people too. Most people would agree that it is permissible to defend yourself if attacked – this is simply the magical version of that type of self-defence.

These spells create a boundary that the subject should not cross. If they *do* attack you once the binding or banishing spells have been worked, then their actions will backfire on *them*, without causing you any harm. In short, they will fall victim to their own spite, as their bad intentions bounce off the magical boundary you have created and hit the perpetrator instead. This is the only way in which a binding or banishing spell can harm the subject, and it is their own bad intentions which cause that harm, rather than the intention of the witch. If they leave you alone, nothing will happen to them. If they don't, these spells will protect you.

WHEN SHOULD YOU CAST TO PROTECT YOURSELF?

Defensive magic should only be cast if you feel that you are being attacked or are under threat. Often, when negative things happen, it is usually no more than a touch of bad luck or a build-up of dark energy that is to blame, which is why you should always cast uncrossing spells as a first response. However, there might be times when you

know that someone is attacking you in some way and if that is the case, then binding and banishing spells could be used to put a stop to their behaviour. Here are some examples of when it could be in your best interests to work some defensive magic:

- If you are being targeted in a narcissistic vendetta.
- If you are the target of narcissistic abuse or rage.
- If someone is deliberating trying to sabotage you in some way, personally or professionally.
- If you are the target of a stalker or harassment of some kind.
- If you are experiencing nuisance phone calls and messages.
- If someone is using coercive control over you.
- If someone is working against you covertly.

In all these situations it would be permissible to work some magic in your own self-defence. It should go without saying that you should back up these spells by informing the correct authorities if someone is targeting you with negative intentions, so you might need to report it to a line manager, the governing body of the subject's profession, the police or all of the above. Do whatever you need to do in order to highlight the subject's behaviour, in addition to working defensive magic. Don't rely on the spells alone. Always back them up in the most appropriate way.

TYPES OF BINDING AND BANISHING

There are two ways in which you can cast binding and banishing rituals. The first way is to cast against the behaviour, while the second is to name the individual or group that you are defending yourself against. Casting against the behaviour is always the gentlest approach, so this should be your first

response. It is also the most effective magic for those occasions when you don't know exactly who is attacking you, for example on social media, as the spell targets the behaviour itself, so whoever is the perpetrator of that behaviour will feel its effects.

Spells that name a specific individual really are a last resort, but they are the strongest form of protection against someone who means you harm. They should be used against repeat offenders, so anyone who has been deliberating targeting you for some time and who shows no signs of going away or listening to reason. Only you will know which way of casting is the most appropriate, so in each of the following spells, it is down to you to decide what to write on the tag – a behaviour or a name – you are simply instructed to write the tag-lock, which is the behaviour or name written on a slip of paper or card or carved into a candle. It is your responsibility to decide how you cast the spells in this chapter and that decision should be based on the level of threat and the number of times someone has crossed you in this manner. All of these rituals will help to restore peace and harmony in your life.

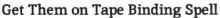

Get Them on Tape Binding Spell

Items required: a piece of card, a black marker pen, black electrical tape
Timing: during the waning moon

This is one of the simplest and most effective forms of binding ritual. It uses few tools, most of which can be found around the house, so it's a great emergency spell if you need to perform a binding quickly. Write out the tag-lock on the card using the black pen, then, starting at one end of the card, attach the black tape and begin to wind it around the card as you say:

> *I bind you with your baneful ways*
> *May your spite return to fill your days*
> *I bind you tight from doing harm,*
> *I bind you, that my days be calm*

Continue wrapping the tape around the card until you have been from one end to the other and back again, finishing where you started. Ensure that every inch of card is covered and the tape overlaps, leaving no gaps. Keep this binding in a safe place or bury it away from your property.

Seven-Day Stick It to 'Em Binding Spell

Items required: a card, a black pen, an empty tub and lid, runny glue such as PVA glue, one teaspoon each of garlic and turmeric powders
Timing: on a waning moon

As the moon first begins to wane, write out your tag-lock and drop it into the tub. Imagine the subject being bound tight, so that they cannot harm you or anyone else. Add the banishing spices, sprinkling them on top of the tag-lock, then pour on enough glue to cover them in a thin layer. Next repeat the incantation three times:

> *Bane and spite is stuck on you*
> *I return it all to stick like glue*
> *No ill intent, no harm can you do*
> *With this spell I now bind you*

Put the lid on the tub and leave it on your altar. Each evening, for the next six days, add a little more glue to the tub and repeat the words three times.

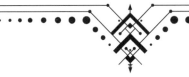

Silent Bramble Binding

Items required: a photograph or business card of the subject or a written tag-lock, garden shears, gardening gloves, garden trowel or spade
Timing: on the first night of the waning moon

Bramble is a plant that is known for its protective attributes and in this spell you are going to use those protective energies to bind your subject tight. This is the kind of spell that should be used when the same subject has targeted you over and over. Get your photograph or tag-lock and go to a place where wild brambles grow. Put on the gardening gloves to protect yourself from the thorns and, using the shears, cut a length of bramble from the bush, choosing one that is pliable. Next, wrap the bramble around the photo or pierce the tag-lock onto one of the thorns. As you wrap the plant, imagine it wrapping around the subject so that they cannot move to do harm to you or anyone else. Once the bramble is bound in place, weave the end under the binding to keep it there, then use the trowel or spade to dig a hole and bury the binding spell in the ground.

Bindweed Spell for Tripping a Foe

Items required: a black candle, a length of bindweed, a lighter, a cauldron or heat-proof dish

Timing: on the dark moon

Bindweed is well known for being a trip hazard, often snagging any unwary walker or gardener. In this ritual we use that power to ensure that the subject fails in their ill intentions. This is a spell that is designed to make the target trip themselves up and bring about their own downfall, similar to the saying *Give them enough rope and they'll hang themselves.* It might be that they become too careless or overly confident in their plotting, but their bad behaviour will be brought to light by their own hand if you cast this spell. Take a black candle to symbolize your subject and carve the tag-lock down the wax. Next take a length of bindweed and wrap it around the candle, using its stickiness to hold it in place. As you do so, say:

Enough rope to hang you
Enough magic to bind you
Enough courage to face you
Enough power to erase you
May you trip and fall, for all to see
This is your downfall, cast by me

Secure the candle in the cauldron and light the wick. As the candle burns down, it will burn through the bindweed, freeing you from this person and their malice. This spell can be quite smoky, so make sure that you do not leave it unattended.

Poison Apple Withering Spell to Banish Malice

Items required: a small apple, a large jar and lid, a piece of paper, a black pen, an apple corer, three belladonna seeds, surgical gloves (or three blackthorn thorns)
Timing: during the waning moon

This ritual is for use when someone has malicious intent towards you. Usually this is the result of envy. It might mean that they are waging a vendetta against you for some reason, or that they are trying to sabotage your life in some way, perhaps trying to undermine you at work in the hopes of taking your job for themselves, or maybe they are interfering in your relationship. Whatever the nature of their malice, this withering

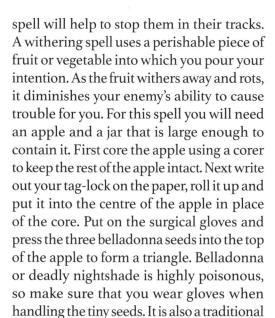

spell will help to stop them in their tracks. A withering spell uses a perishable piece of fruit or vegetable into which you pour your intention. As the fruit withers away and rots, it diminishes your enemy's ability to cause trouble for you. For this spell you will need an apple and a jar that is large enough to contain it. First core the apple using a corer to keep the rest of the apple intact. Next write out your tag-lock on the paper, roll it up and put it into the centre of the apple in place of the core. Put on the surgical gloves and press the three belladonna seeds into the top of the apple to form a triangle. Belladonna or deadly nightshade is highly poisonous, so make sure that you wear gloves when handling the tiny seeds. It is also a traditional ingredient in banishing spells. Put the apple into the jar and put on the lid. Holding the jar, say:

> As this poison apple withers away
> Your malicious spite will end this day
> Deadly nightshade seals the core
> That you may trouble me no more

Dispose of the gloves carefully and then wash your hands. Keep the jar outside your property, on a doorstep or by the garden gate, and monitor its withering. Once it has turned fully brown, you may dispose of it on

the compost heap. Note: if you prefer not to use belladonna seeds, you can substitute them for three blackthorn thorns instead and modify the incantation to suit.

Sour Spite Withering Spell to Bind a Slanderer

Items required: a lemon, salt, a piece of paper, a black pen, an athame or knife, a pentacle, black cord or string to bind
Timing: on the waning moon

If someone is speaking against you, telling lies about you or otherwise slandering your good name, use this spell to bind their tongue. Write out the tag-lock, then take the lemon and cut part of the way through it. Press the tag-lock into the opening and add a little salt. Now begin to bind the lemon, by wrapping the black cord around it and tying it tightly as you say:

> Those who slander know no joy
> By this spell I stop their ploy
> Backbiter, traducer, maligner of my name
> Let the vilifier be vilified, I silence their
>   game

Once the lemon has been thoroughly bound up tight, tie off the cord and leave the lemon on the pentacle until the new moon, then place it in the compost or bin or bury it in the earth. For an extra-strong spell, use this ritual in conjunction with the uncrossing spell from the last chapter to stop the rumour mill (see page 240).

Freeze Them Out Banishing Spell

Items required: a piece of card, a black pen, an empty tub and lid, spring water
Timing: on the waning moon

This spell is great when you need to stop someone in their tracks quickly. It is a containment spell which uses the power of ice to bind their actions against you, then banishes them from your life. To begin,

write out your tag-lock and put it in the tub. Fill the tub with water and put on the lid, then place the tub into the freezer. As the spell water freezes it will put a stop to any movement against you. Leave the tub in the freezer until you are sure that the conflict has passed, then take it out of the freezer and turn it upside down over a drain. As the ice melts and drains away, it banishes the subject. To finish, rip up the tag-lock and throw it away.

Flush Them Out Banishing Spell

Items required: nine pieces of toilet paper
Timing: whenever you need to be rid of someone who is causing trouble for you

This simple banishing spell is so easy and yet very effective. Take nine pieces of toilet paper and, one by one, screw them into a ball as you imagine your foe going away and leaving you alone. Throw each crumpled tissue into the toilet with the words:

Banished, banished, banished be!

When all nine tissues are in the toilet, flush them away, saying:

By the strength of three times three
Banished, banished, banished be!

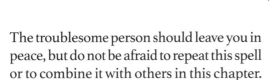

The troublesome person should leave you in peace, but do not be afraid to repeat this spell or to combine it with others in this chapter.

Move Along Banishing Spell

Items required: blessing seeds, cayenne pepper, dried basil, a mortar and pestle
Timing: at midnight, on the first night of the waning moon

Often the best outcome in any conflict is that your enemy will simply move on with their life and stop their negative behaviour. This is a great little spell which encourages just that, so use it if someone is deliberately attempting to stand in your way or place obstacles in your path to prevent you from getting ahead or achieving your goal. Place half a teaspoon of the following ingredients into the mortar – cayenne pepper and dried basil for banishing and blessing seeds for making your goal manifest. Grind them all into a fine powder using the pestle. As you do so, visualize the person moving away and disappearing from your life while you chant:

> *Go away, do not stay,*
> *Move along, get out of my way*

Once you have ground the ingredients to a powder, go outside and put a pinch of the powder into the palm of your hand. Repeat the chant once more, then blow the powder out of your hand and into the air. Repeat this step daily until all the powder is gone. Circumstances should force your enemy to move on within six months.

Dark Mirror Banishing Spell

Items required: a dark obsidian mirror or crystal ball, paper and pen
Timing: on the dark moon

A dark mirror is usually made of obsidian crystal. It can be a flat circle or a crystal ball. Try to keep a dark mirror just for banishing spells – don't use the same mirror for scrying with; have two separate ones. Write out your tag-lock, place it underneath the dark mirror and say:

> Black as night, you are gone from my
>   sight
> Surrounded by darkness, you know no
>   light
> Black as night, be gone from my sight
> I banish you this darkest night

Leave the tag-lock in place until you are sure that your foe has moved on, then tear up the tag-lock and throw it away. Remember to cleanse the dark banishing mirror so that it is ready should you need it again. This spell works well in conjunction with the Move Along spell above.

A Simple Candle Banishing Ritual

Items required: a black candle and holder, a lighter, clove oil, garlic powder and dried agrimony leaves, an athame or carving tool, kitchen paper
Timing: during the waning moon

This is a basic candle-burning ritual that you can use to back up any of the other spells in this chapter. Take the black candle and carve it with your chosen tag-lock, then anoint it with clove oil. Next mix together a generous pinch of the banishing herb dried

agrimony and garlic powder, and sprinkle the mixture onto the kitchen paper. Roll the anointed candle through the herbs, pushing the candle away from you as you are working to banish something. Visualize your opponent accepting defeat and leaving you alone. Then set the candle in the holder, light the wick and allow it to burn all the way down. This can take several hours so be sure to pick a day when you have the time to watch over the candle.

Paper Poppet Banishing Spell

Items required: a sheet of black card, scissors, a silver pen, black cotton, a cauldron or heat-proof dish, a lighter
Timing: during the waning moon

As the moon wanes, go to a quiet place and think about the thing that you need to banish and why you want to banish it. Cut a humanoid shape from the black card and write a tag-lock on the paper doll with the silver pen. Name the doll for the behaviour you want to banish. Now fold the arms and legs in to the body of the doll, followed by the head, and bind in place using the black thread. Say these words:

Hear these words and heed my voice
I bind and banish you because you've
*   left me no choice*
Take your bane and leave me be
By these flames, so shall it be

Light the doll and allow it to burn in the cauldron. Once the ashes have cooled, scatter them outdoors to the four winds.

BLASTING TOOLS

Blasting tools are crafted to provide the strongest protection for the witch. Although they have been misrepresented in literature and film, the main objective of a blasting tool is to create a magical boundary to ward away threats. If that boundary is tested, say by an enemy directing malice towards the witch, the blasting tool would repel and return that malice with great force. Traditionally blasting tools would be fashioned from the wood of the blackthorn tree, but they can also be made from other thorny woods, such as hawthorn, bramble or rose. They are thought to have originated in Celtic culture.

blasting star, empower it to its purpose with the following incantation:

This dark star blasts you from my sight
Trouble me no more, offer me no slight
Blasted away, now get thee gone!
By this charm, so it is done.

Take the blasting star and bury it beneath a yew tree if possible, or wait until you are sure the spell has worked to banish your foe and then burn it.

Blasting Star to Banish a Saboteur

Items required: four blackthorn or hawthorn twigs, each 13cm (5 inches) long, a ball of red wool or string
Timing: during the waning moon

This ritual is good for dealing with those troublesome individuals who participate in harassment or sabotage and just won't leave you alone. To begin with, you will need to create a blasting star. Be sure to visualize your subject being banished as you work this charm. Take two of the blackthorn twigs and fashion them into an equal-armed cross, securing them with red yarn. Take the other two twigs and place these in an X shape, turning the cross into a star, and secure with red yarn. Once you have your

Seven-Day Spell to Invoke Karma on a Foe

Items required: a black candle and holder, a lighter
Timing: on the dark moon

Invoking karma really is a last-resort spell, because the karmic laws are indiscriminate, so if you are in any way to blame for your current situation, karma will deal you a blow too. Bear this in mind before you cast this spell. Take a black candle and carve your subject's name into the wax. Set the candle in the holder and light the wick. Focus on the flame and say:

In seven days all your malice returns
In six days your dream burns

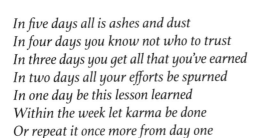

In five days all is ashes and dust
In four days you know not who to trust
In three days you get all that you've earned
In two days all your efforts be spurned
In one day be this lesson learned
Within the week let karma be done
Or repeat it once more from day one

Allow the candle to burn for 30 minutes, then blow it out. Re-light the candle and repeat the chant each night for the next six nights. On the final night, allow the candle to burn down completely.

Spell for Victory

Items required: a gold candle and holder, patchouli oil, dried rosemary, dried bay leaves, kitchen paper, an athame or carving tool
Timing: on the full moon

Coming under attack in any way is not a fun experience, but rather than giving in to a victim mentality, train your mind to think like a victor instead. Cast this spell to ensure that you defeat your enemies and emerge so victorious that they never make the mistake of picking a fight with you again! To begin with, spend a few minutes imagining what victory looks like to you. You need to build up a clear picture of this victory so that it will be clear when you have won the battle. Then take a gold candle and carve the word *Invictus*, meaning *unconquerable* in Latin, down the length of the wax, then carve your name on the other side. Anoint the candle in patchouli oil, then sprinkle some dried rosemary on the kitchen paper and roll the candle through the herbs, pulling it towards you, in order to draw victory to yourself. Place the candle in the holder and light it. Finally, lay a circle of bay leaves all around the candle, to symbolize the wreath of a winner. Now say:

Pick a fight and call me out
My enemies I will always flout
I face them down, every foe
For victory is all I know!

Let the candle burn down naturally.

CHAPTER TWENTY

· · · · · ◦ ◉ ◦ · · · · ·

CASTING EVERYDAY SPELLS

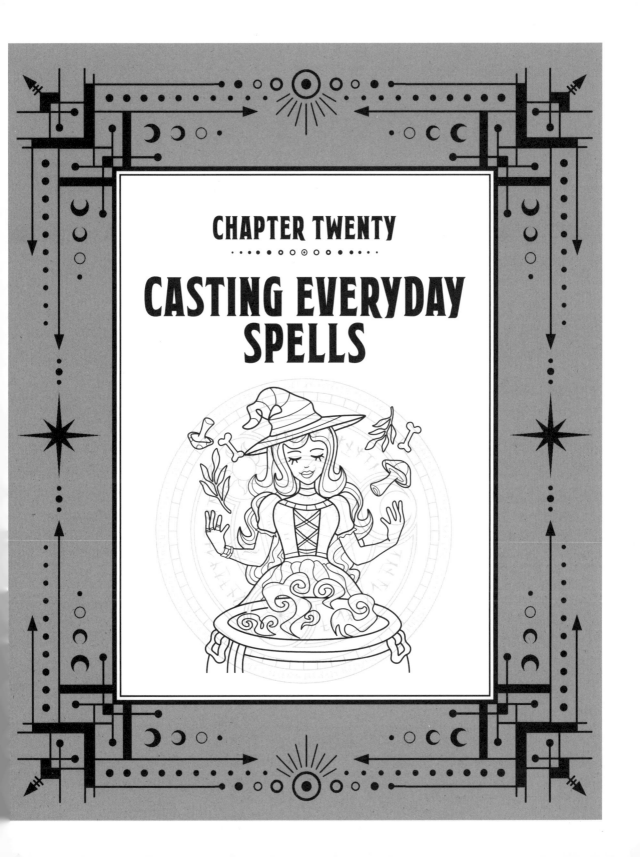

Life can be full of little niggles which can all add up to accumulated stress and mental health problems further down the line if you are not careful. As people dash from one place to the next, dropping children off, running errands, going to work and so on, there are a myriad of minor irritations that can put a blight on the day. Use the spells in this chapter to iron out life's little wrinkles and make everything run more smoothly.

Spell to Find a Parking Place

Items required: a small fairy statue, picture or keyring
Timing: on the waxing moon

To give yourself the best chance of always finding a parking place when you need one, call on the help of the elementals with this spell. First find a small fairy that you can keep in your car or hang on your car keys. Name this your parking fairy and enchant it with the following incantation:

Fairy of earth and elemental grace,
Locate for me a parking space
Make it safe and make it close
To wherever I choose to go
So mote it be

Whenever you are driving round, ask your parking fairy to guide you to the perfect parking place.

Spell to Locate Your Car

Items required: none – but memorize your registration number!
Timing: whenever you can't find your car in a car park

Losing your car in a busy car park can be a very distressing experience as you find yourself wondering if it has been stolen or if you simply can't find it! Getting worked up won't do any good, so if you have lost your car, stand still for a few moments and take three deep breaths.

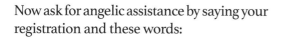

Now ask for angelic assistance by saying your registration and these words:

Angels, help me to locate my vehicle
*   quickly*
Fly above and find it for me
Then guide me there, so mote it be

Green Light Go!

Items required: none
Timing: whenever you need to

This simple chant can help to clear your path ahead and keep all lights at green as you drive. It is good if you need to get somewhere quickly when in the car, and it can be adapted to clear your life path of obstacles too. Simply adjust the visualization to suit your objective. Take a deep breath, imagine a good journey of clear roads and green lights, and say in your head or out loud:

Clear the way I need to go
Green lights all the way
Driving forward on quiet roads
Neither held up nor waylaid

Ritual for Forgiveness

Items required: paper and pen, honey, an
empty jar and lid
Timing: at the time of the new moon

On the night of the new moon, sit quietly and consider what it is that you wish to forgive or be forgiven for, and the person or people who are involved. Write the nature of the transgression on the paper and drop it into the jar, then add a little honey and say:

By Mother Nature's honey dew
As you forgive me, so I forgive you
By the gentle hum of honey bee
Please forgive me as I forgive thee

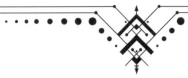

Put the lid on the jar and leave in place until the moon wanes, then wash it clean, washing away the transgression with the honey.

Truth Spell

Items required: a white candle, a bowl of sand, a charcoal block, dried juniper leaves, a lighter
Timing: on the full moon for strongest power

If you feel that you are being kept in the dark or suspect that someone is being deceitful, a truth spell can help to shed light on the situation. Bear in mind that truth spells work to enlighten the caster as to what is really going on. If you ask for the truth, then that is exactly what you will get and it won't be sugar-coated. As the full moon rises, light the charcoal block and place it in the bowl of sand, add a teaspoon of juniper leaves to the smouldering block and say:

> *Juniper cleanses all lies and deceit*
> *That the knowledge of truth I will soon*
>   *receive*
> *As the leaves burn on this altar, let the*
>   *smoke now clear*
> *That the truth be revealed from one who*
>   *is dear*

Next light the white candle and meditate on the flame for a while, then say:

> *I work with the light, I welcome it in*
> *It brings forth the truth, hidden within*
> *All secrets are told, as all lies unfold*
> *I am safe in the light, brought in from*
>   *the cold*
> *And by the turning of the Wheel*
> *By this rite let the truth be revealed*

Allow the candle and the herbs to burn out naturally and be prepared for the truth to come out. This spell usually works quite quickly, within a few days, and while there is no guarantee that you will like what you discover, you will be able to plot your next move with the full picture in mind.

A Fury Spell for Justice

Items required: a white candle, lavender oil, dried agrimony
Timing: on the new moon

This spell calls on the Furies of the Greek pantheon to bring justice to a perpetrator, or to win a court case. Carve the word *justice* and the date of the hearing into a white candle and anoint it with lavender oil, then roll the candle in the dried agrimony, rolling it towards you to bring out a favourable outcome. Light the candle and imagine that the court finds in your favour while you say:

Ladies of justice, beings of fury
Luck be with me from the jury
I summon justice for the one who
*   wronged me*
Let their fate be sealed by the Furies!

To further empower this spell, cast it in conjunction with the Victory Spell from the last chapter (see page 258).

Spell to Prick Someone's Conscience
Items required: *a grey candle, a pin, a lighter*
Timing: *on the full moon*

If you think that someone is acting without good conscience, you can use this spell to gently help them reassess their motives and actions. It can also bring about a confession of guilt if that is required, and would work well alongside both the Spell for Justice and the Truth Spell (see above for both), if that were the desired goal. Take a grey candle and press a pin into the wax about halfway down. Push it in far enough that it remains firmly in place, then visualize the person thinking better of their behaviour and changing their ways. Light the candle and say:

A flame to shine a light upon the ashes of
*   a wrong*
This pin that pricks a conscience helps
*   the guilty now confess*

No more to bear the burden, no secret to
*   suppress*

Allow the candle to burn all the way down. As it does, the pin will eventually drop from the wax, releasing the power of the spell. The guilty party should come forward with a confession within a moon phase.

Spell to Summon Lost Belongings
Items required: *a frankincense incense stick and holder*
Timing: *whenever you have misplaced something*

If you have lost something, use a quick incense ritual to help you to find it. Light the incense stick, place it in the holder and pull the smoke towards you as you say:

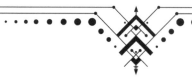

Smoke of air let my memory flare
Bring that which is lost back to me
As I recall where it is with clarity

Soon after the incense has burnt out you should remember where the lost item is or someone will find it for you.

Spell to Bend Time

Items required: *none*
Timing: *whenever you need to*

Bending time is the art of using time to your own advantage. If you are running late or you need to finish work early, you can use a time-bending chant to help time work in your favour. Of course we cannot actually change the flow of time, but chants like this one work to ensure that we are not penalized for being late! Simply repeat this chant in your head to bend time to your will, imagining time passing faster or slowing down, whichever suits you best.

Spirit of the hour, show me grace
Move with me through time and space
Speeding up or slowing down
Time works for me with no rebound

Silent Problem-Solving Spell

Items required: *a notepad and pen, an envelope, dried mugwort*
Timing: *in the evening*

If you have a problem that you need to solve, write it down in detail just before you go to sleep at night. Place the note in an envelope and add a pinch of mugwort for prophecy, then seal the envelope and sleep with it beneath your pillow. The mugwort will help to send prophetic dreams your way and you should dream of possible solutions within the week.

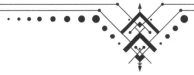

A Blessing to Accept Change

Items required: a large pillar candle, rose oil
Timing: on the first new moon following a change

Change can be difficult to accept, especially if it was brought about by circumstance rather than something you planned for. Moving into a new day-to-day reality can be unsettling and it takes time to adjust. Use this blessing spell to help make the change easier to transition into. Take a pillar candle and anoint it with rose oil, for self-love and compassion. Light the candle and say:

All things must turn and turn about
Change must be faced without self-doubt
The catalyst through which we grow
I accept each day and go with the flow

Let the candle burn for an hour and re-light it each day until you begin to accept and feel comfortable with the new circumstance.

A Spell for Wisdom

Items required: a tea-light and holder, a picture of an owl or of Athena
Timing: at the new moon

Wisdom is something that we acquire as we age, learning from mistakes as we go and building knowledge from experience. There may be times, however, where you feel that you need a little boost of extra wisdom and for that you should invoke the aid of the Goddess Athena, who was the goddess of wisdom in Greek mythology. Her sacred animal was the owl, so find a picture or statue that represents Athena or her totem owl and light a tea-light beside it, then say the invocation to bring her energies into your life.

Great goddess Athena, I invoke you!
Lend me your wisdom in all that I do
Inspire me with strategy, let my tactics
*   prevail*
Grant your wise counsel, that I will not
*   fail*
With mental agility and inner strength
Impart your wisdom onto my
*   wavelength*
So mote it be

Spell to Protect Your Computer and Tech Devices

Items required: amethyst, clear quartz and haematite crystals
Timing: on the new moon

To protect your computer and workspace from negative energy, place the following crystals on or near the PC or laptop: amethyst to soak up electromagnetic energy, clear quartz to keep communication flowing easily and haematite for protection of the device. Leave these crystals in place on your workspace and cleanse them with smoke or running water every dark moon, to keep them working efficiently.

A Spell for Courage

Items required: a charm that means something to you, pine oil
Timing: on the full moon

There will be times in life when your courage is tested. To stand your ground in the face of adversity, take a charm that holds significance to you and anoint it with pine oil for strength, then say:

When times are tough I will not flee
I stand my ground for all to see
My heart has courage, my spirit is true
I show great strength in all I do
When battle comes I hold my own
As each day my bravery is honed

Wear or carry the charm whenever you have a battle to face and need an extra boost of courage.

A Silver Moon Wishes Spell

Items required: three silver coins, a dried bay leaf, a lighter, a cauldron or heat-proof dish
Timing: on the full moon

Making wishes is one of the oldest and most traditional forms of magic as you are asking a boon from the universe. This spell uses the power of the full moon as a focus and should

Place the three silver coins in a triangle shape on the floor and set the cauldron in the middle. Say:

I offer this silver to the moon above,
In perfect love and perfect trust
With this spell I request a boon
That this wish be granted within three
    moons

Write a word that symbolizes your wish on the bay leaf, then light it and allow it to burn in the cauldron. Leave the silver in place as an offering and blow the ashes to the wind. Your wish should come true within three months.

be cast outdoors if possible. On the evening of the full moon, take all the items outside.

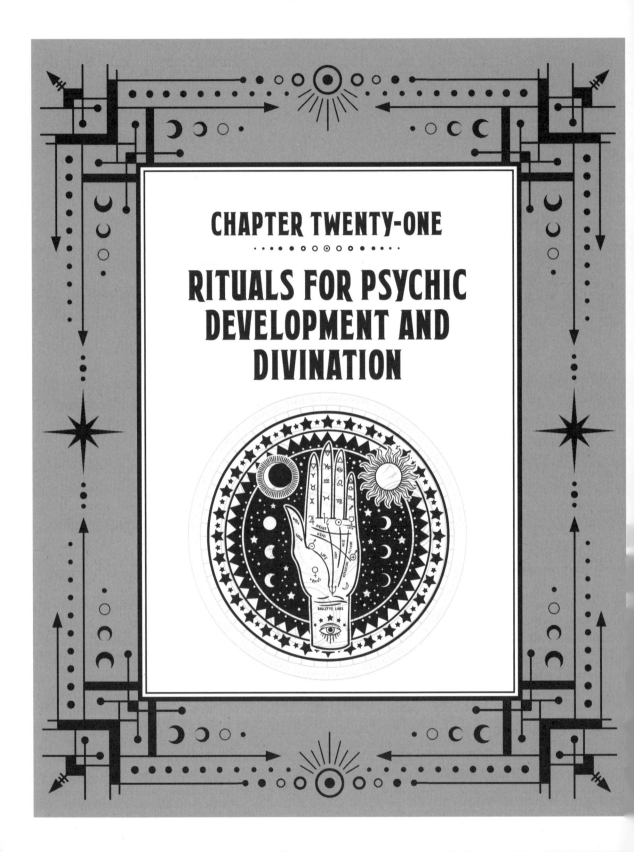

CHAPTER TWENTY-ONE

· · · · · · ○ ◎ ○ · · · · · ·

RITUALS FOR PSYCHIC DEVELOPMENT AND DIVINATION

Psychic powers and magic go hand in glove, and most magical practitioners also work hard to develop their psychic ability. Being psychic can sometimes feel a bit spooky, but there is nothing supernatural about it – it is simply your sixth sense or intuition at work. The more you trust it, the stronger and more reliable it will become; intuition is like a muscle in that it needs to be exercised and developed. Furthermore, psychic power is entirely individual, so you won't have the exact same ability as your sister or best friend. It is also not uncommon for people to have a combination of psychic abilities, and for additional abilities to manifest, the more you use these powers of intuition.

AM I PSYCHIC?

Everyone has intuition, which means that yes, everyone has some degree of psychic ability. In many people this is a latent power because they frequently dismiss whatever their intuition is telling them, meaning that the power never gets a chance to develop. In paying attention to your gut feelings, however, you are taking the first step towards developing your psychic powers and bringing this sixth sense to the fore.

Intuition is a natural aspect of the psyche and both humans and animals have it. It is a vital part of the survival instinct. Even soldiers are told to listen to their gut when out on patrol, to remain alert to possible threats of ambush and attack, to use their intuition as well as their training, because both those things working in parallel provide the best chance of survival. Developing these skills should in no way be viewed as dabbling in the supernatural – intuition is the most natural instinct in the world and without it we simply wouldn't survive as a species. So how do you begin to develop this skill? Here are some tips for using your intuition in daily life.

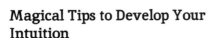

Magical Tips to Develop Your Intuition

- Listen to your instincts when meeting strangers; try to pick up on their vibe. Is it positive or negative?
- Before you set off for work each day, ask your intuition which way you should go. Pay attention to any niggling doubts and change your route accordingly.
- When out shopping, ask your intuition to guide you to the best bargains so you get a good deal – this might not be in a place where you usually shop.
- Go outside at night (pick a safe environment such as your garden or balcony) and see if you can pick up on the presence of another living creature – is it human or animal? Or something else?
- Go to a park or forest and try to connect with the spirits of the trees. What do they feel like and what are they telling you?
- When the phone rings, see if you know who is calling before you answer, without looking at the phone.

All these tricks will help you to hone your skills in ways that fit easily into a busy life, using day-to-day activities to boost your psychic powers.

TYPES OF PSYCHIC ABILITY

There are different kinds of psychic ability, and you will need to discover which one might be yours. Working with the ability that you are the most drawn to, and which you find the easiest, is the best way to begin honing your skills. Having a natural aptitude for precognition means that divination is likely to be easier for you to master, while someone with a clairvoyant ability will be more drawn to scrying. Here are some of the most common psychic abilities. See which one resonates with you the most and begin working with that.

Precognition

Precognition is the ability to see or to know things that are outside of your current awareness. This could mean that you automatically know that your child is having a bad day in school, even though you're not there. It could also be that you can predict things before they happen, or experience flashes of the past when visiting old buildings. Precognition is often called fortune-telling, but there is far more to it than that. While premonition, or the ability to see things before they happen, is a part of it, precognition encompasses the ability to see both forwards and backwards in time, as well as having an awareness of what is going on with your loved ones in the present moment, even if they are miles away. This ability can manifest in dreams, visions, emotions and instincts. It can appear as visual or emotional flashbacks or premonitions.

Mediumship

Mediumship is the act of communicating with the dead. This is something that lots of people shy away from and it should certainly be approached with caution, because when you open the door to the dead, you don't know what else will turn up. Even with protection magic in place, dealing with souls who have unfinished business, or who simply want someone to act as their messenger, can be very draining and upsetting to the medium. This skill manifests in dreams, visions, scents and unconsciously mirroring behaviours

that the deceased was known for, whether this be a turn of phrase, a way of moving, a slight tic or something else. Visitation dreams from deceased loved ones is the mildest form of mediumship and the one most often experienced, along with unexplained scents connected with the deceased.

Clairvoyance

Clairvoyance is also known as the Sight or Second Sight and people who have this skill are called clairvoyants or seers. It is related to the skill of precognition, but clairvoyants may also see spirits, ghosts, auras, elementals and so on. Clairvoyants may have the further skill of remote viewing, which is when they see something that is happening miles away, usually through

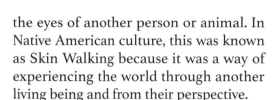

the eyes of another person or animal. In Native American culture, this was known as Skin Walking because it was a way of experiencing the world through another living being and from their perspective.

Clairaudience

Clairaudience is the ability to hear words, music and sounds that do not come from the local environment in any way. These sounds could be the voices of spirits wanting messages to be carried to their loved ones, or it could be music or sounds from the past – say, for example, the sound of the old shipyards on the now barren River Clyde in Scotland. This skill can take some practice to become adept at because all too often it is like playing a game of Chinese Whispers: the sounds and words become distorted as they travel between the source and the psychic. It is best used in conjunction with another skill to improve both accuracy and clarity.

Clairsentience

Clairsentience is the ability to sense things that are not fully present, for instance picking up on a ghostly presence or the residual energy from a past event. It is a very common skill and most people have this ability to some degree. When you walk into a strange house or building and you immediately pick up on the atmosphere, be it good or bad, then you are using your powers of clairsentience. It can also manifest as the power of psychometry, which is tuning in to the energy of an item and discovering things about the person it belongs to. People with clairsentience can frequently pick up on the residual energies left over from violence, war, abuse and suicide. It can be disconcerting and disorientating, but it cannot harm you. It simply works to highlight the energy field and atmosphere of a place or person.

Psychometry

Psychometry is the practice of picking up psychic impressions using touch. By holding a belonging or a photograph of the subject, it is possible to discern things about that subject. Psychometry can also be used in places, by touching sacred stones, ancient castle walls and so on. This is a skill that works well in conjunction with any of the abilities above, but is especially compatible with clairsentience. However, you should be careful where you try to use this skill. Avoid battle sites if possible, or buildings that housed a lot of pain and suffering, such as old prisons, hospitals and asylums, until you are used to feeling and grounding the dark energies that gather in such environments.

BECOMING PSYCHIC

Throughout this chapter you will find spells and rituals that will help you to hone your psychic powers, allowing you to work with each one of these skills. You can pick and choose the ones that work best for the ability which resonates with you the most. Having a basic understanding of what these skills are and how they are used is essential for you to develop them, because you need to know how they work before you can use them correctly. Remember to always cast a circle of protection before you begin to work with any of these psychic energies and before you cast any of the spells in this chapter. At the end of your psychic studies, be sure to use the grounding spell provided at the end of the chapter, so that you can shake off any

excess psychic energy. Honing any psychic skill takes time and practice, so be kind to yourself and remember that no one gets results every single time.

Spell to Open Up the Third Eye

Items required: one teaspoon of carrier oil such as almond or olive oil, two drops each of clary sage and ylang ylang essential oils, a shallow bowl or offering dish
Timing: best on a full moon

Use this spell to gently open up the third eye, which is the psychic eye located in the centre of the forehead. It is from here that visions and precognition will flow. On the night of the full moon, pour a teaspoon of almond or olive oil into a shallow offering bowl and mix in two drops of clary sage and two drops of ylang ylang essential oils, which are thought to increase psychic ability. Stir this mixture with the index finger of your receptive hand – i.e. the one you don't write with – to receive psychic experiences. Using the same finger, anoint the third eye on your forehead with the oil and say:

Open the eye and show me the way
Psychic visions come hither and stay
Let me see and let me know
All that the spirit realms wish to show

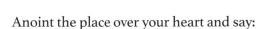

Anoint the place over your heart and say:

In perfect trust and perfect love
I receive psychic visions from above
I welcome them, they help me see
All the power that manifests in me

Use this spell just before you perform divinations or any of the spells in this chapter, then when you are finished, close the third eye again with these words:

I thank the spirits for the sight
I close my eyes without a blight

Wax Divination
Items required: *a pillar candle, a glass bowl, spring water*
Timing: *during the waxing moon*

Wax divination is the practice of interpreting the shapes made when melted wax is poured into cold water. It is one of the easiest forms of divination to practice, perfect for beginners. Fill the bowl with cold spring water, then light the candle and allow it to burn for a while, until the melted wax pools at the top. Carefully pick up the candle and pour the wax into the bowl. See what shapes the hot wax makes as it hits the cold water and try to interpret them, using your intuition. Here are some typical meanings to get you started:

- **Star** – a wish will come true.
- **Arrow** – you are being guided on your path.
- **Flower** – a time of growth and beauty will unfold.
- **Heart** – love and friendship will blossom.
- **Bird** – a time to nest.
- **Ship** – your ship has come in, bringing abundance.
- **Horse** – a journey is coming.
- **Leaf** – plant seeds of growth and set new goals.
- **Tree** – achievement, a goal is coming to fruition.
- **Cat** – nurture your independent spirit.

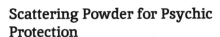

Scattering Powder for Psychic Protection

Items required: sea salt, blessing seeds, black Himalayan salt, a mortar and pestle, an empty jar and lid
Timing: on the new moon

Use this mixture to make your circle of protection extra strong. In the mortar mix one tablespoon each of sea salt, blessing seeds and black Himalayan salt. Grind them to a fine powder and keep in an air-tight jar. Once you have cast your circle in the usual way, sprinkle a little of this mixture round the perimeter to enhance the protection.

Vision Quest Ritual

Items required: dried mugwort, a bowl of sand, a charcoal block, a lighter, camomile tea
Timing: during a full moon

Vision quests are an aspect of many ancient cultures, including Native American and Aborigine. They are a way to request a psychic vision which can show you your true path or help you to make a decision. First make yourself a cup of camomile tea. This will help you to relax in mind, body and spirit. Next light the charcoal block and place it in the bowl of sand. Put one teaspoon of dried mugwort leaves on the block to burn.

Mugwort is a traditional witch's plant that is associated with prophecy and psychic visions. Pull the smoke towards you and up over your head, as you say:

A vision quest I would take
A spirit journey I would make
Guide my steps and lead the way
Show me dreams of future days

Sip the tea and meditate for as long as you can. Make note of any symbols, animals or people that pop up in your mind's eye, or any places that you are shown. Use your intuition to interpret these signs.

PSYCHIC CONNECTIONS

Some people claim that they have a psychic connection with close friends, lovers and family members. This connection can mean that they know what the other is thinking or doing at any given time. It can also happen that if one is in danger, the other automatically knows that something is wrong. Often these connections are formed accidentally over a period of time. Such a connection can be a great comfort if you are separated, say if someone is deployed or working away, because the psychic connection can offer a way to check in with each other, without distracting them from their work. Usually this will happen through dreams, when the

mind is controlled by the subconscious, but it can also be experienced while you are awake, depending on how strong the connection is.

It can be quite surprising when it happens, but if you suddenly find yourself thinking of a particular person, or dreaming about them repeatedly, it could be that there is a psychic connection linking your mind and emotions with theirs. Accidental links like this can be triggered when one of you is experiencing a stressful time and it can come as quite a shock, particularly if you find yourself psychically linked to an environment that you have never personally experienced – the theatre of war, for example.

There are also ways in which to develop a psychic link with someone from scratch, but you will need their permission to work with them in this way. The two spells below can

help you to facilitate a psychic connection with someone you know, but you will need to work as a pair, both giving consent and equal time to the practice.

Ritual to Create a Mind Connection
Items required: something that belongs to the person you wish to connect with, a white tea-light and holder
Timing: anytime

First find a partner to work with. This should be someone whom you know well and trust. They should be someone who wants to develop their own psychic abilities too. Decide on a time and day that suits you both, but work in separate locations. Also decide who will send the vision and who will attempt to receive it. At the appointed hour, go to a quiet place and sit comfortably. Light the tea-light and take hold of the item that belongs to your friend. This will serve as a physical link to them. Close your eyes and either concentrate on the vision you are sending or open your third eye to receive a vision from your friend. Choose something simple to send and receive. Here are some examples:

- A colour of the rainbow
- A number from 1 to 20
- An emoji
- A tree

- A flower
- An animal

Once you have spent an allocated amount of time sending and receiving this information, have a chat and see if your psychic connection was successful. Were you both seeing the same image in your mind? Take turns both sending and receiving information to build up a psychic link. Remember that these things can take time, but with practice it will get easier. You might also find that you connect at random over the following days, for example texting or calling each other at the same time. Take this as a sign that your connection is getting stronger, so keep working at it.

Dream-Walking Ritual

Items required: an item that belongs to the person you wish to connect with, lavender oil or pillow spray, a sachet of dried mugwort
Timing: anytime, but a full moon will enhance the ritual

This ritual is designed to create a connection between one person who is sleeping and one who is awake, therefore it works best between people who are in different time zones, or who work opposite shift patterns. The spell is conducted from the sleeper's perspective. It is based on the Native American practice of dream-walking, or skin-walking, which

is the psychic equivalent of walking a mile in someone else's shoes. It could best be described as your spirit taking a piggyback on another living person, which is why it is essential to have their consent.

With this ritual, you will experience all that your loved one is experiencing; although you will be asleep, your senses will be fully alert and you will see, hear, smell and taste all that your partner does. You will also experience the same feelings, both physically and emotionally. Unless you are an experienced practitioner, do not attempt to connect with someone in this way if they are in a negative environment, such as a war zone or a prison. Dream-walking can be unsettling for both parties, so be sure that you are both in agreement before you proceed. Also be aware that once such a connection is forged, dream-walking can occur accidentally as well, so be prepared for this too and make your partner aware of it.

To begin with, fill a small pouch with dried mugwort to aid in psychic dreams and place this beneath your pillow, then spray the pillow with generous amounts of lavender spray. This will help to ensure that you sleep well enough and long enough for the connection to be experienced. Place the item that belongs to your partner under the pillow or beside your bed. Then say this incantation to activate the connection:

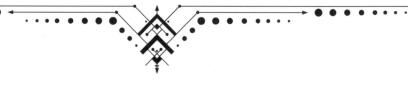

In my dreams I see you, I know exactly
* where you are*
I see all that you do, be you near or far
I taste all that you taste, hear all that
* you hear*
I dream-walk towards you, just to be near
I feel all that you feel and when it's time
* to wake*
I know you felt my spirit too, through
* this connection that we make*

Get into bed and go to sleep as usual. Make a note of your dreams as soon as you wake so that you can discuss and clarify with your partner whether the dream-walking connection was successful or not. Again, take turns with this and give it time. This is deep magic that you are working with, and you need to be patient with yourself and keep practising.

To Summon an Ancestor

Items required: a photograph of the person you wish to connect with, a white candle and holder, a sandalwood incense stick and holder
Timing: on the full moon

Sandalwood is also known as ancestor incense because it is said that burning it can help to facilitate a connection with those who have lived before us. This could be your immediate relatives who are now deceased, such as parents and grandparents, or the ancient ancestors of your bloodline. Why would you need to summon an ancestor? There are lots of reasons why you might choose to connect with a spirit in this way – for protection, guidance, strength or courage being just a few. It is also polite to let ancestors know of big life events such as pregnancy, the birth of a baby, marriage and so on. This ritual will help to forge a psychic connection between you and your ancestors. Light the candle, put it in the holder and place this beside the photograph of the ancestor you want to connect with. If you want to connect with your ancient ancestors, use something that represents them instead of a photo. Light the sandalwood incense and wave the smoke all around the representation as you say:

Ancestors I call you, come into my
* space*
Let me feel your energies, surround me
* with your grace*
When lost show me the way, when
* saddened lift me high*
When joy fills my heart, though far
* apart, I know you help me fly*
By blood of my blood and bone of my
* bone*
Ancestors I call you, I welcome you
* home*

Place the incense in the holder and perform any divinations or meditations you want to, asking your ancestors for their guidance, then give them thanks and release them by saying:

Ancestors I thank you for coming here this day
I release you with gratitude, love will light your way

Spell to Invoke a Spirit Guide

Items required: a sage smudge stick, a bell, a white candle and holder
Timing: on the waxing moon

Spirit guides are spiritual helpers who can assist you on your quest for enlightenment. They can be people, elementals, angels or animal totems. You can work with many spirit guides if you want to, but most practitioners work with just one or two. Often they make their presence felt through dreams, or through hints that a certain culture could be of interest to you, leading you to find books, music and documentaries about that culture. We all have spirit guides, but just like angels, they cannot intervene in your life without your permission, so use this simple invocation if you would like to get to know your spirit guide better. First smudge your working area with the sage to cleanse away any negative energy and purify the space. Light the candle and place it in the holder, then ring the bell three times. Now invoke your spirit guide in the following way:

Guiding spirits hear my cry
Send to me my spirit guide
Let me see and let me know
All the wisdom they can show
Guide my steps throughout each day
And teach me to live in a spiritual way
Blessed be

Ring the bell once more and perform any kind of magic or divination practice that you choose. When you are done, release the spirit guide with these words and another three rings of the bell to finish:

Blessed Spirit I offer you thanks for being with me
Go if you will, stay if you choose
In love and trust
So mote it be

THE ART OF SCRYING

Scrying is the practice of gazing into a reflective surface to see psychic images and visions. Those who are just beginning to learn this skill are more likely to see these visions in their mind's eye, rather than in the scrying vehicle. Given time and with practice, you may start to see images in the scrying vessel itself. The first hint that this is going to manifest is when the scrying vessel seems to fill with cloud or smoke. Wait for the smoke to clear and the vision will then be revealed. This takes practice because the appearance of the smoke can be such a shock that the seer breaks their concentration and has to begin again, but once mastered it is a very useful psychic tool. You can scry using mirrors, crystal balls, dark mirrors and crystals, or a simple bowl of water from the kitchen.

Find a vessel that appeals to you and create a routine whereby you spend time scrying at the same time each day. This will help to train your subconscious mind to open itself to psychic visions. Use the following spell to help in your practice; it is based around a bowl of water, but you can use it for crystal and mirror scrying too.

Scrying Ritual
Items required: a cauldron or bowl of water, a candle and holder
Timing: at any time, but dark or full moons work well

Fill the cauldron with water, then light the candle and place it close by, ensuring that the candle flame is not reflected in the water. You need a clear surface with which to scry, so turn off the lights and work by candlelight only. Sit comfortably and say the following scrying chant before you begin:

Light of wisdom in cauldron dark
Bless me with enlightened spark
Show the turning of the wheel
In visions which are now revealed

Gaze into the vessel and allow your eyes to softly focus. Blink when you need to, don't stare and – although it sounds counter-intuitive – don't try too hard! The best visions come when you are in a relaxed and dreamy state of mind, so just gaze at the water and see what comes up. Make this a nightly practice if possible to make progress quickly and achieve the best results.

PENDULUMS AND BEYOND

Pendulum work is one of the easiest forms of divination, though it has its limitations. It's a great way to become more in tune with your natural psychic ability and you can use it to gain insight and answers to closed questions – that is a form of questioning which elicits a yes or no response. You can ask the questions out loud or in your head.

Silent Pendulum Ritual

Items required: a pendulum of your choice, or a ring suspended on ribbon or chain
Timing: whenever you choose

Hold your pendulum lightly in your dominant hand, the hand you write with. Pendulums work in different ways for different people, so you will need to determine how the pendulum responds to you, by asking it a question to which you know the answer is yes and seeing which way it swings – this swing is your pendulum saying *Yes*. Next ask it a question to which you know the answer is no, and notice how it changes direction. This new way of swinging is your pendulum saying *No*. When the pendulum seems to swing in circles, that generally means the answer to your question is unclear and you should ask again later. You can also use a pendulum board, which has a vertical line drawn on it for *Yes* and a horizontal line drawn on it for *No*. You can easily make one of these yourself at home, or they can be purchased online, and while they are not essential, they can make pendulum scrying easier for beginners. Use your pendulum for enlightenment and general questions. Have fun with it!

A Silver Coin for Insight

Items required: a silver coin
Timing: whenever you need to

If you don't have a pendulum handy then you can use a silver coin to the same effect. Hold the coin in your hand, close your eyes and ask your question, then flip the coin in the air and see how it lands. Heads would indicate that the answer to your question is yes, while tails means no. A spinning coin indicates that the situation is still unfolding and the final response could change with time.

Blessing to See the Future

Items required: a mugwort incense stick and holder
Timing: on a full moon

About an hour before you go to bed, burn a little mugwort incense in your bedroom. Allow the scent to permeate the room, then as you climb into bed say the following incantation to bring about prophetic dreams of the future.

> *In my dreams I wish to see*
> *A vision of a future me*
> *Take me forth within my sleep*
> *And when I wake the vision I'll keep*

Have a notebook and pen next to the bed so that you can write down your dreams as soon as you wake and interpret the signs and symbols as an indication of where your future lies.

TASSEOMANCY

Tasseomancy is the art of reading tea leaves to see signs and symbols of what the future might hold for the tea drinker. Sadly, it is less common now than it was in the past, largely because the invention of the teabag means that fewer people use the loose leaf tea that tasseomancy requires. Although it is a skill associated with tea, it can also be performed using coffee grounds or wine sediment in the bottom of the glass. Tea is generally the preferred medium though. You can purchase special tasseomancy cups and saucers that have symbols and their meanings on them, but they are not essential and an ordinary teacup and saucer will suffice.

First make a pot of tea using a loose-leaf blend of tea leaves. Allow the infusion to steep then pour out a cup of tea for yourself, or whoever you are reading for, without using a tea strainer. Do not add sugar or milk as this can affect the reading. Sip the tea as you ponder a question or dilemma. Once you have drunk nearly all the tea, leaving about a teaspoon of liquid in the bottom of the cup, swirl the cup three times to distribute the leaves. Place the saucer on top of the cup then quickly turn the whole thing upside down. Turn the cup right way up and hold it with your dominant hand. Now read the tea leaves that are in the cup, looking for symbols and shapes. Symbols on the nearest side of the cup refer to the next six months, while those on the far side refer to the next twelve months. Use your intuition and these interpretations as a guide. Tasseomancy is a lovely thing to do with like-minded and magical friends during an enchanted tea party.

- **Anchor** – security, a safe harbour calls you home.
- **Heart** – love, success in relationships.
- **Broken heart** – a break-up is on the cards.
- **Arrow** – direction, motivation, achievement.
- **Broken arrow** – lack of direction and motivation, sabotage of your goals.
- **Bird sitting** – feather your nest.
- **Bird flying** – spread your wings.
- **Cross** – spiritual guidance and protection.

- **Dagger or sword** – conflict and back-stabbers.
- **Flower** – growth, beauty, grace.
- **Money sign** – wealth and prosperity.
- **Plane** – travel, holidays, working away.
- **Church** – a spiritual awakening.

SCRIBE WITCH RITUALS

A scribe witch is one who uses the power of the written word as her main tool. This could be writing petition spells, secret codes or, as in the case of the rituals here, automatic writing and the power of runes. Scribe witchery is a form of practice that appeals to those who love words – writing them, reading them, learning new alphabets and languages. Here we look at two ways to use scribe witchery for the purposes of psychic development.

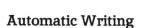

Automatic Writing

Automatic writing is often linked to the skill of the medium and, while it can be used to communicate with spirits, it is also an effective way to communicate with your higher self as well as your own personal spirit guides. What is more, it uses very few tools. All you need is a pen and notepaper. You can light candles and incense if you want to, but it is not essential. Lay the notepad before you and close your eyes. Think about who and what you want to commune with. Are you connecting with your higher self, a deceased relative, a spirit guide? Next pick up the pen and hold it lightly with the tip against the page. Do not try to direct the pen, just let it move as it will. It may begin to move quite slowly at first, before picking up speed. Just let the pen do what it wants. Continue for as long as you want then put the pen down. Read what you have written – or what you have channelled from a higher power. The page might be covered in words or pictures, just see what you have and what it means to you. Repeat as and when you want to.

RUNE STONES

There are lots of different runic style alphabets from different cultures. The Celtic Ogham is one kind and the Norse runes are another. Both are used as divination tools and in spell-craft. Here you are going to make a set of Norse Rune Stones, also known as the Elder Futhark.

How to Make and Use Rune Stones

Items required: 25 pebbles, a marker pen, clear varnish, salt, spring water, an offering bowl, a pouch to hold the stones
Timing: make on the full moon, use whenever you want guidance

Gather 25 pebbles and bring them to your altar. Pour spring water into the offering bowl and add a little salt. Use this mixture to cleanse each of the stones, then set them out to dry. Once dry, draw one of the runes listed below on each stone. One stone should be left completely blank. Varnish all the stones to protect them and let the varnish dry. Put them in the pouch and bless them by holding the pouch and saying:

Spirits of air, of forest and sky
Bless these stones of the third eye

To use the stones, gently shake the bag as you ponder on your question or dilemma, asking for guidance, then draw out three stones and lay them in a row. Read them from left to right as representing Past, Present and Future, using your intuition. The interpretations below will help you with this and give you a starting point to work from.

Wryd – the blank rune, the unknown, darkness, death, an ending of something.

Fehu – abundance, peace and plenty, a sign of joy and happiness to come.

Raidho – travel, an important journey which could be physical or spiritual, a needed change of scene.

Hagalaz – things will come to a head, completion of something, harmony.

Eihwaz – great strength and resilience, trust, dependability, reliable friends.

Tiwaz – leadership, direction, drive, motivation, authority.

Laguz – healing powers, renewal, rebirth, regeneration, resurgence, psychic ability.

Uruz – freedom, independence, free spirit, energy, motivation, emancipation, courage, direct action.

Kenaz – vision, creativity, inspired action, applied knowledge.

Nauthiz – endurance, survival, bravery, fortitude, stamina, loyalty, commitment.

Perthro – initiation, destiny, precognition, premonition, future building.

Berkano – fresh starts, new beginnings, regeneration, shedding an old skin.

Ingwaz – common sense, family bonds, virtue, morality, standards, compassion, home life, sustenance.

Thurlsaz – great change is coming, be prepared, protect your nest ready to weather the storm.

Gebo – gifts, accolades, achievements, honours, promotions, graduations.

Isa – a challenging time to be endured, inner strength, mental clarity.

Algiz – defence, warrior spirit energy, shielding, protection, guardian spirits watch over you.

Ehwaz – a flurry of movement, forward action, teamwork, loyalty, positive change.

Dagaz – self-direction, a change of heart or career, forge your own path.

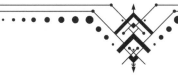

Ansuz – communication, public speaking, non-verbal communication, signalling, enthusiasm, manipulation, word play.

Wunjo – the happy rune, joy, excitement, exuberance, pleasure, comfort, fellowship, friendship, good times ahead.

Jera – efforts paying off, things coming to fruition, abundance, harvest, goals achieved, success.

Sowilo – step into your power, use it for positive change, know your worth, value yourself.

Mannaz – intelligence, information, skills, adaptability, critical analysis, growth.

Othala – security, stability, increased wealth and comfort, safety, a safe harbour.

GROUNDING PSYCHIC ENERGY

When you have completed your psychic studies for the day you will need to ground your energy. This ensures that no excess energy is attached to you, which could upset the balance of your own energy. Grounding is a simple visualization technique.

Visualization to Ground Psychic Energy

Items required: none
Timing: use after your psychic spell workings and practices

Sit on the floor and picture the psychic energy that you have raised with your practice. Imagine this energy being sucked into the ground and away from you. At the same time, imagine that white light comes down from above your head and fills you with cleansing energy. To complete the grounding process, you should eat and drink something to reconnect with your physical, earthly body.

CHAPTER TWENTY-TWO

· · · · · ◦ ⊙ ◦ · · · · ·

BLESSINGS FOR MAGICAL LIVING

Life is a series of ups and downs, but a magical life is always one of gratitude, where each and every little win is celebrated, where change is welcomed or at least accepted, and where the losses are honoured, even the little ones. Achievements and losses that go unacknowledged can often be a source of low mood or resentment towards other people. As a witch, you can take charge of this acknowledgment yourself, by casting blessings for all of life's milestones, from birthdays to secret anniversaries of the heart that no one else knows about. You can also use blessings to determine the perfect holiday destination, to honour the seasons and to bless a lost loved one. In this final chapter, you will find simple candle blessings for all of the above and more besides!

HOW TO LIVE MAGICALLY

Learning to live magically can take some adjustment. If magic is a new concept to you then even after reading this book, it still may not be your first response. If you are stressed, you may feel so stuck that the concept of magic as a possible solution evades you completely and it is only when your mind is calmer that you ask yourself *why* you didn't think to cast a spell at the time to smooth things out and move things along? It can take some time before magic comes naturally,

even longer before you know exactly what kind of magic needs to be cast for whatever situation you find yourself in, so don't worry if it takes you a while to get into the habit of daily blessings, or casting for crisis control and damage limitation.

A magical life is one that you will create over time and there is no rush to perfect it all at once. After all, magic isn't going anywhere! It has been around for centuries and it will always be there when you need it most. Don't worry if the teachings of this book and others like it don't resonate with you right away. It's okay to feel your way into a magical life slowly and cautiously, so if things don't click for you immediately, it doesn't mean that you are doing it wrong. Just go at your own pace, working the kind of spells that you feel comfortable with. If you don't like the idea of banishing spells, don't do them. If candle magic doesn't suit you, work with crystals instead, or herbs, or petitions. Use whatever magic appeals to you the most and work up from there. You have the rest of your life to perfect your magical art.

It could also be the case that you feel so at home with spells that you are casting them for everything, even when a mundane response is more appropriate. While it's great that you are in tune with your power, magic is not an excuse for laziness. Remember what we said right at the beginning of the book – magic takes work and if you misuse it, it will come back to rap you on the knuckles! If this sounds familiar, learn to moderate your magical output. Don't over-cast or you will end up burnt out and exhausted.

Magical living, like most things, is all about balance. Not too much, not too little, but just enough to make your days run smoothly, your problems fade quickly and your dreams come true, because there are few things in life that magic can't help you with. Sometimes all it takes is a simple blessing, while at other times you will need to work a more complex ritual and a whole series of spells to affect the outcome that you want. Just remember that a spell a day goes a very long way!

Birthday Blessing

Items required: a birthday candle, a cupcake, an old spoon or sealing wax ladle, a lighter, greaseproof paper, glitter in your chosen colour

On your birthday, place a birthday candle in a cupcake and light it. Make a wish for the coming year as you blow out the candle. Remove the candle from the cake and put it on the spoon, then use the lighter beneath the spoon to melt the birthday candle. Remove the wick as the wax melts, then pour it onto the greaseproof paper, repeating your birthday wish. Add a sprinkle of glitter and repeat your wish for the third and final time. Allow the wax talisman to set as you eat your cupcake. Finally remove the paper

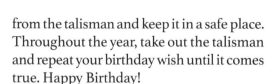

from the talisman and keep it in a safe place. Throughout the year, take out the talisman and repeat your birthday wish until it comes true. Happy Birthday!

Graduation Blessing

Items required: a gold or silver candle and holder, bergamot essential oil
Timing: one week before graduation

Graduations can be exciting yet also nerve-wracking occasions. Your mind may be imagining all the things that could go wrong, such as tripping over your gown, falling over on stage or knocking off your mortar board! Use this blessing to put a little magic on your side and ensure that everything runs smoothly. Exactly one week before your graduation, anoint a gold or silver candle with bergamot oil, both of which symbolize success. Light the wick and say:

> *A life of study has got me here*
> *Sacrifices I have made*
> *Now I come to graduate*
> *All nerves away will fade*
> *As I go forth to accept my scroll*
> *All things will smoothly run*
> *I will emerge a graduate*
> *My success has just begun!*

Allow the candle to burn itself out.

This blessing can also be used for work promotions, weddings and so on – simply rewrite the incantation with your own achievement as the focus.

Blessing for the Perfect Holiday Destination

Items required: a yellow candle, a pinch of blessing seeds
Timing: best on the new moon

Fancy a holiday but not sure where to go? Let magic help you to decide, with this blessing for spiritual travel guidance! Light the yellow candle, close your eyes and visualize the style of holiday you want – is it an adventurous ski trip or a relaxing beach holiday? See yourself enjoying the kind of holiday that feels wonderful to you, then say:

> *A perfect holiday I summon now*
> *One that gives me all the wow*
> *Take me on a magical vacation*
> *And lead me to the right location*

Leave the candle burning, while you take a pinch of blessing seeds outside or to an open window and complete the spell by blowing the seeds to the wind and saying:

> *East, south, west, north*
> *Show me the way and guide me forth*

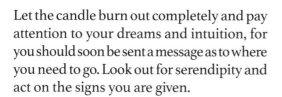

Let the candle burn out completely and pay attention to your dreams and intuition, for you should soon be sent a message as to where you need to go. Look out for serendipity and act on the signs you are given.

Blessing to Follow Your Nose

Items required: none, just your nose!
Timing: use whenever you want to explore

This spell works well anywhere, but it is especially fun to use when you are on holiday or in a place that you are not too familiar with. Stand for a moment and close your eyes, then say in your head or out loud:

> *Guardians and guides, lead me to a magical place in this area, one which will bring me joy and happiness and which will enhance my stay here in this place. I trust your guidance and will follow where you lead, knowing that you keep me safe. Blessed Be. Now, which way should I go?*

Remain standing for a while until you feel a tug or a pull in a certain direction, then head that way. Whenever you are not sure where to go, simply ask again *Which way?* and follow your gut. If your nose is tingling that is also generally a sign that you are on the right track. This blessing could take you

to a museum, a nice restaurant or a witchy New Age shop on a tiny back street, but in any case it usually carries you to a place that you wouldn't have found otherwise and which is perfect for you, so enjoy your magical explorations and see where you end up.

To Bless and Ward a Mirror

Items required: tea tree oil, a black marker pen
Timing: on the full moon for best effect

Mirrors can act as portals, meaning that negative energy can become trapped within them and seep back into your environment. Some people also believe that mirrors can be used by spirits to gain access to your home. While you might never have experienced

this yourself, it's always better to be safe than sorry, so it makes sense to bless the mirrors in your house. You spend time in front of a mirror every day when you are getting ready, and you don't want any trapped energy to darken your mood or blight your day through your reflection. This simple blessing spell will keep all the mirrors in your home positive and clear of dark energy. If possible, draw a pentagram on the back of the mirror to ward it and keep the portal closed. Alternatively, you can draw a pentagram in the air in front of the mirror too. Then dab a little tea tree oil, which is good for protection and cleansing magic, onto each compass point of the mirror – north, east, south and west – and allow it to dry as you say:

This magic mirror reflects only good
    cheer
No evil may use it to enter here

Repeat this blessing every month, more frequently if you have been going through a tough time or someone in your household has experienced a trauma of some kind. In this case you might want to bless the mirrors daily, especially the ones most frequently used, such as the bathroom mirror.

Blessing for the Recently Deceased

Items required: a white candle, black lace or veiling
Timing: soon after the death

Because they are viewed as portals to the spirit world, in many cultures mirrors are covered after a death. This is the case in Celtic, Jewish and Indian traditions. The reason for this was so that the spirit of the deceased did not become trapped in the mirror and also so that dark spirits would not be drawn through the mirror by the sorrow of a house in mourning. Many people still continue this tradition. It is a way of blessing and protecting the spirit of the person who has passed away. First light a candle and say:

We light this flame to guide the way
For _____ (name) who could not stay
Feel our blessings beloved spirit
As we bless this house and all within it

Leave the candle in the centre, or hub, of the house and go around covering all the mirrors with black lace. Keep the mirrors covered until after the funeral has taken place, when the deceased will have crossed over. Let the candle burn down naturally.

Blessing for a Material Loss or a Lost Love

Items required: a black candle
Timing: on a waning moon

People suffer losses every day, from big losses such as a bereavement, a relationship or a job to smaller losses like a lost purse or a lost opportunity. Whether large or small, any loss can have an impact on you, so cast this spell to bless yourself as you come to terms with it. Light a black candle and, as you focus on the flame, say:

(Name that which is lost)
This loss is mine, I feel the pain
I acknowledge the void left in its wake
I sit with the hum of grief's refrain
For a new beginning I must make

Blessing for a Secret Anniversary of the Heart

Items required: a tea-light and holder, paper and a pen, a cauldron or heat-proof dish
Timing: on the anniversary itself

What is a secret anniversary of the heart? It is a sadness which comes from a secret you keep deep in your heart. This could be an abortion, a miscarriage, an assault, a break-up etc. It could also be a nostalgia for a happier time that is long past, say a holiday romance or a fling, or perhaps it's a reminder of a lost love as their birthday draws near. Whatever it is, use this blessing to acknowledge the emotions it brings up for you. On the date it happened, light a tea-light and write down what your secret sadness is, then roll up the paper, light it in the candle flame and let it burn in the cauldron, saying *I remember, I remember you.*

Blessing for a Pregnancy

Items required: tea-lights and holder
Timing: daily throughout pregnancy

A pregnancy can be a very exciting time for soon-to-be parents. It can also be fraught with worry and anxiety, especially in the first weeks and months. To alleviate some of this worry, cast this blessing spell each

day to bless the pregnancy through to full term. Light a tea-light and say:

Blessed be the seed that is sown
Blessed be the babe that grows
Blessed be the womb that protects
Blessed be the love we project
Blessed be the mother and child
Blessed be the symptoms mild
Blessed be this babe so dear
Until and beyond, the day we welcome
   you here!

Blessing for an Elder
Items required: *a tea-light and holder*
Timing: *from new to full moon*

Watching a loved one growing old and frail can be very upsetting, especially as the roles begin to reverse and someone who once took

care of you now needs taking care of. This blessing is for the elders of your family, to give them a boost of magic and to give you time to come to terms with their mortality. It honours the aging process as a natural part of life. Light the tea-light and say:

Blessed be the bones now frail
Blessed be the ears that fail
Blessed be the eyes growing dim
Blessed be the strength within
Blessed be one worn with care
Blessed be the wisdom they share
Blessed be our Elders true
Blessed be, for I love you

Blessing to Welcome Spring
Items required: *a yellow candle, spring flowers*
Timing: *on the spring equinox*

To welcome spring, place a yellow candle on your altar and surround it with a circle of spring flowers, which you can leave in place as your seasonal altar decoration. Light the candle and say:

I welcome spring's blessings of lighter
   days
Of watery sunlight and gentle rays
Gifts of renewal and rebirth are near
I ask that these blessings now settle here

Blessing to Welcome Summer

Items required: a gold candle, summer blooms
Timing: on the summer solstice

To welcome summer, place a gold candle on your altar and surround it with summer flowers, which you can leave in place as your seasonal altar decoration. Light the candle and say:

*I welcome summer's blessings of hot
    golden rays
Of sun, sea and sand and holidays
Gifts of growth and achievement are
    near
I ask that these blessings now settle here*

Blessing to Welcome Autumn

Items required: an orange or brown candle, autumn leaves
Timing: on the autumnal equinox

To welcome autumn, place an orange or brown candle on your altar and surround it with a circle of autumn leaves, which you can leave in place as your seasonal altar decoration. Light it as you say:

*I welcome autumn's blessings of harvest
    days
Of rain and fog and misty haze
Gifts of abundance and richness are
    near
I ask that these blessings now settle here*

Blessing to Welcome Winter

Items required: a green candle, evergreens
Timing: on the winter solstice

To welcome winter, place a green candle on your altar and surround it with a circle of evergreen boughs, which you can leave in place as your seasonal altar decoration. Light it as you say:

*I welcome winter's blessings of darker
    days
Of cold frosty mornings and snowflake
    haze*

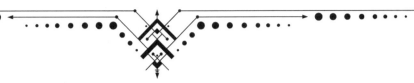

Gifts of deep slumber and festive cheer
I ask that these blessings now settle here

Blessing for Hogmanay

Items required: seven birthday candles and holders, some kind of festive cake, salt, a silver coin, bread, a tray, a symbol of something you want the next year to bring to you
Timing: just before midnight on New Year's Eve

New Year's Eve, or Hogmanay, has always been steeped in magic and superstition. It is said that the first person to enter a house in the New Year should be a dark-haired man, which ensures that good fortune will follow in his footsteps, especially if he comes bearing gifts. This became the tradition of *first footing* in Scotland, which is when symbolic 'gifts' are left on the doorstep, to be carried across the threshold by a friendly neighbour after the midnight chimes have struck. It was also said that burning seven candles in the house on this night would bring good luck for the next year, but they must be burning from one year to the next and they must not be blown out.

This blessing draws on both those traditions. To begin with, place the bread, salt and money on a tray. Add the symbol of what you're hoping the new year will bring – this could be a heart for love, a business card for promotion, lavender for health etc. At about 11pm, put the tray outside the main door to your home and leave it there. Go back inside. Then at 11.50pm, light the seven birthday candles in their holders, push them into the cake and say:

> *A blessing on this house this night,*
> *As the clock strikes twelve and all comes*
> *   right*
> *Farewell to the old year, hail to the new*
> *A year of good fortune and dreams*
> *   coming true!*

Let the candles burn down until they go out naturally, then cut the cake and enjoy it as a midnight snack. Leave the tray on the doorstep until the next day, then bring it indoors to pull in all the blessings, or if you want to be really traditional, have a dark-haired man carry it in for you. Happy New Year!

Blessing for General Gratitude

Items required: a tea-light and holder
Timing: whenever you feel grateful for something

If there is something that you want to bless and give thanks for, but it hasn't been mentioned in this chapter, then use this general blessing for gratitude. Light the tea-light, think of what you are grateful for and say:

Thank you, thank you, thank you for
_____name it)
Thank you, thank you, thank you for
sending it to me!

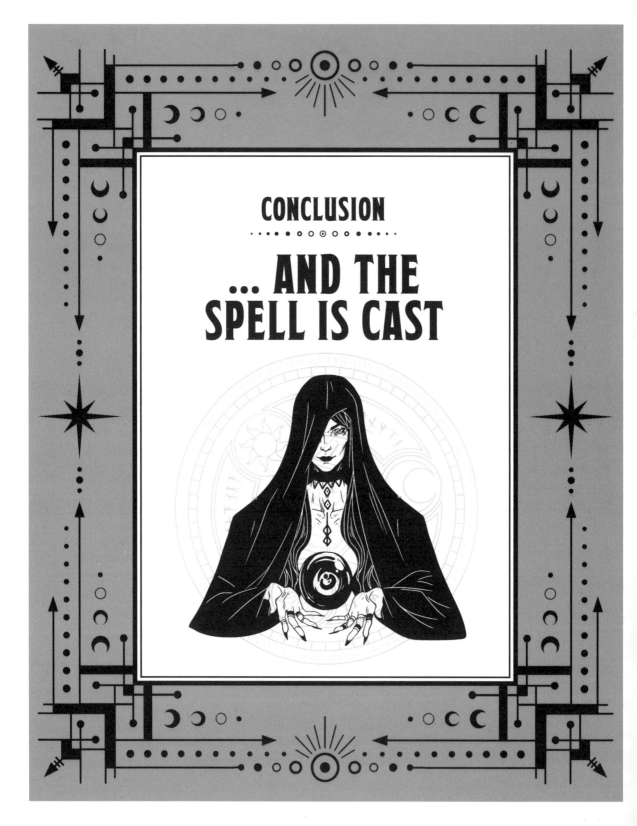

CONCLUSION

... AND THE SPELL IS CAST

I hope that you have enjoyed reading this Book of Shadows and Spells and that you have begun to practise some of the practical magic within its pages. Magic is a natural aspect of life for lots of people and I trust that you will come to reach for this grimoire time and time again, whenever you need to. My aim has been to show you how simple and accessible magic really is, for those who are brave enough to try it.

You now have at your fingertips all the information you need to live a charmed life, and while some of these spells might appear simple, I encourage you to try them nonetheless, bearing in mind that simplicity is a power in and of itself. This book is designed to be a one-stop shop for all things magical. It is also a jumping-off point, something you can be inspired by when it comes to devising your own spells, rituals and blessings.

Of the 250-plus enchantments in this book, I hope that you have found something that has proved useful to you and which has made you feel stronger and more powerful than before, whether that is a piece of psychological information you needed to read or a particular spell you needed to cast. Many of the charms and enchantments here are ones that I have used repeatedly in my own life, while some I have devised specifically for this collection. Keep this Book of Shadows close to your heart and it will serve you well. Be bold in your magic and when life grows dark, reach for these shadows; when you need more light, call on these shadows and when all is well, celebrate with these blessed shadows. Farewell my magical reader, until our paths cross again for our next merry meeting. Live magically!

Serene blessings,
Marie Bruce x

INDEX

FURTHER READING

Buckland, Raymond, *Buckland's Complete Book of Witchcraft* (Llewellyn, 1997)

Cunningham, Scott, *Wicca; A Guide for the Solitary Practitioner* (Llewellyn, 1997)

Cunningham, Scott, *Living Wicca; A Further Guide for the Solitary Practitioner*, (Llewellyn,1997)

Cunningham, Scott, *The Truth About Witchcraft Today* (Llewellyn, 1997)

Curott, Phyllis, *Book of Shadows* (Piatkus, 1998)

Davis, Owen, *The Oxford Illustrated History of Witchcraft & Magic* (Oxford University Press, 2017)

De Pulford, Nicola, *Spells & Charms* (Godsfield Press, 1999)

Greenleaf, Cerridwen, *The Practical Witch's Spellbook* (Running Press, 2018)

Guiley, Rosemary Ellen, *The Encyclopaedia of Witches and Witchcraft* (Facts on File LTD, 1989)

Horne, Fiona, *Witch; A Magical Journey, A Guide to Modern Witchcraft* (Thorsons HarperCollins, 2000)

Hutton, Ronald, *The Triumph of the Moon; A History of Modern Pagan Witchcraft* (Oxford University Press, 1999)

Illes, Judika, *The Element Encyclopaedia of Witchcraft* (Element HarperCollins, 2005)

Illes, Judika, *The Element Encyclopaedia of 5000 Spells* (Element HarperCollins, 2004)

Kane, Aurora, *Moon Magic* (Quarto Publishing Group, 2020)

Jordan, Michael, *Witches; An Encyclopedia of Paganism and Magic* (Kyle Cathie Limited, 1998)

Moorey, Teresa, *Spells & Rituals* (Hodder & Stoughton, 1999)

Moorey, Teresa, *Witchcraft; A Beginner's Guide* (Hodder & Stoughton, 1996)

Moorey, Teresa, *Witchcraft; A Complete Guide* (Hodder & Stoughton, 2000)

Morningstar, Sally, *The Wicca Pack; Weaving Magic into your Life* (GodsfieldPress, 2001)

Morningstar, Sally, *The Wiccan Way* (Godsfield Press, 2003)

Saxena, Jaya & Zimmerman, Jess, *Basic Witches* (Quirk Books, 2017)

Van de Car, Nikki, *Practical Magic* (Running Press, 2017)

ACKNOWLEDGEMENTS

I am not the kind of author who involves lots of other people in her work. I don't participate in any writing circles or allow close friends and family to read my works in progress. This is because I believe that the editor who commissioned the work should be the first person to see the finished result. That said, there are several people who have been key figures in the progress of my writing career over the years whom I would like to thank.

I am very grateful to the team at Arcturus, for welcoming me so enthusiastically and for turning my work into such stunningly beautiful books! Special thanks go to Nathalie Dehaye, for her professionalism and efficiency in dealing with emails and making sure that they reach the right people. Thank you so much, Nathalie! Without your help at the start this book, and others like it, simply would not exist. You play a valuable role and I appreciate it.

I am indebted to my editor, Tania O'Donnell, for her continued support of my career over the last two decades. It is always such a joy to work with you, Tania. You have opened more than one publishing door for me and welcomed me with so much warmth. Your enthusiasm for my work never wanes and I know that my ideas are safe in your hands. You are a fantastic champion for your authors and their work, and I can't wait to see what we come up with next!

I would also like to thank the Creative Writing course leaders at Sheffield Hallam University, Shelley Roche-Jacques and Harriet Tarlo, who mentored me throughout my Creative Writing Master's Degree. Special thanks also go out to our visiting fellows, Robert Macfarlane, Patrick McGuinness and Cathy Rentzenbrink, for their expertise and encouragement of my work. It was a pleasure being taught by you all and I'm sure that our paths will cross again in the future.

Last, but by no means least, thank you to my mother, Jaqueline Weatherill, who always encouraged my bookworm habits and bluestocking personality, offering me her unwavering support. Thanks for everything, Mum, especially the drive-by food parcels when I was too busy writing and studying to go to the supermarket! I love you so much.

Finally, to all my friends, family, fellow writers and colleagues, and to my loyal readers who have supported my work over the years, thank you so much. I hope that you enjoy this latest book and that there are many more to come in the future. May the light of the Goddess shine bright upon you.

Blessed Be

Marie Bruce x